GAY LIBERATION
AFTER MAY '68

THEORY Q   A series edited by
Lauren Berlant, Lee Edelman,
Benjamin Kahan, and Christina Sharpe

GAY LIBERATION AFTER MAY '68

GUY HOCQUENGHEM

WITH A FOREWORD BY GILLES DELEUZE

TRANSLATED BY SCOTT BRANSON

DUKE UNIVERSITY PRESS *Durham and London* 2022

Designed by Matthew Tauch
Typeset in Alegreya and Helvetica LT Std by Copperline
Book Services

Library of Congress Cataloging-in-Publication Data
Names: Hocquenghem, Guy, 1946–1988, author. | Branson, Scott,
[date] translator. | Deleuze, Gilles, 1925–1995, writer of foreword. Title:
Gay liberation after May '68 / Guy Hocquenghem ; with a foreword by
Gilles Deleuze ; translated by Scott Branson.
Other titles: Theory Q.
Description: Durham : Duke University Press, 2022. | Series: Theory Q |
Includes index.
Identifiers: LCCN 2021034684 (print)
LCCN 2021034685 (ebook)
ISBN 9781478015451 (hardcover)
ISBN 9781478018087 (paperback)
ISBN 9781478022695 (ebook)
Subjects: LCSH: Gay liberation movement—France. | Gay activists—
France. | Social movements—France—History—20th century. | France
—History—1958– | BISAC: SOCIAL SCIENCE / LGBTQ Studies / Gay
Studies | HISTORY / Europe / France
Classification: LCC HQ76.8.F8 H63 2022 (print) | LCC HQ76.8.F8 (ebook) |
DDC 306.76/60944—dc23/eng/20211013
LC record available at https://lccn.loc.gov/2021034684
LC ebook record available at https://lccn.loc.gov/2021034685

Cover art: Design and illustration by Matthew Tauch

THIS WORK RECEIVED SUPPORT FROM THE FRENCH MINISTRY OF
FOREIGN AFFAIRS AND THE CULTURAL SERVICES OF THE FRENCH
EMBASSY IN THE UNITED STATES THROUGH THEIR PUBLISHING
ASSISTANCE PROGRAM.

THIS BOOK RECEIVED A PUBLICATION SUBSIDY FROM DUKE
UNIVERSITY PRESS'S TRANSLATION FUND, A FUND ESTABLISHED BY
PRESS AUTHORS WHO DONATED THEIR BOOK ROYALTIES TO
SUPPORT THE TRANSLATION OF SCHOLARLY BOOKS.

Contents

A Note on Terminology

Throughout the text, where applicable, I use the terminology *trans/transgender/trans people* to keep within the current understanding and articulations of gender. Hocquenghem and Deleuze both use the term *travesti*, which was current at the time, though it has the connotation of *transvestite* or *cross-dressing*. Sometimes this was a contemporary articulation of a political stance, like with *Street Action Transvestite Revolutionaries*, of Les Gazolines. But mostly in this text Hocquenghem (and Gilles Deleuze) are discussing what we understand as transgender or transsexuality. On the other hand, I translate Hocquenghem's reclaiming of slurs used to identify gay people within a similar lexicon.

Translator's Introduction

A Queer Anarchism That Dare Not Speak Its Name

You don't dare say it, perhaps you don't even dare say it to yourselves.
GUY HOCQUENGHEM, "For Those Who Are Like Us"

Already well into his academic and militant life, in 1974 Guy Hocquenghem presented a dissertation in philosophy at the University of Paris VIII, Vincennes. The first half of this dissertation was his first book, previously published in 1972, the theoretical treatise *Le désir homosexuel* (*Homosexual Desire*), which is currently one of the few works by Hocquenghem available in English.[1] The second half would be published independently the same year as his second book, *L'après-mai des faunes*, a translation of which you are now holding in your hands: *Gay Liberation after May '68*.[2] This half of the dissertation primarily consisted of a series of radical journal articles, political communiqués, and manifestos, which Hocquenghem wrote and published in the years after the May '68 uprising.

The year 1968 marked a global wave of uprisings that resonates with today's rebellions. The "events" of May in France felt to many involved like the brink of revolution and the near-toppling of the bourgeois state: emerging from student groups protesting university regulations, French capitalism, and US/global imperialism, the student movement began to occupy buildings. This occupation resulted in violent clashes with the police, which led to widespread labor support and a rash of wildcat strikes across France that brought the economy to a halt. Eventually, the parties and unions came to an agreement with the state, leading to a reimposition of "law and order," though the autonomous militants involved felt betrayed. In the essays and articles collected in this book—starting with pieces from May 1968 at the spark of the revolt and then reflecting on the hopes and failures in the years after—Guy Hocquenghem speaks just as boldly and passionately to those of us engaged in struggle and devising theories of liberation today. Hocquenghem's writing in this book has a sense of urgency, whether it stems from the enthusiasm of recent participation in street blockades and General Assemblies that gave glimpses of another possible world or from anger at movements getting co-opted, militants selling out, and revolutionary commitments coming to nothing. These texts bear witness to the change of life that Hocquenghem experienced as a part of May 1968 and the years after. He continued experiments in horizontal organization, collective living, new connections of desire—all contesting the dominant mode of capitalist crisis, retrenchment, and capture. These are moments for Hocquenghem to envision a world contrary to the dominant one, or as the Zapatista slogan goes, "a world in which many worlds fit."

Submitting a collection of radical communiqués and previously published journal articles as a dissertation could be seen as something Hocquenghem merely threw together in order to get official institutional recognition—and a higher pay rate as a professor at Vincennes, part of his transition into what he called *professional homosexual/revolutionary*. It was certainly a nontraditional dissertation, accepted through a revised process that was part of the educational reforms that came after May '68 as a compromise—the same compromise that created Paris VIII (Vincennes) in the first place. On the other hand, we can see these two parts as more than a tenuous linking of two already written or published books. Specifically, the theory of *Homosexual Desire* only makes sense in the context of the practical militant experience recorded in *Gay Liberation after May '68*.

Now, at last, we can read Hocquenghem's contemporary analysis of the beginnings of gay liberation from an unflagging militant perspective and get a full account of the radical extent of his revolutionary queer politics, situating his theoretical contributions in the larger context of organizing and confrontation with the state. Though *Gay Liberation after May '68* has been long out of print in French, it provides a necessary companion to his better-known first book. If we separate the first book's theory of identity, sexuality, and desire from the action in the streets facing off with cops or the militant organizing and collective life, we run the risk of uncritically assuming the very institutional position as professional fag or revolutionary careerist that Hocquenghem critiques on every page of this book: a queer identity that, instead of aiming to destroy any institution that might contain it, helps buttress its ideological stranglehold. It was this tenuous position between committed militant and professional that Hocquenghem would navigate his whole life.

Homosexual Desire established Hocquenghem as a forerunner in the field of *queer theory*, a term that came later and is associated more with Anglo academic production than its tangential field, so-called French theory. Hocquenghem's first book appeared in both French and English shortly before another foundational French queer theory text, the first volume of Michel Foucault's *History of Sexuality* (which was arguably influenced by Hocquenghem's analysis, though Foucault drew different conclusions that moved away from antistate militancy). Hocquenghem's theory of desire and critique of homosexual identity in *Homosexual Desire* were inspired by Gilles Deleuze and Félix Guattari's attack on Freudianism as part of an anticapitalist analysis: he used much of their theoretical framework and terminology to displace the Oedipal notion of homosexual identity toward a mobile and disruptive homosexual desire with an explicit horizon of collective liberation. That is to say, Hocquenghem's queer theory is explicitly anticapitalist and, stemming from May '68, also antistate and anti-institutional. Thus, even *Homosexual Desire* was a product of Hocquenghem's militant work with the Front homosexuel d'action révolutionnaire (FHAR) and, before that, on the streets during May. As the penultimate chapter of that volume, "The Homosexual Struggle," declares, Hocquenghem's theoretical innovation always served militant liberatory aims.

Unlike *Homosexual Desire*, which is laid out as a theoretical treatise that masks a revolutionary manifesto, *Gay Liberation after May '68* has a less unitary structure. This book is made up of a collection of texts written over six years, mostly pulled from the radical journals that Hocquenghem wrote for and edited, as well as pamphlets distributed outside gay clubs. Still, Hocquenghem's militancy is always the main thrust; remarking on his tone, he notes that he uses "writing in order to persuade, chock full of exemplarity."[3] Along with the multiplicity of texts, Hocquenghem acknowledges a sense of collective authorship, situating his writing in his lived experience among comrades in the midst of struggle. Hocquenghem describes his own writing in this book as a collective experience: "There is an editorial *we* implicit in these texts, since none of them could have been written, debated, revised without the existence of the militant groups, the leftist journals, the people with whom I live. And this *we* hollers its convictions with an urgent tone, with the obvious desire to rally."[4] Additionally, there is a self-criticism in the book: between articles, Hocquenghem reflects on his earlier views, his passions, and the movements. This dialogic aspect leads him to propose an alternative reading method to the one that "seek[s] out the order of causes and of consequences, the logic of convictions, or even the fictive unity of a self."[5] Instead, he urges us to "consul[t] them like the pages ripped out of a diary, guiding oneself by intuitions, images, sensations, on a disorderly course like the swirls [*volutes*] of flames they might feed."[6] The book contains its own movements in all directions: attempts to follow through ideas with the flexibility learned from militancy outside of party structures and determinant theories, simultaneously within and against institutions.

The book begins with a foreword by Deleuze, previously published in English elsewhere, which gives a philosophical rendition of Hocquenghem's queer militancy.[7] The book then moves to Hocquenghem's introduction, "Volutions," one of two major theoretical statements in the book.[8] The book is then broken into seven chapters: chapter 1 deals with the deaths of militants; chapter 2 contains ecstatic texts from 1968 to 1972 detailing the stakes of a revolution that touches every aspect of life, not just labor; chapter 3 offers critiques of militants who betray the movement in pursuit of an "apolitical" cultural revolution of lifestyle, while also trashing the media's representation of militants, and it culminates in the cheeky survey Hocquenghem and others sent out to leftist militants and academics about their private life; chapter 4 discusses drugs, pop, rock and roll, and the rejection of traditional families; chapter 5 comprises a selection of texts Hocquenghem wrote during his time with the FHAR (mostly in 1971), making the argument for a gay liberation that demolishes society and ending with a 1973 interview in which Hocquenghem declares the end of the gay movement; chapter 6 contains two short texts on motorcycles, desire, and anti-automobile organizing; and finally, chapter 7 looks at the tenuous and revolutionary relationship between the women's movement and the gay movement, and closes out with Hocquenghem's other major theoretical text in the book, "A Shameless Transversalism," announcing a possible direction for militant queer anticapitalist movements after May—that is, after the revolution has been recuperated.

Thus, *Gay Liberation after May '68* is less queer theory than it is critical queer liberatory praxis, from May '68 to the MLF and FHAR and beyond— promoting the kind of radical queer actions and style echoed in the US context in groups like Bash Back! and the current work of Black queer/trans abolitionists and anarchists who have made such astonishing contributions to the long project of liberation.[9] Through it all, the reader will feel embedded in the climate of Hocquenghem's day with the same fury and desire, building to a kind of joy that can be brought into our current militant contexts.

Hocquenghem explicitly breaks with the dominant revolutionary tradition, from the various communist formations to Jean-Paul Sartre's "old story of commitment." Instead of enshrining the worker as the revolutionary subject without any texture or content beyond a vaguely masculinist profile, Hocquenghem shows that militancy breaks out at every level of life: "We no longer commit ourselves to just battles, we act through our positions; not out of a sense of men's battles, but through the breaking out of tiny obsessions for no reason: getting high, motorcycles, sodomy, being trans, all these ways of living aren't just an issue of how to be revolutionary, but are the absolute present of the untimely."[10] Hocquenghem's biographer, Antoine Idier, reads this line as a "double rupture: the existence of a politics that no longer has revolution as its horizon and that is no longer Marxist."[11] Idier rejects the attempts by some critics to understand Hocquenghem and the FHAR as a queer Marxism, since the explicit challenge to Marxism is one of the specificities of French gay liberation. This challenge might be one of the important lessons May '68 holds for us today. The initial betrayal experienced by those awakened by May '68, even before the neoliberalization of the former militants, was in the clear failure of the French Communist Party (Parti communiste français; PCF), as well as the various other Marxist and Maoist party formations, to connect with the potential of the moment and listen to the youth in revolt.[12] Instead, on their own, the students and the workers organized along anarchist lines, in the spirit of Spain, under the influence of the Situationists—and, as Hocquenghem emphasizes, with the openness of cruising the Tuileries.

The FHAR came into being when lesbian militants split from the Mouvement de libération des femmes (MLF), or Women's Liberation Movement, in order to bring a focus on sexuality to radical feminist actions. They joined with lesbians from the oldest French homophile group, Arcadie, which had a less political and even assimilationist perspective. The first FHAR actions took place in early 1971 to interrupt an antiabortion meeting and a radio show on the "homosexual question." Hocquenghem was one of the first gay cisgender men to attend the meetings, which eventually encompassed different sexual and gender positions than the original lesbian emphasis.[13] Though the FHAR, like the MLF, was a new formation, it inherited the legacy of the May '68 uprising, where there had already been action committees focusing on feminism and homosexuality from a revolutionary perspective.

Before joining the FHAR, Hocquenghem had a number of years of militant action and study under his belt, even predating May '68. He had come up through a variety of Marxist party formations, more specifically those of Maoist tendencies, and eventually made moves toward a more anarchist strain, though he didn't tend to label his mode this—or any—way. We can't ignore that his political education parallels the development of his sexuality. Hocquenghem met René Schérer, his philosophy teacher at the Lycée Henri IV, when he was fifteen. According to Hocquenghem, his teacher (also his onetime lover and lifelong collaborator) was the one who taught him about both sex and politics.[14] Thus, for Hocquenghem, revolution and sexuality were never separate phenomena.

Later, as a student at the elite École normale supérieure (ENS), Hocquenghem was notorious for his militant tendencies. His persona and voice were clearly identifiable during the May '68 uprising, not only because his writings in political journals began cropping up at the time but also due to his participation in the streets and disruptive interventions on campus and in meetings. Over the ensuing years, Hocquenghem continued to write and agitate within revolutionary, anticapitalist formations like the FHAR and to participate in experimental living arrangements while attempting to eke out minimal stipends as a student at the ENS and then later with income as a teacher at Vincennes.[15] Even after May, unlike many of his fellow *soixante-huitards*, Hocquenghem did not give up his radical commitments to anticapitalism, despite keeping his university post until his death in 1988.

The limited English reception of Hocquenghem's work in the field of queer theory has deemphasized his militant involvement. *Gay Liberation after May '68* therefore restores the context of militancy to our reception of Hocquenghem. While queer theory had its birth in gay liberation, we are still working through what this legacy means in the aftermath of the revolutionary moments of the 1960s and 1970s. Michael Moon's beautiful introduction to the reprint of the English translation of *Homosexual Desire* remarks on the uniqueness of the book in fusing gay liberation and French theory. I would echo Moon's comment that even Hocquenghem's first book "still requires to be read not only as a treatise but also as a manifesto, a powerful incitement to join an intense political struggle whose time has come."[16] Until now Hocquenghem's work available in English has been relegated to the realm of theory that can be easily taken out of context, essentialized, removed from on-the-ground struggles. But his writing always takes a clear stance, explicitly anticapitalist, anticolonial, antiracist.

For many Anglo readers of queer theory, Hocquenghem might be best known as an early precursor to what became known as the "antisocial thesis." In the acclaimed roundtable published in PMLA in 2006, featuring Robert L. Caserio, Jack Halberstam, and José Esteban Muñoz, Tim Dean writes that Hocquenghem precedes both Leo Bersani and Lee Edelman in articulating an understanding of homosexual desire as a threat to social order.[17] Importantly, Dean highlights that homosexual desire, as "the killer of civilized egos" as Hocquenghem puts it, "betokens not the end of sociality but rather its inception."[18] Here Dean emphasizes the utopian aspect of Hocquenghem's thinking, beyond mere shattering. The *utopian* epithet may ultimately be the shameful mark that has put Hocquenghem's militancy out of reach, making it seem dated.[19] For Hocquenghem, (homosexual) desire points to the possibility of destroying capitalism along with colonialism, racism, misogyny, and sexual repression. In a field dominated by Foucauldian discursive analysis and concepts of power, the understanding of an inherently liberatory queer sexuality gets easily dismissed along with the "repressive hypothesis" as a naive or even immature position.

In a way, it seems like queer theory has "grown up" and out of the revolutionary fervor that animated militants like Hocquenghem. Still we must find a way to relate to this legacy, especially as so many of us try to reclaim that enthusiasm in our current struggles. Kadji Amin makes a helpful and subtle distinction between Hocquenghem's articulation of his theories and the influence they have had on later queer theory, calling Hocquenghem's strand "liberationist negativity," as opposed to the "psychoanalytic negativity" typified by Bersani, Edelman, and Dean.[20] While theorists like Bersani reject the redemptive quality to sex that liberationists like Hocquenghem were so passionate about, Amin points to the ways that psychoanalytic negativity also invests (queer) desire with an equally utopian dimension in its self-shattering effects. Amin acknowledges the animating motive of liberationists like Hocquenghem toward an anticapitalist, antiracist, anticolonial "erotic coalition" but also marks their shortcomings in actually living out these hopes given "the imperfect and messy relations . . . between queer eros and the political," or in any "alternative socialities."[21] Amin thus pushes for a deidealization when it comes to thinking queerness, which can allow us to access this history realistically—and perhaps aside from our own liberatory hopes for our future movements.

In other words, our utopian, liberatory commitments often diverge from the work we get caught up in organizing, which not only comes up against the force of the state but also against the internal policing and disagreements among comrades. In this book, Hocquenghem shows us both the utopian dreaming of a militant fag and the messiness of splintering so familiar to those involved in the long-term struggle for liberation. But instead of a "growing up" that leaves behind our liberatory dreams and instead of a pessimism that sees the failure of the liberation movements of the 1960s and 1970s as the inevitable and eternal triumph of capitalism, we can take up Hocquenghem's urgency as a call to aim our sights on liberation explicitly and continuously. We can do this without a nostalgia for a revolution that never occurred, perhaps even in the key of the kind of queer "failure" that Halberstam theorizes.[22] But I also want to point our attention to the untold and unremembered histories of fags and dykes and trans people living out these "alternative socialities," in all their messiness, against the dominance of the state. What I read in these texts as Hocquenghem's queer anarchism parts ways with all the preconceived leftist strategies and demands a constant calibration, an ethical choice, to imagine liberation as an act of solidarity across differing forms of oppression and to keep doing it better until we get there.

This translation of Hocquenghem's second book, then, can help restore for today's militant, theoretically inclined queers a different lineage that resituates queer militancy at the foreground of theory, where queerness is not only what is done between the sheets but in the streets (though of course queer sex also happens on the streets, a longtime phenomenon and provocation). A revisionism that fits all resistance into the mold of civil and human rights protests has forgotten (or worse, intentionally obscured) the militancy of the liberation movements of the 1960s and 1970s—Black liberation, women's liberation, gay liberation, the American Indian Movement, and the global decolonial movements—all of which posed a real threat to the nascent neoliberal order.[23] Today's students of queer theory, along with today's movements, are relearning that this militancy—its active threat to the state—is what helped achieve whatever minimal steps toward "equality" racialized, gendered, and economically excluded groups have received. More important, today's queers are walking in the footsteps of militant homos like Hocquenghem in their agitation. Reading Hocquenghem today can help us rethink our queer militant lineages, expand our chosen elders, and revive a strain of thought that is ever more needed in an age of global uprisings; the increasing threat of repression, violence, and devastation; and the ever-present possibilities of liberal recuperation.

After May '68, the question of recuperation was particularly pressing. This is true for every radical movement in confrontation with the state. The institutions and agents of the state will grant symbolic victories that shift the demands from dismantling to reform in order to pacify one identity group with concessions while actually strengthening the tools of oppression. The compromise that led to Vincennes and Hocquenghem's eventual doctoral thesis is one example. To avoid such recuperation, some militants aim for a "purity" politics that avoids any entanglement with the current power structures, trying to exist altogether outside. But instead of letting the fear of recuperation stop action dead in its tracks, Hocquenghem here asks us to turn the idea of revolutionary purity on its head, asking, "How can we generalize 'recuperation,' sink the boat by overloading it, instead of emptying it in order to uphold 'purity'?"[24] We might even say that if we took it seriously, what we now call *queerness*, and what Hocquenghem described as *homosexual desire*, would necessarily destroy all ideas of purity along with the surrounding institutions and eventually itself.

As for the tradeoff of becoming a professional revolutionary or on-duty fag, Hocquenghem suggests that instead of an ascetic revolutionary vow, "Let's organize in order to have enough to live off of and to sustain what we like."[25] Hocquenghem speaks out against the midcentury communist piety that demands the bourgeois youth implant themselves in factories as workers. And against the student dedication to a false appearance of pennilessness, Hocquenghem advocates for an engagement in the oppressive systems and bourgeois professions that imagines ways to turn them to our needs and their ruin: "The only thing we could change here is not to demand everyone quit or blame themselves for constant 'recuperation.' . . . It's often uptight and shameful leftists themselves who argue for the elitist character of these jobs and in this way unconsciously defend their status. So what? Anyone is capable of being a designer; anything goes in journalism today; pirating university degrees could be organized on a grand scale. Everyone gets a PhD; it's not impossible."[26] One has to make a living in this current system, but it makes no sense to invest professions and labor with any romantic or revolutionary value, whether you are a manual laborer or a leftist intellectual. Better to use one's position to degrade everything that supports the system.

In "The Good Life of Leftists," results from the survey Hocquenghem and his comrades sent out to well-known figures, he writes unsparingly about the hypocrisy with which people approach their work life: "No one admits to having a profession, yet they've been doing the same things for ages. . . . What does this mean? The shameful leftist social climb?" He concludes with the "surplus value" that a revolutionary pose gives the intellectual: "To be a leftist is also a way to be different, to stick your nose out of professional drabness. That doesn't always mean getting paid. . . . There are some for whom the way of life just lets them get famous: Sartre lives like an ex-student in a dorm-style studio."[27] Being a leftist is another process of individuation, a CV line that makes you hirable.

And yet Hocquenghem also questions the revolutionary moralism that calls even having a job "recuperation" and proposes instead to invert the relationship. Instead of allowing the institutions of power to co-opt revolutionary excitement or drain the ideas of their danger, he suggests that people with access to the resources of these institutions could instead engage with them in a radical liberatory way. The delightful image of manufacturing PhDs in order to sink the elite status of holding such a degree actually provides a strange case, however, considering the state of the university today. Still, Hocquenghem's thought has resonance with the way Fred Moten and Stefano Harney motivate the Black radical tradition in *The Undercommons*, toward collective organizing "in but not of" the university: "One can only sneak into the university and steal what we can."[28] Hocquenghem would agree that our allegiances ought never to lie with the institutions, but with the movements: an escape plan, or what Moten and Harney theorize as "fugitivity."[29]

The fact of gay liberation's various recuperations into homonormativity seems definitively to show that nonnormative, or deviant, marginalized sexuality and gender are not simply revolutionary in and of themselves. To understand deviant gender and sexuality as revolutionary, we might think of "gay sex" as a form of liberation. Consider the following forms of nonmonogamous, nonheteronormative relationships: cruising and other forms of public sex; multiplicity of partners; or, as Hocquenghem would argue in his more theoretical mode, the public, desublimated anus. We can further imagine genderfucking until the binary of forcibly assigned gender disappears. For Hocquenghem and other gay revolutionaries, these forms of sexuality and gender enactment literally entail the downfall of capitalist society and its enforced hierarchies.

But if homosexuality is liberatory, Hocquenghem sees it as something to be eventually cast off, "destroyed," since as it becomes a settled and recognized identity, it comes to serve a purpose for the state. Thus he moves beyond the seemingly immature position of a simple utopian idea of gay sex. A liberal movement aiming for an acceptable version of homosexuality only achieves a token of progress, while forcing the rest (particularly trans people or racialized queers) to remain in the territory of dangerous perversion, subject to violence from the state and its agents. Instead, Hocquenghem insists that homosexuality as a liberatory force must explicitly dislodge misogynist patriarchal culture, as well as racial capitalism and colonialism. Liberation comes through living the perversity and deviancy of sex and gender that are excluded by heterosexual family life in order to maintain hierarchies of domination: queer sex is a form of refusal, an ethical action that specifically aims to undermine domination and destroy society. Hocquenghem was already witnessing the splintering of gay liberation into assimilationist demands for rights, in an attempt to prove that "we are just like you." In the end, focusing on different forms of desire as identity markers plays right into market logic. As Hocquenghem writes, "The desiring fascism that marks the annals of the great libertines of the Western world is also the great big sense of being in one's place, dressed up to look like the most absolute radicalism and revolutionary apoliticism."[30] For Hocquenghem, this pose is the ultimate betrayal of May as it concerns gay liberation, "as if the whole journey since May could be summarized in the move from the world of slaves to the world of libertinized masters."[31] In other words: turning the revolution into a job, capitalizing on oppression. The social expenditure of a liberal pursuit of desire (bourgeois gays) reinstates the major class distinction by framing desire as a luxury, an expensive dessert on the menu of actual revolution. Instead, Hocquenghem envisions a nonhierarchical desire that dissolves all distinctions of bodies, types, and identities.

Seeing the trends of the movements, Hocquenghem quits revolution, but not for recuperation. He critiques the very notion of revolution in the introduction, "Volutions," and so when we use the traditional term *revolution* to describe his positions, we aren't fully comprehending his project. In his foreword, Deleuze teases out *volution* as the critical term for Hocquenghem's methods: "Imagine a fast-turning spiral: Hocquenghem is at several levels at the same time, on multiple loops at once, sometimes with a motorcycle, sometimes stoned, sometimes sodomized or sodomizing, sometimes trans. On one level, he can say *yes, yes I am a homosexual*; at another level *no, that's not it*; at yet another level, it's another thing altogether."[32] The volution becomes a strategy to turn away the methods of identification, what Hocquenghem calls being "pinned down by social entomology."[33] Deleuze's description might also outline Hocquenghem's efforts to escape recuperation, a nondialectical dialectic with no telos except liberation, whatever that means. (I leave that definition empty on purpose, to allow for new navigation to take on different commitments and solidarity, and also because whatever is outside of society and civilization risks recuperation immediately upon being represented.)

To a certain extent, Hocquenghem's removal of the prefix *re* from *revolution* stems from a wariness of the famous Marxian maxim that history repeats itself, first as tragedy then as farce. This sums up, for Hocquenghem, the betrayal of May: "They were right to baptize May a 'dress rehearsal.' There is no Re-volution, we no longer want to share the prefixes that moor the flight of our wills, their overflow dissolving our powers. Above all when these prefixes reinfect us with their sickness of the past: the tradition of the worker movement, their stupid idea of change; we rehash other ideas and restart civilization—the same civilization we want to forget. Changing words while keeping the prefixes—and thus *Revolution* becomes reactionary."[34] He discusses such reactionaryism in his article claiming solidarity with the Bengali Liberation Army, in the face of French Maoists siding with China and the ultimately genocidal actions of the Pakistani government.[35] We see "leftist" groups taking such reactionary measures today, when different Marxist-Leninist groups, for example, defend murderous states such as Syria or Iran for "strategic geopolitical reasons" or even defend US military operations cloaked in liberation, as if there isn't a way to be antistate, anti-imperial, and antiwar—in other words, supporting people's self-determination.[36] As Hocquenghem notes, these parties ignore riots and uprisings when they don't "do" revolution in the right way, or when the parties can't seize the momentum of the uprising for their own ends. Militants must fear recuperation from revolutionary leftists just as much as they fear state power and capital. And ultimately the professional revolutionaries will crush movements that don't fit their agendas, don't make specific demands, and won't broker with state powers.

When you take away the repetitive prefix, you are left with the link to desire that in Hocquenghem's view is the actual force for liberatory, or utopian, aims. This utopian strand of Hocquenghem's thinking is grounded not only in gay liberation, queer theory, or the revolutionary practices of cruising and sodomy but also in a (queer) reading of Charles Fourier, the utopian socialist whom Hocquenghem pits against Karl Marx as the more important "revolutionary" thinker of the nineteenth century—a thinker who doesn't offer a continuation of tradition but, rather, "an interruption in the rhetoric of the classroom greats" (i.e., an overlooked text).[37] I call this a queer reading in part because Hocquenghem writes alongside his former teacher and lover, René Schérer, making this a work that emerges from a gay context. Furthermore, Hocquenghem and Schérer insist on "redoing" Fourier since the utopian socialist starts with desire as a form of production, thereby displacing a classical Marxist separation of production and consumption. For them, Fourier breaks out of the prison of civilization, to which Marxist progressivist thought is still confined, and also understands production and desire outside of the narrow framework of economy. In other words, as Hocquenghem reflects back on this essay, Fourier is nondialectical, untimely, "detemporalized, simultaneous like two television sets projecting their clips side by side . . . neither before nor after, but a constellation."[38]

Given Hocquenghem's love of Fourier, Ron Haas claims him not as a Marxist or even a leftist but instead as utopian. Haas understands how Hocquenghem tries to retain queer tradition and elaborate its utopian possibilities: "For Hocquenghem, the rich, tenebrous homosexual worlds of the past pointed to an infinity of other avenues for the expression of human desire and human fellowship—not just for homosexuals—avenues that were slowly being blocked for the sake of bourgeois respectability."[39] Hocquenghem can claim homosexual love as "the only love that aims at equality because, being marginalized, it has no *social use*."[40] A liberationist commitment, then, would deploy this disruptive, even nonhuman desire against the cisheteropatriarchal and capitalist shackling of desire through repression, guilt, and sublimation.

But Hocquenghem is always ready to leave behind any political position as soon as it gets recuperated. This happened quickly with "the homosexual" position after a militant gay movement was born. Just as the contemporaneous decolonial movements got folded into liberal humanism through the idea of "human rights" (alongside proxy wars and Cold War manipulations), gay liberation was shuttled toward assimilation and inclusion. Homosexuality, according to Hocquenghem, is entwined with humanity as one of its obsessions: "Homosexuality haunts humanity, like the guilty conscience of sexuality."[41] Hocquenghem the utopian wants to do away with civilization and its inventions, like the human, the homosexual, and economics. Hocquenghem's Fourierist idea of liberation is the liberation of desire, the flux of desires that circulate differently from Marxist capital. The ultimate utopian dissolution is of identity, pointing to the "transindividual": the exchange of desire "reveals that *the individual is not the full human being*."[42]

Hocquenghem's "revolutionary" stance goes beyond mere reclamation of the negative, the transgression for transgression's sake that Marxist thinkers would dismiss.[43] As Hocquenghem says in an interview with Georges Danjou, "Every time we try to make homosexuality respectable, we push up against the same obstacle: how to remove fags from criminality, without ruining the libidinal or erotic relationship between fags and criminals?"[44] In fact, he claims, "The criminal aspect of homosexuality offers an opportunity": "it's this relationship between fags and criminals that makes homosexuals a group of people beyond redemption for society, a quite amazing revolutionary movement."[45] The emphasis, then, is on a group "beyond redemption for society"—Hocquenghem's whole game is to tear down society; today we might call his approach anarchism or abolition. He argues that we must continually reaffirm a practical commitment to oppose capitalist cisheteronormativity because that monster continually swallows up resistance. Hence, those who oppose it must also shift territory. In fact, for Hocquenghem, quitting is a strategy. The willingness to quit protects the revolutionary from recuperation, even for those whose identities have been demonized as unnatural.[46]

In "Against the Gendered Nightmare," the anonymous authors state: "[Hocquenghem's] writing represents some of the earliest queer theory which explicitly rejects Civilization—as well as the families, economies, metaphysics, sexualities and genders which compose it—while also imagining a queer desire which is Civilization's undoing."[47] Hocquenghem argues that queer positionality itself produces the conditions for liberation that ultimately dissolve the position as a fixed identity along with the structures that force these identities onto us. But importantly, as the authors of *Baedan* insist, the goal isn't to replace the structure with another system, which would just be one more step in the history of oppression. The authors of *Baedan* ground their understanding of Hocquenghem in his militancy. In particular, the authors draw "important ties between Hocquenghem's project and the insurrectionary anarchist project as we conceive it," through the emphasis on desire and the spread and dissolution of autonomous groups: "Only by avoiding the old-forms of 'revolutionary' or 'working class' organization can we side-step the traps which are laid out by recuperation. To orient ourselves around desire, and to pursue the 'blissful enjoyment of the present,' would mean to disavow the progressive ideologies of reform, inclusion, movement building, or incremental change."[48] The radical critique of *identity*, of gender and sexual roles as prescribed by cisheteropatriarchal racial capitalism, gave way to what we might now call a form of *identity politics*, transforming revolutionary disruption into neoliberal demands for recognition and rights. However, the way we understand this term today in its mainstream use is already the neoliberal recuperation of the movement work of marginal groups.

In fact, at the same time that Hocquenghem was critiquing his experience with the limits of the FHAR and MLF formations as groups formed around "identities," the US-based Combahee River Collective, a group of Black lesbian feminists, was articulating what the collective called *identity politics* along similar lines to Hocquenghem's critique: "We are actively committed to struggling against racial, sexual, heterosexual, and class oppression, and see as our particular task the development of integrated analysis and practice based upon the fact that the major systems of oppression are interlocking."[49] The Combahee River Collective developed its position from a disappointment with militant groups similar to what Hocquenghem describes in *Gay Liberation after May '68*. The group insists, "Our liberation is a necessity not as an adjunct to somebody else's but because of our need as human persons for autonomy."[50] Black people, women, and queers can't be tacked on to the "workers' revolution." At the same time, the Combahee River Collective understands that it isn't something called "biological maleness" that produces the violence of patriarchy; furthermore, patriarchy itself works in tandem with anti-Blackness, homophobia, and class struggle. Ultimately, the freedom for those in the Combahee River Collective would mean collective liberation because it would derive from "the destruction of all the systems of oppression."[51]

Hocquenghem is aligned with this understanding of *identity politics* when he writes that gay militants are "not revolutionaries who specialize in the sexual problem" but instead, "precisely because they live by embracing the most *particular* situation[,] . . . what they think has *universal* value."[52] In the French leftist context, to focus on gender and sexuality as movement work was seen as either a form of bourgeois decadence or a deflection from the economic priority of a proletarian revolution, an "adjunct" as the Combahee River Collective calls it. In fact, in France antihomosexual laws were relatively recent, stemming from Vichy and then reconsolidated by Charles de Gaulle's government. It may not sound quite right to bring into conversation someone so committed to the destruction of identity positions with a group articulating a position stemming from what it calls identity. Still, *identity politics* has been taken up by modern-day electoral politics and targeted advertising in a way that does not reflect its militant origins. Idier suggests that with *transversalism* Hocquenghem is working toward what we might today call *intersectionality*, a specific inheritance of the Combahee River Collective. *Transversalism* would then articulate an intersectionality that destroys identity.[53]

Hocquenghem's ideas resurface in the current anarchist trans militancy grounded in the abolition of gender, family, and prison—forms of destruction that he advocates in this book—and, importantly, tie into decades of queer and trans movement work.[54] Though Hocquenghem himself is a cis gay man, in his enthusiastic manifesto that closes this book, "A Shameless Transversalism," he sees transness as the beginning of the destruction of gender and sexual hierarchies, which are themselves tangled up in the racial capitalist-colonial machine. Hocquenghem launches an appeal to stymie academic comprehension, political capture, and individualistic concepts of identity: "A shameless, slutty transversalism, having lost all modesty—i.e., all sense of what's appropriate—that endlessly tries to put square pegs in round holes, losing its identity while gaining it, lewd when accepted as theoretical, 'untimely.' . . . Confusing the order of causes and consequences."[55] There are no sanctified objects, and logic is put in distress; the only worthwhile theory is "lewd," tarted up, and ready to go. Hocquenghem had already announced this horizon of an abolition of gender and sexual identities at the end of *Homosexual Desire* as "a slope toward transness through the disappearance of objects and subjects."[56]

The fullest understanding of transness that Hocquenghem gives in this book is the following: "*Transgender*, for example, is not the middle between man and woman, or the universal mediator (man into woman, woman into man); it's one part of a world transferred into another like we pass from one universe to another universe parallel to the first (or perpendicular, or askew . . .); or rather, it's a million inappropriate gestures, transferred features, events (growing breasts, removing hair) happening in as untimely a way as the appearing or disappearing of a feline smile in *Alice in Wonderland*."[57] Hocquenghem puts transness—I won't say trans identity—in an analogous destructive position to homosexual desire in the liberation of features, gestures, and events from the grounded, essential body, from the subject—women subjected to the relationship of penetration, the man wielding the phallus.[58]

Hocquenghem is writing in the context of trans-led uprisings in the United States like Stonewall and the radical trans group Les Gazolines creating situations and disruptions in France. Thus, he also notes in his new term a slippage, from *transversalism* to *transness*: "Transversalism, transgender, versatility [*transversalisme, transvestisme, versatilisme*]."[59] Deleuze shows how transversalism moves toward a destruction of gender, from the specificity of homosexual desire to a new position: "Wouldn't the homosexual be, not the one to stick to the *same* sex, but the one who discovers countless genders that we have no idea about?"[60] The liberatory disruption of homosexuality gets us to the point where, as Deleuze writes, "there is no longer a homosexual *subject*, but homosexual productions of desire, and homosexual arrangements that produce utterances, that swarm everywhere, S&M and transgender, in love relations as much as in political struggles."[61] Hocquenghem calls this point the "homosexual view of the world":

> We homosexuals refuse *all* the roles: because it is the very idea of Role that disgusts us. We don't want to be men or women—and our transgender comrades can explain that best. We know that society is afraid of everything that comes from the deepest parts of ourselves, because it needs to *classify* in order to rule. Identify in order to oppress. This is what makes us know how to clock people, despite our alienations. Our inconsistency, our unsteadiness, frightens the bourgeois. We will never be able to freeze ourselves, even in the position of the proletarian revolutionary: we have suffered the role of man that they have forced on us in the flesh.[62]

The important thing, then, is the betrayal of the masculine imperative; being a man and being gay are disciplinary measures, ostensible police orders. In breaking with the MLF, he calls out the feminists for excluding trans women, a problem that persists in some so-called feminist groups today: "As if feminine qualities were not basically trans to begin with."[63] Hocquenghem acknowledges here what we now might call the *performativity* of gender, where the feminine position is on the one hand a project of masculine domination; but he goes further, in a liberatory push, to show that transfemininity displaces essentialist underpinnings, presenting a "queer" femininity that slips transversally through the masculine grasp.[64]

Although Hocquenghem himself doesn't engage here with Black liberation, if we want to understand his message for today's militants, we must look toward the more radical work in Black/trans theory and movements. The most important currents in Hocquenghem's militant theory must be articulated in relation to the Black radical tradition, specifically a Black queer/trans feminist thinking, and Black anarchism. In *Black on Both Sides*, C. Riley Snorton also uses the term *transversality*, with reference both to Guattari and Édouard Glissant, to elaborate an understanding of Blackness and transness in relation to each other. Snorton refuses biologizing or essentializing definitions to show that transness forms "conditions of possibility for the modern world," but also announces escape from modes of domination, in "the transitivity and transversality of fungibility and fugitivity of gender/sexuality and Blackness."[65] Along with Snorton, Fred Moten emphasizes a fugitivity and escape that help formulate an understanding of Blackness beyond skin color as an intentional, radical taking of sides, against domination and toward freedom. Like Hocquenghem's militant transversality, there is a sliding, a moving from one position to the next to escape being fixed and understood, confined and labeled, all toward the horizon of something radically outside, elsewhere.

In Hocquenghem's reflections on the aftermath of May, I suggest that we discover a queer anarchism that doesn't quite say its name, underlying his experiences of collective life and struggle and his dedicated refusal of power and identity. I am inspired here by recent work that reads an often unspoken affinity between Blackness and anarchism. In *Wayward Lives, Beautiful Experiments*, Saidiya Hartman proposes a misreading of the studied forms of anarchism to discover "the radical imagination and everyday anarchy of ordinary colored girls." Underneath the official labels of "deviance, criminality, and pathology" applied to the Black women whom she follows, Hartman discovers "an insurgent ground," "open rebellion," "waywardness, refusal, mutual aid, and free love," "queer and outlaw passions."[66] Hartman frees anarchism from political ideology toward an embodied enacting within racialized, gendered, sexualized positions against the state and its power. This radicalized position is what William C. Anderson and Zoé Samudzi describe as "Black in anarchy": "a reflexive understanding of our existence within a color-based caste system [that] can predispose us to be more readily primed for radical politics."[67] I don't want to remove the specificity of Blackness in any of these conceptions of anarchism, but simply hope to borrow the flexibility in theorizing a queer anarchist practice beyond our standardized understanding of politics. This helps us situate the nonutopian utopianism of Hocquenghem's gay militancy, born from struggle, in a desire for and toward disruption, within the larger context of ongoing liberation struggles that we inherit, combine, and inhabit in the current moment. Hocquenghem's elaboration of a liberatory queerness starts from a place of anarchy imposed by its exclusion from normality. Still, in this book, Hocquenghem mostly lacks an analysis of racism, and only hints at an anticolonial critique. A true anarchist queer/trans struggle will be explicitly tied to collective liberation, taking its cues from radical Black feminism and Indigenous resistance.

Hocquenghem's anarchism takes the sodomist's approach, from behind, trembling with desire, to open the "utopian" space: "We don't tackle the big questions that concern humanity head-on. We slip sideways between two layers of guilty conscience, crumbling the frameworks where they try to confine us from behind into multiple quiverings of the social body in its infinite urgent places."[68] The "sideways," "from behind," is a queering of that monolithic revolution that would sum up each person's needs in the will of *the people*, giving up individual and communal autonomy for one thinker's dream of liberation. Hocquenghem and his comrades embody strategies developed from a sense of autonomy, mutual aid, and self-management that many groups discover works best in moments of heightened confrontation, crisis, community defense, or even in cruising grounds. Refusing the state along with "revolution," Hocquenghem rejects names and identities, except the most degraded, like *fag*; his search for new horizons with words like *volution* and *transversalism* articulates a transgender undoing of social positions—this urge and tendency evoke a queer anarchism that cannot speak itself, since to speak is to represent and get caught back up in the play of politics. And so it goes on in its critical practice of destroying and creating, eluding capture by refusing to be seen.

I am finishing this manuscript in 2020, in the wake of ongoing global uprisings that seem to outstrip the revolutionary moment of May '68 with an insurgent fire that has been spreading at least since the Arab Spring, Occupy movements, and Black Lives Matter uprisings in the early 2010s. We are in the midst of an unquelled global surge of rage and unrest. The COVID-19 pandemic has illuminated the inherent violence of a racial capitalist world system, whether in sheer indifference to mass death, promotion of environmental collapse that occasions new diseases and global spread, insistence on economics over care, or in the imperialist and racialized impacts of incompetent health-care systems. In this context, the police killings of George Floyd, Breonna Taylor, and Tony McDade have sparked a widespread uprising, with many US cities becoming sites of siege where a multiracial, Black-led coalition faces off with violent police and federal authorities. We have witnessed beautiful moments of liberation: burning down a police precinct, reappropriating resources held in chain stores, and distributing forms of mutual aid, whether providing support to arrestees or just helping people find food and shelter. As people who are new to militant actions take to the streets to demand not just the end of unaccountable racist police killings but the end of police and prisons as a whole, only to be tear-gassed by their local police with the support of their local representatives, they can no longer ignore the fact that the state runs through police order. The daily functioning of the state means the constant threat of death and physical harm, particularly targeting Black queer/trans people, all in the service of a very few.

The experience of May '68 has echoed periodically over the decades. May '68 can thus be seen as an initial sounding, *untimely* as Guy Hocquenghem would call it, part of a decades-long series of delinked, anarchist uprisings that continue to push across the globe against all forms of state oppression. We can't fail to see the brutal violence, embodied by the police, that the state enacts against its (purportedly protected) citizens in the name of liberal democracy and racial capitalism. But what necessarily gets left out is the collective experience of momentary liberation. Anyone who is familiar with or who has participated in street movements over the last twenty years—but more importantly over the last decade and, increasingly, over the last few years—might claim the overlooked legacy of May. To us, Hocquenghem's words in this book will sound as if they are describing the latest street actions and collective discussions. Like the students and workers and fags and dykes on the front lines in 1968, we've had the immediate experience of that other world—the elsewhere, escape, fugitivity, abolition, anarchy.

In *Gay Liberation after May '68*, Hocquenghem's youthful utopian excitement mixed with his bitter resentment is particularly infectious because of his unflagging commitment to a collective liberation, no matter his blind spots, whether in terms of his ability to speak in an informed way about certain positions or the way history has ultimately borne out his ideas. Hocquenghem refused capitulation; he refused recuperation; but he also didn't fuck with ideas of purity. It would be wrong, even dangerous, to dismiss the fury with which we are rising up against this civilization, willing to tear it all down, like Hocquenghem. The English translation of *L'après-mai des faunes* will therefore hopefully infuse the language of contemporary queer theory with a volutionary insistence that takes a flexible and ethical stance toward liberation and the destruction of racist capitalist institutions. In Hocquenghem, today's movements recognize a comrade. Reading him, we can be cruised by a man who lived revolution in its momentary state, its timeless presence, its slip of the wrist. He knew enough to say that the revolution had to be gay, it had to be lesbian, it had to be trans—and we must add, it has to be Black and Indigenous. It has to be honest in its solidarity with the struggles of everyone across the globe who counter the state, and it has to spell the end of humanity, civilization, and the institutions it holds dear, no looking back: "Here we see the after-May as a multiple life change. The after-May of fawns is made of leaps in all of the fields of the possible, not in faithfulness to a fixation. It is an after without a backward glance at a May, otherwise well-behaved, a horny myth notwithstanding—without kids' nightmares about the Crisis. It's like a summer afternoon."[69]

GAY LIBERATION
AFTER MAY '68

Foreword

Gilles Deleuze

The foreword: no one can escape it, not the author of the book, not the edi-tor, nor the foreword writer—the true victim—even though there is no need of a foreword. This is a gay book. It could have been called: "How the Existence of Homosexuality Began to Be Doubted"; or, "No One Can Say 'I Am a Homosexual.'" By Hocquenghem. How did he get here? A personal evolution that can be read in the ordering of the texts in this book and their varying tones? A collective revolution due to a group effort, a becoming of the FHAR?[1] Obviously, it's not by changing, by becoming heterosexual for example, that Hocquenghem beings to doubt the soundness of ideas and claims. It's by remaining homosexual *for ever*,[2] staying homosexual by being more and more so, or better and better, that we can come to say, "but after all, no one is." Which is a thousand times better than the boring and drab verdict that claims everyone is, everyone would be, an unconscious latent fag. Hocquenghem is not talking about evolution or revolution, but about volutions.[3] Imagine a fast-turning spiral: Hocquenghem is at several levels at the same time, on multiple loops at once, sometimes with a motorcy-cle, sometimes stoned, sometimes sodomized or sodomizing, sometimes trans. On one level, he can say *yes, yes, I am a homosexual*; at another level *no, that's not it*; at yet another level, it's another thing altogether. This book does not repeat the previous book, *Homosexual Desire*; it spreads it, mobilizes it in another way, transforms it.

First volution. Against psychoanalysis, against psychoanalytic interpre-tations and reductions: homosexuality understood as a relationship with the father, with the mother, with Oedipus. Hocquenghem isn't against any-thing; he even wrote a letter to his mother.[4] But that won't work. Psycho-analysis has never been able to handle desire. It must always reduce it and make it say something else. Among Freud's most ridiculous passages, there are those about "fellatio": a desire so bizarre and so "shocking" couldn't be taken literally, it must refer to the cow's udder, and thus to the mother's breast. We'd get more pleasure sucking a cow's udder. Interpret, regress, reverse. It all makes Hocquenghem laugh. And maybe there is an oedipal homosexuality, a mommy-homosexuality, guilt, paranoia, whatever you want. But that homosexuality drops like lead, weighted down by what it hides and by what the combined advice of family and psychoanalysis wants to make it hide: it doesn't hold to the spiral, it doesn't stand the test of lightness and movement. Hocquenghem settles for presenting the specificity and irreducibility of a homosexual desire that is in flux,[5] without end or origin, a matter of experimentation and not of interpretation. You are never homosexual based on your past, but on your present, once it has been shown that childhood was already presence without reference to a past. For desire never represents anything, and doesn't refer to something else hidden in the background of a domestic or private drama. Desire arranges, it schemes, it makes connections. Hocquenghem's wonderful essay on the motorcycle: the bike is a genital. Wouldn't the homosexual be, not the one to stick to the *same* sex, but the one who discovers countless genders that we have no idea about?[6] But first Hocquenghem tries to define this specific, irreducible homosexual desire—and not as a regressive interiority, but as the present traits of an Outside, of a relation to the Outside: the specific movement of cruising, the way of meeting up, the "anular" structure,[7] the interchangeability and mobility of roles, a certain betrayal (plotting against one's own class, as Klossowski says?: "They told us we were men, and we were treated like women; yes, to our enemies, we are traitors, sneaky, dishonest; yes, in any social situation, at any moment, we let men down, we are snitches and we are proud of it").[8]

Second volution: homosexuality does not produce desire without creating utterances at the same time. Indeed, producing desire and creating new utterances are the same thing. It's obvious that Hocquenghem doesn't speak like Gide, nor like Proust, even less like Peyrefitte:[9] but style is political—and so are generational differences, and the ways of saying *I* (see the gaping difference between Burroughs father and son, when they say *I* and talk about drugs).[10] Another style, another politics: like Tony Duvert's importance today, a new tone.[11] Today, from the depths of a new style, homosexuality produces utterances that are not about, and should not be about, homosexuality itself. If it were a question of saying "all men are fags," there would be no interest at all—it's a useless proposition that only entertains fools. But homosexuals' marginal position makes it possible and creates the need that they have something to say about *what is not* homosexuality: "The homosexual movements have brought the entirety of men's sexual problems to the surface."[12] According to Hocquenghem, the utterances of homosexuality are of two complementary types. First, about sexuality in general: far from being misogynist, the homosexual condemns the singular phenomenon of phallocentrism in both the subjugation of women *and* the repression of homosexuality. Indeed, phallocentrism operates indirectly and, by creating the heterosexual framework of our societies, casts boys' sexuality onto girls to whom it gives the role of simultaneously being the first hunter as well as the first prey. Therefore, whether there is a mysterious connection between girls who prefer girls, boys who prefer boys, boys who prefer a motorcycle or bicycle to girls, girls who prefer, etc., the key is not to insert a symbolic or pseudosignifying relationship in these plots and conspiracies ("a movement like the FHAR seems closely tied to ecological movements . . . *even though this is unspeakable in political logic*").[13] That's why, just as well, the second type of utterances concerns the social field in general and the presence of sexuality in this whole field: by escaping from the heterosexual framework, from the localization of this framework in a type of relationship as well as from its spreading into all places of society, homosexuality is able to pursue a micropolitics of desire, and to act as indicator or as sensor of the entirety of power relations to which society submits sexuality (including the case of more or less latent homosexuality that permeates manly military or fascist groups). Specifically, homosexuality breaks free not by smashing each power relation, "because, being marginalized, it has no *social use*; because power struggles are not initially imposed by society; because here the roles man/woman, fucked/fucker, master/slave are unstable and reversible at every turn."[14]

Third volution. We believed Hocquenghem was establishing himself, burrowing into his place on the margins. But what is this margin? What is this specificity of homosexual desire? And these counterutterances of homosexuality? Another Hocquenghem, at another level of the spiral, denounces homosexuality as a word. *Nominalism* of homosexuality. And really there is no power in words, but only words in service of power: language is not information or communication, but prescription, decree, and commandment. You will be on the margins. It's the center that makes the margins. "This abstract division of desire that allows control over even those who escape, this placing within the law what is outside the Law. The category at issue, and the word itself, are a relatively recent invention. The increasing imperialism of a society that wants to give social status to everything unclassifiable has created this particularization of the disparity. . . .

Dividing so as to rule better, psychiatry's pseudo-scientific idea transformed barbaric intolerance into civilized intolerance."[15] But here is the bizarre thing: the less homosexuality is a state of being, the more homosexuality is a word, the more it must be taken at its word, accepting its position as specific, its utterances as irreducible, and behaving as if . . . In defiance. Out of near-duty. Through a dialectically necessary moment. By passing through and by progress. We will act like queens because you want it. We will outflank your traps. We will take you at your word: "Only by making shame more shameful can we progress. We reclaim our 'femininity,' the very kind that women reject, *at the same time we declare that these roles have no meaning.* . . . The practical form of this struggle—we can't avoid it—is the passage through homosexuality."[16] Another mask, another betrayal, Hocquenghem ends up Hegelian—the necessary moment through which we must pass—Hocquenghem ends up Marxist: the fag as the proletarian of Eros ("It is precisely because they live by embracing the most *particular* situation that what they think has *universal* value").[17] This surprises the reader. Tribute to the dialectic, to the École normale supérieure?[18] Homo-Hegelianism-Marxism? But Hocquenghem is already somewhere else, in another spot on his spiral, saying what he had in his head or in his heart, which can't be separated from a kind of evolution. Who among us has not had to kill the Hegel or Marx in ourselves, and along with them the infamous dialectic?

Fourth volution, final figure of the dance for the moment, final betrayal. We must follow Hocquenghem's texts, his position regarding the FHAR and within the FHAR, as a specific group, the relations with the MLF. And even the idea that the splintering of groups is never tragic. Far from being shut up in "the same," homosexuality is going to open itself to all sorts of new possible relations, micrological or microphysical, essentially reversible, transversal, with as many sexes/genders [*sexes*] as there are arrangements, not even excluding new relationships between men and women: the mobility of certain S&M relations, the strengths of trans people, the thirty-six thousand forms of love according to Fourier, or n-gender people (neither one nor two genders).[19] It is no longer about being neither man nor woman, but about inventing genders, which means that a homosexual man can find the pleasures a man would give him with a woman and vice versa. (Proust already countered exclusive homosexuality of the Same with this increasingly multifaceted and more "localized" homosexuality that includes all sorts of transsexual communications, including flowers and bicycles.) In a beautiful passage about transness, Hocquenghem speaks of a transmutation from one order to another, as if from an intensive *continuum* of substances: "Not the middle between man and woman, or the universal mediator. . . . It's one part of a world transferred into another like we pass from one universe to another universe parallel to the first (or perpendicular, or askew . . .); or rather, it's a million inappropriate gestures, transferred features, events . . ."[20] Far from closing itself in on sameness of gender/sex, this homosexuality opens itself to a loss of identity [*loin de se fermer sur l'identité d'un sexe, cette homosexualité s'ouvre sur une perte d'identité*], to the "system enacted by non-exclusive connections of polyvocal desire."[21] At this exact point of the spiral, we hear how the tone has changed: it is no longer at all about the homosexual being recognized, and being posited as a subject endowed with rights (let us live; after all, everyone is a little homosexual . . . demand-homosexuality, recognition-homosexuality, homosexuality of the same; oedipal type, Arcadian style).[22] For the new homosexual, it is about insisting on being this way, in order to be able to say at last: *No one is, it doesn't exist*. You call us homosexuals, sure, but we are already something else. There is no longer a homosexual *subject*, but homosexual productions of desire, and homosexual arrangements that produce utterances, that swarm everywhere, s&m and transgender, in love relations as much as in political struggles. There is no longer a defeated divided Gide-subject, nor even a still guilty Proust-subject, even less the pathetic Peyrefitte-Self. We understand better how Hocquenghem can be everywhere on his spiral, and say all at once: homosexual desire is specific, there are homosexual utterances, but homosexuality is nothing, it is only a word, and yet let's take the word seriously; we must pass through it, in order to restore everything that it contains of otherness—which is not the unconscious of psychoanalysis, but the progression of a future sexual becoming.

Volutions

An attitude that would no longer even be revolutionary in the sense
of reversal return . . . but volutionary, in the sense of Wille [will], in the
sense of willing whatever is possible.
J.-F. LYOTARD, "A Fanatical Capitalism," *Critique*, November 1972

We will no longer do *Re-*, the laurels are cut.[1] Recap, resent, rehash, repeat—
they were right to baptize May a "dress rehearsal."[2] There is no Re-volution,
we no longer want to share the prefixes that moor the flight of our wills,
their overflow dissolving our powers. Above all when these prefixes reinfect us with their sickness of the past: the tradition of the worker movement, their stupid idea of change; we rehash other ideas and restart civilization—the same civilization we want to forget. Changing words while
keeping the prefixes—and thus *Revolution* becomes reactionary.

That is to say that here we are not recapitulating or making a revolution.
The desired disruption can't be reduced to repainting in red, to returning
everything to its place, to paying off the debts of the proletariat—in short,
to making a revolution, a world turned upside down, showing the real
truth of its hypocritical intentions, merely turning the wheel around the
untouched center: Man, his wife, and his children.

WITHOUT LAW OR SELF

The revolutionary side only exists "in relation to": in relation to the bourgeois world against which it wants to rise up. Its existence only lays claim to
the assumed debts of the exploiters. An especially fake claim since capital
tends toward a cynicism where it drags along a growing part of the population that is mesmerized by the media. Why invoke justice, demand so-
called rights for the oppressed, when the system answers, "the real guilty
ones are the victims and not the assassins"? When, in the USA, members of
the military who are guilty of genocide, like Lieutenant Calley,[3] get called

misunderstood heroes? When we see leftist campaigns face not the incomprehension, but the actual hostility of the "people"? . . . We can't—we can no longer—count on bourgeois guilt. The revolutionary side plays the game of morality while capital cheats and wins.

To be revolutionary or not, to take it or leave it, to be in or out. Leftist superiority, the irrevocable judgment of revolutionary normality. Sacred words—*revolution* more than any other . . . It's not even about choosing between bourgeois vice or its opposite, the virtue of revolutionaries. This is what the latter hide from us, with their mythology of the "revolutionary subject," "the proletariat," and their sacrosanct "strategy": the immense number of paths unexplored, untraveled, or abandoned too early.

If we add up the tracks in question with the encompassing term *cultural revolution*,[i] we might win the respect of Leninists and the bourgeois, whatever the case may be. But we then lose the invaluable splintering of all the false alliances. We lose it because this packaging kicks off the game of representation, where they speak in the name of and in the place of the so-called totality about the results of an exploration they haven't even made. Above all, we lose hopelessly if we are blackmailed by revolutionary bias and accept the lowest common denominator: revolutionary politics as the phallic culmination of all the local organizing.[ii] This universal currency makes all strategies interchangeable; this steady compromise between ideological imperialisms consolidates the revolutionary side like gold consolidates the bourgeois side, where we can count, measure, compare the forces of each.

We have no need to measure our upheavals by this abstract universal standard, the "Revolution," which invariably lets the bourgeois see the level

---

i In *Counterrevolution and Revolt*, Herbert Marcuse uses the term *cultural revolution* to capture the protests in the United States. Respectable enough to become the theme of reflection for a great philosopher, *cultural revolution* enables "integrating the universal." Therefore, for example, the sexual revolution would only be a revolution if it becomes "a revolution of the entire human being, which converges with political morality." By affirming the cultural revolution as total against an economic-political reduction, one finds oneself again with the Totality, the "Human Being."—GH.

ii Artaud writes, regarding Art, this phrase that is also true for revolutionary politics: "Making Art is depriving a gesture of its echoes in the organism," cutting the vibrations in order to seal off what is frozen.—GH. Antonin Artaud (1896-1948) was an influential experimental writer and theater director, known for his Theater of Cruelty, who influenced writers like Jean Genet as well as Deleuze and Guattari, who took the idea of the "body without organs" from him.—Trans.

of danger—measures it, localizes it, and confines it. Instead, we should be going in all directions. Shaking off the civilizing power that tails us. Digging up the structure wherever one can undermine it. Always surprising the enemy from behind. Never being exactly where they expect. And so it becomes obvious: there is no revolutionary subject, *no subject at all*. There are historical drives that make this piece of our social skin bristle, that make that organ of our social body quiver. By breaking away from our identities, we are without limits to our passions.

Of course, at first we invoked our multiple selves against the despotic Grand Subject of History, treating them as irreducible. But when brought fully into light, this self—which they have used to scare and shame us—actually describes our real strengths, which spring up, wild and unsuspected. The trap of subjectification—which puts all of reality under the domination of the subject—vanishes. By looking at ourselves instead of hiding and whimpering, grumbling, fighting against the misery of the world, we have seen our image decompose, our self shrivel, crack, shatter into pieces thrown to the four corners of the universe right before our eyes.

CIVILIZATION: THE NERVOUS BREAKDOWN

But at the heart of its troubles the dying civilization finds an effective venom to inject in us: the arsenic of the Crisis. For minds immune to the fascisms, the wars, consumerism and other even stronger emotions, only the scene of the millennium can still control the bleeding of the old world's credibility. The form of the apocalypse is a convenient representation to give to the wish to be done with the old codes, to contain, drown, and defuse possible outbreaks.

A horror show. Strange shocks quake a fissured ground. Noxious gases escape, heralding the mysterious birth pangs that gasp from below, creating inconceivable monsters for us. In the minds of the elderly, wars without a Red Cross; for much of the youth, the end of capitalist growth and the return to an ecological prehistory. The Crisis steps up its theatrics: only pompous speech can pull together a decomposing social body in the midst of terror, and breathe the semblance of a soul into the rule of Capital.

No more controlling history. After the misfire of revolution, after the failure of the hope born after-May of fashioning a social reality by will alone, comes the great black hole "from which we will never return," the doomsday device of a crisis that no one can do anything about, even the militants advocating "human responsibility." Farewell, progress of Man, enlightened and scientific. Farewell also to his mirror image, the Revolution as pinnacle of social progress, the highest realization of humanity.[iii] Greetings to the monsters of the historical unconscious, a procession of unused pyres and slums, pyres and mysticisms, comets and regressions.

The wheel of history turns like mad, with the danger of dislocating or decentering the earth's axis. It will turn backward from now on toward a new Middle Age. The end of dialectical temporality: who would dare brag again that Crisis breeds Revolution? There's no point in acting, fighting, writing, the tragic voice screams: what will remain when the hell of Crisis is unleashed? Impossible to wish when all that remains is for the rats to find a calm corner in the ship tossed about by the hurricane. The repetition of terror, not of orgasm, takes hold.

This is what the most shocking geopolitical management is trying to establish today, a social energy crisis that could empty hearts and bodies. An extraction of the new energies unveiled by the outbreak of deconstructive desires. A good dose of collapse, of pileup, of weakening of productive forces but also of forces of desire. A grand battle in our brains on a planetary scale, and the stakes are no longer only the pumping of black gold, but also the hijacking [détournement] and—why not?—the drying up of desire.

The great multinational soft machine tries to achieve dehumanization in the face of the desiring flood, to outstrip it by eroding vital power through a brutal devaluation of hopes. A terrible branding is restored. The law of the great transcendent power, which must be terrible and imposing since in the end the supposedly orgasmic fires of consumerism have only heated up volutionary desires instead of satisfying and sedating them. Since you don't want to be sated, you will be bludgeoned [matraqués][4] by that shadowy repression emerging from nowhere, the Crisis. The thrill of the great unknown we were promised only turns out to be the forerunner of a long bed rest. The little desires are put to bed—here comes the great corpse.

We already knew that we didn't know what awaited us—and that is what inspired us. Give to this unknown the mask of the Crisis, and game over,

---

iii   The old Right joins the progressive Left in the fear of seeing their common world collapse: Louis Pauwels (*Paris-Match*, January 5, 1974) endorses Roland Leroy when he denounces "the Grand Capital . . . that completely repudiates rationalism and optimism . . . [that] develops ideologies of the end of the world . . ." (*Nouvelle critique*)—G.H. Pauwels (1920–97) was a French journalist and editor. Roland Leroy (1926–) is a French journalist and Communist politician—Trans.

the enemy exorcized. Tragic superiority and historical fatalism—those old and repulsive fogeys—replace the coming attraction. The Crisis is Mr. Thiers suppressing the commune of our desires, the Versailles of difficult necessity gunning down the hopes of after-May.[5] Man is once again wolf to man—moreover, he had never ceased being a wolf according to the phony appearances of indefinite progress. You know it well, you have shouted about it enough, so what are you complaining about?

Besides, the Crisis is the ultimate cure for boredom—Viansson-Ponté's topic.[6] The refreshing and merry Crisis for those rallied by a new Bastille Day. New scam. A con trick to trap the desire for change. The final manipulation of desire for jouissance turned into desire for repression and apocalypse. Civilization and its discontents instead of liberation of flux. The last seduction: the multinational octopus brings you its new show, melodrama where farce failed. The face of the death drive tops off the dance of civilization. Through the looking glass of the end of history, our eyes do not see Alice's field of speaking flowers, but instead the bitter return toward the difficult periods of humanity.[iv]

There are also the perverts of the Crisis, those who anticipate the orgy of the great catastrophe. The old morality buried, here come the cynics, sequined and made-up, ready to drink champagne in the ruins. Decadents like Bowie, bittersweet salon queens, snobs of the latest fashion, who come to lick the feet of the great collapse.[7] Confusing decryption and decadence, apostles of the fin de siècle trend of an end of world ideology, they turn the call for the transversal into a scandal in the halls of the Académie française. They get the nervous pleasure of believing in their elegance during the crisis of civilization. Glorifying the corrupt. In short, just another way of re-attaching to the civilized world and its fantasies. Even if it means playing the unworthy children, wasteful heirs participating in the furious potlach of the collapse of values: debilitating and egotistical claim of being the last debauchees, and not the first mutants.

Enough of the hopeless ones easily softened by their own fates. Ex-militants doomed to getting high joylessly, who have already seen every-

---

iv   A good echo that truly sets the tone of the current campaign, by way of denial: regarding the crisis, Olivier Guichard writes, "We see a constipated moralism bloom again, similar to the one that saw fit to say that in 1940 the invasion came to punish us for our collective sins. Today, scarcity will come to punish the sensualists"—GH. Olivier Guichard (1920–2004) was a French Gaullist politician—Trans.

thing but not lived at all. In their own eyes, born too late in a world too old—already an old tune. Ridiculous like children born late to that elderly couple, fascism and fashion. In a new 1929, we have new Cocteaus; it's once again "Surprise me, Jean,"[8] without surprise but drunk with remorse. Pleasure is reclaimed from failure by those who find themselves agreeably kept by the future fascisms, failed copies of a Maurice Sachs[9] or of those women shaved by the Liberation, swimming in caviar that tastes like ashes. Images only good for selling the idea of "no longer believing in anything," as if it were a question of belief. Not beyond, but on this side of Good and Evil. The allure of an unhappy consciousness nurturing its unhappiness with the pleasure of dancing on the volcano. Such is the libidinal charm of the fascism cropping up today.

But why bother enjoying the leftovers and burning their ships in the final party of ressentiment? We are talking about going elsewhere, leaving the ideological rot still studded with glitter; splitting, no longer giving in to the civilized neuroses tasting of angst. The fumes of the contemporary nervous breakdown only affect weak heads. That doesn't mean taking pleasure in the chance of being born during an epoch doomed to decay. On the contrary, let's speak, let's take action, let's cut into this flaccid reality of twentieth-century daily life. Let's get rid of the embittered implications heavy with meaning that give our actions the perfume of disillusioned, aged youth. Putting on makeup, dancing, making love, should not imply merging into the sickening slime of the suffering of the final days.

FOLLOWING MAY

Leaving behind the choice between a revolutionary moralism and the affectation of the new libertines—such is, for the author, the question posed by this book right now. The articles that make it up are so many attempts to tear away the ruptures of a daily life outside the Law from the dictatorship of revolutionary superiority. Prism of one path among others, multiple trails littered with sparks of an enduring May. We don't want to come back to these trails, like a dog retracing its steps to smell the places where it has pissed. Moreover, we don't want to unfurl pretentiously the dialectical red carpet of consecutive states of consciousness that lead toward some more general truth over the grand staircase of progress. The following sketches work by erasures, bumps, resets. Thus, no single direction, and above all not the rancid result of sneering disenchantment where desire dissolves.

Yes, with this multiplicity (presented here only in part) we want to kill the god Revolution, bring an end to the use of a single Will whose giantlike strength would come from giving up all kinds of little desires. The will of a battering ram to break down the largely mythical center of a Capital more supple than its enemy (the revolution is always stuck in the previous war). Instead, these thousands of little desires, partial drives, tiny obsessions, will remake the world for us with jouissance at its head.

No, we don't believe that the new scarcity makes our volutions obsolete, except to infantilize them with the paltry leftovers of superfluous decadence. There is nothing to be learned from the talk about consumerism, nothing special in the discussion of the Crisis, if not to learn new possibilities of transversal invention. And it's not by cutting back after having faked an opening that they will keep us prisoners. If we experience jouissance and luxury without bitterness, who cares about the price of gas? To stir up the forces of the imagination, there is no need to believe in a society of abundance.

———————

Here we see the after-May as a multiple life change. The after-May of fawns[10] is made of leaps in all the fields of the possible, not in faithfulness to a fixation. It is an after without a backward glance at a May, otherwise well-behaved, a horny myth notwithstanding—without kids' nightmares about the Crisis. It's like a summer afternoon.

There likely remains in this book a manner of writing in order to persuade, chock full of exemplarity, a utilitarian and not very orgasmic habit of writing that broadly renews the law of the revolutionary signifier. There is an editorial *we* implicit in these texts, since none of them could have been written, debated, revised without the existence of the militant groups, the leftist journals, the people with whom I live. And this *we* hollers its convictions with an urgent tone, with the obvious desire to rally. The way this voice speaks here, piling up naïvetés, it bursts out in multiple positions. Thus there are two ways of taking these pages: either by seeking out the order of causes and of consequences, the logic of convictions, or even the fictive unity of a self; or by consulting them like the pages ripped out of a diary, guiding oneself by intuitions, images, sensations, on a disorderly course like the swirls [*volutes*] of flames they might feed.

JANUARY 1974

01 Black November

There are deaths covered with the red roses of remembrance, such as Gilles Tautin's or Pierre Overney's;[1] overdoses without flowers or wreaths; deaths inside the four walls of the prison. In 1972, when the following article was written, a sensational series of suicides in prisons shook the leftist belief that we only die at the enemy's hands.

Deaths on behalf of the revolution, it seems, must be preferred to "private" deaths, without name and without future. As if, in its own way, the revolution enshrines the civilized Moloch,[2] about whom we never speak, other than building it new statues along the royal road of sacrifices: dedicated to the memory of generations to come who will no longer need suicide, where repression will no longer kill.

Revolution and Death: these two institutions meet at Père-Lachaise[3] with their sculptural faces, a tragedy for the civilized, who are happy to rediscover the collective heritage of humanity. The same refrain, the same capital letters serving new causes. God is always there to make sure nothing disturbs the magnificent arrangement of sacrificial, spectacular Death, distant but respected like the beyond.

Here begins the brashness of approaching god to watch his oneness decompose into countless aspects. Sometimes funny deaths, like this friend in a community who invites the neighbors over on the day when he throws himself from a roof; sometimes arousing deaths, like a spasm of too powerful orgasms; sometimes dreamy deaths . . . There is no longer "one" Death, not even an individual death, which would be like the mark of one's uniqueness, but thousands of deaths tangled up in other drives. The Death that shows up for a meeting with History is finished: instead deaths at every turn, every moment, fragmented deaths, lived one hundred times, scattered beyond the people for whom they are no longer even the judgment and the end.

The recurrence of these suicides in prison leans toward a death made banal, de-civilized, like for a masochistic Sade:[4] a shred of an event passes through us, cracked into a thousand pieces.

Don't lose time turning the other cheek, and other accommodating
tricks. If you seek a seat your size, death will fit like a glove.
JACQUES RIGAUT, *Écrits*

We don't want to depart before putting ourselves at risk; as we go,
we want to take with us Notre-Dame, love, or the Republic.
JACQUES RIGAUT, "Je serai sérieux comme le plaisir . . . ,"
in *Agence générale du suicide*

Youth of 1972, it is not certain that you will ever grow old.[5] Where are those
who told us only a few years ago, "You'll see, you'll get old and wear a tie,
you will settle down . . ."? Well, rather than accept the vile law of required
aging, more than one of us today feels the morbid and comforting flower of
the suicidal dream growing inside, both poisonous and beloved. Others become immobilized, hold their breath as if stuck and stalled, weighted down
with the need for everything to stop, already frozen by this unsettling voice
that whispers in our waking nightmares: being caught like this, before it
all blows over, while the backwash of May can still be read on our tortured
faces. Let history be framed like a snapshot that still captures us in a heroic
gesture the day after an eve of revolution.

Still others have already felt the very gentle suppression of desires, the
softening of a drift that ends by scuttling at port. They have gradually sunk
into the silent abysses. Like a film that slows down and puts you to sleep . . .
This film is *Repeated Absences* by Guy Gilles,[6] where our brother sinks into
himself like this. They call it "drugs."

Even a year ago, more than one leftist saw the suicides of young prisoners as merely the hideous failing of a penitentiary system that ought to be
denounced in its own right. And indeed, this reaction—since this was a reaction, not an action—while understandable, is nonetheless unfortunate.
It is an essentially individual reaction, while everyone knows the problem
is to unite to win . . . Thus, I can't stop myself from restating the sharp concern I had for these prisoners who died by suicide, and for one of them in
particular, Gérard Grandmontagne.[7] I can't stop myself from noticing that
around me the principal leftist "activity" that remains for us in this time
relates to his and these other suicides.

Yes, today, a chain of suicides inextricably binds us to those who injured themselves, hung themselves, killed themselves in prison. Otherwise, we wouldn't even dare to speak of them. We have dreamed too much, we walk on a carpet made from the scales fallen from our eyes.

We have torn off, one by one, the Nessus tunics we wore.[8] And every time we undress some more, a bit of our flesh is taken away too.

We have desired politics. Politics tainted us, chewed us up, and spit us out, and we've torn it out like an overly invasive cancer. After-May, the outgrowths of willful leftism [*gauchisme volontaire*] were too heavy to bear.[9] Farewell Trotskyism, anarchism, Maoism, awkward constructions of badly raised adolescents; shameful, poorly masked desires for power. Many countries, entire continents have sunk within our memory: the Algeria of the war, Mao's China, Vietnam, have all passed like express trains, in the thundering sound of bombs and brawls. We've hardly had time to bring our fantasies to these countries before they've left us. Boumédiène reigned, Nixon visited Peking, peace begins tomorrow in Vietnam.[10] It might be horrible to say, but had these legendary lands only existed in our imagination, it wouldn't have made a difference to us . . .

So we sought to live while fighting, not to fight in order to hide our lives. But we spoke about the life we wanted to build. Indeed, in each one of our communes, a different disguise has fallen off. We have torn the fabric of the family, the shameful little secrets that let them live in private until everything became public. But the throat dries out from too much talking; wanting to say everything, we find that perhaps we have nothing to say. And the communes split up, and we leave a bit less armored. We imagine ourselves to be completely naked. We were discovering our bodies, that's the truth, we finally got to the bottom: desire! This time, we were there: women, homosexuals . . . That song already bores us, the nursery rhyme we all can recite from memory. Sure, that's all true: but we don't just live off truth, here and now. And when, as a homosexual, I rediscover every day that I don't like or desire homosexuals, like a frightened insect that buzzes and slams itself against the window, I panic . . . Not too much, of course. But still, was it worth it, all of that?

That could only be the fruit of the unrepentant narcissism of disappointed militant leftists, the archaic dream of a literature of the self. But still, suicide was taboo. There were always enough reasons to hope. Leftists, communists, bourgeois, everyone still agreed to say that tomorrow would be pink, red, and self-managed. From the *Year 01*, dear to Gébé,[11] up to the new society of Chaban,[12] there were plenty of brighter futures.

Yet, today, suicide spreads itself across the front pages of the newspapers.

But what is the death drive except the individual returned to the self and even nurturing its anxieties—a horrible and mournful Oedipus? The dear little Ego flares up and contorts itself, earthworm dug up by May's shovel. The fear of death, they explained to us, makes it so that each person, reduced to their own ego's perspective, feels weaker and more ephemeral than the social institutions that surround them. Perhaps this is what we are all suffering today: we have beaten our fists and heads against the walls of bourgeois society; we were injured before knowing if we had even shaken them. Everything is always there every day. And we have so little time . . . Of course, it is only I who die. Nothing dies around us: one cop replaces another, the modernist prof replaces the old asshole at the Sorbonne, the industrial psychologist replaces the foreman. But as long as a group stronger and longer lasting than the surrounding institutions doesn't exist, it will be this way. We have yet to build the grave of Oedipus, where our personal anxieties vanish. And if Oedipus doesn't perish, it's we who will kill ourselves.

The sewers overflow, carrying along the badly digested chunks of our history of the last four years. And not only for us, but for all of those touched by the hope of May, sometimes long after. Perhaps we will discover a community unlived until now: for the leftists, frustration was just a strategic opportunity to seize, a rallying cry to broadcast, a stage to complete, and they knew all the ins and outs. For the youth of Argentré—remember the suicide there two years ago—for the bikers of the Bastille, for the drunks working at Renault, frustration was something entirely different. Not "the hope of another life," or of another society, but impotent rage against society, without the compensations of the leftist imaginary. This time, we don't even have *Sick and Tired*,[13] with its pretty capital letters and slogan. Quite simply, we've had enough. Just like with drugs, it's already been said . . . it was progressive because it was collective, transgressive insanity, schizo—who knows? . . . Today, we find out it is perhaps also simply the desire to disappear: everything mixes into a cocktail given in honor of Morpheus-Thanatos.

Then here we all are in it together, a chain of suicidal people, strayed from our direction, lost to the revolution, our dreams thinned out in preparation for the grand winter that begins.

ACTUEL, NO. 26, DECEMBER 1972

02 Cultural Revolution

May, *the 1960s, just like a sack dress or a song by Frank Alamo.*[1] *And the 1960s are over, except for the revivals. For a long time, the reference to the events of May has been ambiguous. So much so that we must actually wonder: Was May the birth of an "opposition"? Or was it the end of something, like a final somersault?*

Enough references to May. Enough costumes forced on this miserable month. Enough exalting interpretations—for the greater good, of course. The text of Action,[2] *even if it announced the end of the rule of law's monopoly of violence, is as fraught with a certain foolishness of May.*

Students, the conscience of the nation. Revolutionary rags waved like in a Godard film.[3] *The red flag, the general strike, CRS-SS:*[4] *a wide, faded range that only lets you glimpse the face of after-May with difficulty, trying to reconstruct it—just see the distortions between this text and the next. May is closer to the nineteenth century than to us in many respects, and we don't have to hide it just because the bastards say it too. Perhaps the last insurrection to unfold following the old schema that goes from tragedies to comedies: incitement-repression-revolution, student-ignited and workers on strike.*

The day after May, the orthodox Leninists announced their delight: they had said that your dad's Marxism was over, but here it is again, reappearing with the red standard flying over the universities. However, it's a pyrrhic victory: against modern capitalism it asserts an older tradition from a safer territory, the Paris of the barricades, from the cobblestones to the Place de la République and from the Sorbonnes to the Billancourts . . .

Perhaps also the last humanist revolt: the students dressed in disinterestedness and bravery, even in the media's eyes. The respectability of the movement, stuck on self-defense, which will abandon the Katanga people[5]*—since they don't fight for theoretical values. The students of May valiantly take up obsolete beliefs once again: Man against the machine, the lavish ideal against dirty materiality. A race long extinct from the university departments where from now on cynicism teems.*

Therefore, the discontinuity comes no doubt from after-May, breaking with the secular chain that links 1848 to 1871, 1871 to 1936, and 1936 to 1968.[6] *Discontinuity is primarily the failure of May. Not that we should redo it better, but rather do something else. In the after-May, May hangs about for too long with its glorified injured face, exhausting itself in desperately protecting a myth that frays, a superficial agreement about a common origin. The different leftists consider themselves brothers; they don't stop taking count of the family agreements and disagreements on the basis of a strengthened revolutionary certainty. Elsewhere, underneath, slinks a long and sinuous crack, which will end up separating those that remain preserved in May and those that drift in the after-May.*

Students, those old adolescents with zits and glasses, have spawned an antiquated, pubescent revolution. Of course, May is also action committees:[7] *demanding everything, right now—but an everything without content, a "real life" filled with photocopiers and general assemblies. And also, let's say it, a sexual repression without end, at most livened up by those obligatory dirty jokes. May's sex is pretty sad, with the head of a Wolinski drawing.*[8]

The joys of May: across the front page of the newspapers the always defeated toy soldiers play, counting on transforming the "military defeats" into "political victories," while trying to gamble on the compassion of a paternalistic society. It's a matter of politics, in this series of mirror images with false windows. Everything is political, they claim, as if the fact of giving everything access to the sacred field of politics were a win.

In reality, May is a sensible political protest, which explains the easy victory of the Communist Party. Even if the bourgeoisie continues to fear its memory, for us May is over.

....

WHY WE FIGHT

The press and the radio told you: hundreds of troublemakers interrupted the operation of the university. The press and the radio told you: these people are outside agitators. The press and the radio told you that hundreds of the "enraged"[9] made violence reign in the Latin Quarter, and thus prevented serious students from working in peace. *The press, the radio lied to you.*

Peyrefitte and the ministers lied to you.[10]

It wasn't for fun that the students clashed with the riot police [*les gardes mobiles*], helmeted and armed to the teeth. It wasn't for fun that the students met with police violence during exam time.

It is never for fun that one fights against a stronger force.

For years, students protested against the authoritarian measures that the government wanted to force on them. In calm times, they *protested* against the Fouchet reform, against the Peyrefitte measures.[11] In calm times, but also times of general indifference: for years, those in power ignored their protests just as they ignored the workers' protests. For years, this protest remained in vain, unheeded.

Today, the students *resist*.

Their only crime is to refuse a University whose only aim is to train the bosses of tomorrow and the willing tools of the economy. Their only crime is to refuse an authoritarian and hierarchical social system that denies any radical opposition; their crime is to refuse to be the servants of this system.

This sole crime got them beaten by police and put in prison.[12]

If the college and high school students have mobilized, if they have faced repression, it's because they wanted to *defend themselves* against police repression and bourgeois power. The students act in *self-defense*.

They want you to believe that this is only a few solitary agitators letting off steam, who, of course, come from Nanterre.[13] All the evils come from Nanterre. Power is clutching at straws: the "troublemakers" from Nanterre aren't, have never been, solitary. Otherwise how do we explain that, across all of Europe, the students are demonstrating? General causes bring forth general unrest.

To stop the student revolt, chopping off Nanterre would not be enough: the revolt born today in Paris knows no boundaries; in Berlin thousands of students have thwarted a strong and reactionary state power. The SDS (Socialist German Student League) was also nothing but a few agitators to them:[14] today it represents the only grand opposition movement to the fascistization of West Germany. In Italy, thousands of students have asserted their right to challenge the social system. To violent repression, they responded with demonstrations that were even more violent than those that took place last Friday. In Spain, in England, in Brazil, in Louvain, across Europe and the world, students have confronted the forces of the bourgeois order in the street. Everywhere, including Paris, the violence of the repression has shown that the governments fear these movements, so weak in appearance, but which have begun to shake the existing order. However, the press campaigns have attempted to separate and to discredit the movements: if the student revolts occupy the newspapers' first page, it's not due to the journalists' soft spot for them. If anything, they only seek to make the hate campaign proportionate to the potential danger the current order faces.

THE SAME BATTLE

In Paris and in Nanterre, they don't fight alone; they don't only fight for themselves. In Germany on May Day, tens of thousands of students and workers met up *together* at the instigation of the SDS in the first anticapitalist demonstration that Berlin has seen since Nazism. The "few agitators" became a mass movement. Those who fight against the capitalist university find themselves beside those who fight against capitalist exploitation.

In France, we know that our battle has just begun; we know that the youth are sensitive to the capitalist crisis, to the crisis of imperialism that oppresses in Vietnam, Latin America, throughout the third world. In Redon, in Caen, young workers violently rose up—more violently than us.[15] This the press let pass silently—the same press that attacks us today. In spite of the state, in spite of the silence and the manipulations of a press at its service, our fights will converge with theirs.

Today students are aware of what is expected of them: to become the executives of the current economic system, paid to make it work better. Their battle involves all the workers, because it is also their fight: they refuse to become professors in the service of an education that chooses the children of the bourgeoisie and eliminates others; sociologists manufacturing slogans for the electoral campaigns of the government; psychologists charged with making the teams of workers function according to the best interests of the boss; executives tasked with enforcing against the workers a system to which they too are subjected.

The young workers, high school and college students, refuse the future that today's society offers them; they refuse unemployment, ever more threatening; they refuse today's university, which only gives them an ultraspecialized training without value; which, under pretext of "selection," reserves knowledge for the children of the bourgeoisie; which is only a tool of repression against all the ideas that don't conform to the interests of the dominant class.

When the youth revolt with violence, they know they make this refusal clearer and more obvious; they know that their battle will only succeed if the workers understand the significance and make it their own. That's why we continue today; that's why we call on you.

ACTION, NO. 1, MAY 7, 1968

....

May '69: end of May's action committees. Their remnants in the university depart-ments form "Base Groups." In the meantime, we discovered two words in China, "Cultural" Revolution, which seem to capture the after-May better. It's also the end of de Gaulle.[16] *The new presidential election was between Poher and Pompidou.*[17] *May's actors had already left the stage. Big "politics" showed itself for what it is, a repressive splintering of "revolutionary" action.*

....

THE CULTURAL REVOLUTION DOESN'T JUST HAPPEN

May '69 is the televised caricature of May '68: electoral sparring instead of class struggle, the choice of a new representative of power instead of the fight against power. The traditional political stage, where mediocre and outdated actors put on a show, completely masks the reality of the revolt of the masses.

Since de Gaulle = May—in other words, for the bourgeois unconscious, a confused and awful blend of an authoritarian State and the revolt against all institutions—bourgeois politicians are trying to make us believe in a return to the blessed era where a true division of powers was reflected in Parliament. That's why Poher is the rotten fruit of May; and Pompidou, re-made in Poher's image, is the doubly rotten fruit of June, bringing us the

Grenelle Accords with the French Communist Party (PCF), along with more repression.[18] History only repeats itself as farce. The bourgeoisie hopes that this temporary fix will allow them to maintain their domination until the integration of Europe, the only mythical future that it can envision: drowning one or two European revolutions in the European order. Pompidou and Poher, Marcellin and Edgar Faure,[19] the threat of force and the silly use of deception—never again will the French bourgeoisie escape this vicious circle. Losing their last illusions along with de Gaulle, the French bourgeoisie showed itself for what it was: caught between imperialisms that are too powerful for it. On a world scale, it is no more than a haunted petite bourgeoisie: beware the ideas of May!

Our project is to refuse the "grand politics," the shape and form of bourgeois domination; to systematize the new ideas that appeared in May; to strengthen our revolutionary forms of anticapitalist struggle. In May, the masses refused to limit their activity to what their enemy defined as politics or what the unions defined as demands. Before even knowing what agenda they fought for, the workers occupied their businesses, the students their departments. Thus they cast off managerial and academic authority. The "agenda" that the PCF, the business unions, and certain University groups forced on the movement of May was only a mask on the face of the proletarian revolution. The revolutionary activity of the masses has begun to operate in all areas: ideas, customs, habits of life, institutions. Students and workers have struck head-on the bourgeoisie's stronghold: the ideas that centuries of bourgeois domination have entrenched. The idea of the *cultural revolution* doesn't just happen. Today, the path of cultural revolution is:

- in the university, to fight, not for everyone's access to bourgeois knowledge, an impossible dream that reinforces submission to this knowledge, but for the destruction of bourgeois ideas;

- in businesses, to fight not only for a new organization of labor, but also against the bourgeois conception of labor as a separate activity (from "politics," from "private life," from "leisure"). The restoration of the bourgeois ideas and system in the so-called socialist countries has taught us that by only attacking the bourgeois State apparatus and neglecting what supports and underlies it in ideas and institutions, we halt the revolutionary process and we prepare the counterrevolution.

Cultural revolutionization breaks with strategies that reproduce the image of past revolutions. In a world marked by the collapse of imperialism, the crisis of bourgeois ideology at the heart of imperialist metropolises, the appearance of revisionism as a complement to bourgeois domination, the only revolutionary path today is the path of cultural revolution, the finally discovered form of proletarian power, just as it was launched in China.

The cultural revolution is a struggle for power. It aims to establish proletarian power throughout: the question of central power, of local power, of the style of leadership, of customs, of morals, of ideas. The cultural revolution—the only social revolution possible today under the conditions in which the bourgeoisie uses its power—will only succeed with the destruction of the bourgeois state. In France, there is no longer a first step along the way that will lead to the dictatorship of the proletariat; we must take on all the tasks at the same time, or give up trying to accomplish any.

RÉVOLUTION CULTURELLE, NOS. 1–2, JUNE 1969

....

May '70: the revolution is either all of life, or it's nothing. The distinction between private and public life is the source of all our troubles. However, while the Maoists set themselves up in the factories, some ex-students from Censier and some workers from Renault, more or less unemployed, attempt living together. Leading to three essential updates.

———————

First, domesticity, in Fourier's sense, emerges as the key to politics and to the public. Or rather, the interpellation of the private by the public-political, and vice versa, proves to be as effective as on March 22 (when everything had already begun with a tale of hookups in the Nanterre dorm).

Another break to discover behind pompous terminology: "fusion of revolutionary masses." Language that tends to restore a strategic totality, a method of democratic Leninism named Maoism. But which also entails the critique of politics as a fusion of the vanguard, of representatives. Implementing direct communication. Setting up particular circuits, particular fluxes not encoded in revolutionary strategy.

What might in fact turn out to be dangerous: the student-worker communes dramatically split. But at least we refused the stereotyped forms of political society: we ask intellectual men, spokesmen for the proletariat, "Where are you speaking from?" By ignoring the convenient assignments that only immobilize a fluid reality and make the sanitizing megaphone of political consciousness necessary in order for a pseudoworker to be able to speak to a pseudostudent.

Third update: the most important, without a doubt, is what kind of civilization we are talking about from now on. A current flows from the fight for civilization, in the sense that young Americans speak of Youth Culture,[20] to the Fourierist critique. Wildness: radical critique (uprooting) of civilization, absolute deviation, as long as we avoid the political reinterpretations of it. No doubt a certain after-May begins here.

....

TO CHANGE LIFE

The meaning of the European cultural revolution does not leave any of the bourgeois institutions and morals outside the critique of the masses. Whoever isn't moving forward in this area is inherently moving backward, and paves the way to revisionism in safeguarding the unchallenged domain where the bourgeoisie exerts control. An example: the critique of the family, which the practice of the *crèche sauvage* would have been able to establish, has not even been tackled.[21] The parental function, pillar of oppression, has not been called into question for tactical reasons (it's necessary to have parents on your side to preserve the *crèche sauvage* against the administration).

What threatens the attempts of revolutionary practice on this or that aspect of bourgeois life is their scattering: when they haven't been repressing them, the revolutionary groups and militants that make up the revolutionary Left have been incapable until now of synthesizing these scattered revolts. When we don't talk about the family, medicine, psychiatry, we settle for allowing bourgeois ideas and morals to survive; we condemn ourselves to turning revolutionaries into their opposites, into protectors through neglect or laziness of the habits that have embedded the rule of the bourgeoisie.

With regard to daily life, too many comrades shrink from tackling the problems with the necessary spirit of revolt. Too often, because they are good comrades, we shrink from critiquing such and such method of obviously reproducing those of the dominant class. We thus demonstrate liberalism and the kind of contempt of the masses conveyed by a pedagogical misunderstanding inherited from the bourgeoisie, summed up in this phrase: "There will always be time to tackle that later." (Later = after the revolution. But which revolution? Made by whom?)

Example of the principle, "Who does not move forward moves backward": the issue of the destruction of the University. Some advanced groups of the revolutionary Left have destroyed the credibility of knowledge and the university's operating procedure; but, as we can tell, the destroyed university reproduces itself every day in disenchanted indifference and cynicism; in the academic departments, it drags on and it rots. Students no longer go to classes; or if they go, they make paper airplanes or sleep. After four or five experiments of transforming their course into a mini-AG,[22] more than one leftist lecturer has become a systematically embittered sneerer who no longer believes in anything. Out of weariness, the University has returned through the back door, for example the door for student presentations. The university has diarrhea, but it shits itself and bathes in it. It is only truly destroyed for those dozens of individuals who have permanently quit.

What went wrong is that the militants believed it was enough to say, *let's destroy the university*, without explaining to the student masses that it wasn't a phase, but a part of the strategic revolutionary project. In a way, they gave the impression that it was necessary to begin by destroying the obstacle that separated students from the reality of class struggle, the institution of the university; then they'd be able to join the worker and peasant struggles, which would have at the same time separately destroyed their own oppressive institutions. This is how at the university the revolutionary enthusiasm of May partially mutated into its opposite, generalized disgust. We ought to be able to show to students who are becoming revolutionized that the destruction of the university is also the concern of workers, and the destruction of the factory is also the concern of students; to show that the fusion of revolts partially precedes the destruction of the institutions that separate them; to show at last that the revolution begins every day with the ability to do something else besides hanging out on the lawns of Censier and Nanterre, without this something else limited to being a militant for a few hours a week.[23]

What threatens us in our tasks of revolutionization and synthesis of scattered revolts is not only indifference and liberalism, reproducers of the bourgeois system of oppression. It is also the distorted image given to the *cultural revolution* when it is reduced to an *individual moral development* of the militant. There are people who can speak of the cultural revolution and give this expression a content that is perfectly repressive, not to mention counterrevolutionary. For us, the cultural revolution does not mean the ideological struggle to repress the bad instincts of the radicalized petit-bourgeois student, who could then be transformed into the exact copy of the ideal communist militant. This image of the ideal communist militant they want us to identify with carries along with it all the qualities given to the working class through revisionism: discipline, spirit of sacrifice, etc.

In Italy, the group that has pushed this line the furthest is the Unione comunista italiana, an example that militants in all the European countries ought to consider.[24] The militant becomes the plaything of organization, the principal problem becomes individual transformation, the central keyword is "to serve the people" and, in order to serve them, to identify with the image one has of them: marital fidelity, consistency at work, etc. In the line defended by Liu Shaoqi, Mao attacked "individual perfectionism of the communist," the replacement of the glorification of revolt with submission to a pseudomodel of proletarian life.[25] Militants are first separated from the masses and then trained for obedience and self-repression.

The experience of comrades from Censier at Renault-Billancourt is highly revealing:[26] the violent debate they had with other comrades revolved around being criticized for having organized as groups in an attempt at beginning collective life alongside worker comrades. Two assumptions ground this out-of-date Marxist-Leninist analysis:

1   Life in groups separates militants from the masses, transforms the political group into a discussion group [groupe affectif].[27]

2   A revolutionary student who refuses to work in the factory like the workers, to "settle themselves" [s'établir] (a telling term for the protection thereby procured) is merely a progressive petit bourgeois.[28]

In our view, this reasoning that many revolutionaries still accept is the final refuge of the French Khrushchev-China supporters.[29] It is marked by politicism [politisme]; that is, by the assumption that there is an absolute break between politics (meetings, photocopying, putting up posters, etc.) and daily life. People don't only live off of meetings—the rest of the time they go home to their spouses, legal or not, to the cinema, and engage in social relations. The militant is therefore cut off from the masses during most of life. The two paths available to us today are clear: change the individual through inoculation with the proletarian vaccine that will immunize them, through a fantastical self-repression, against their own desires; or else change the situation and relations within the group and between the group and the masses.

In the context of the fight "against egoism," the Italian Unione has gone so far as to demand that young workers work more in order to enable the old to respect their pace; some French comrades have gone so far as to glorify the formative quality of factory discipline and assembly-line work. As far as we're concerned, the expression "sharing the life of the masses" ought to be abandoned for the slogan "sharing the revolt of the masses." We students and revolutionary workers want to break with the image of the disciplined working class, the love child of revisionism and of the dominance of capital.

The positive contribution of those who begin as a student but come to deny their identity as a student over the course of the revolutionary process is not to become one more of the oppressed at the factory. Students do not have to repeat the whole cycle of proletarian oppression in order to become revolutionary. Their role is to contribute their experience of revolt in fusion with militant workers; to advance their revolt through coming into contact with the place where all forms of revolt are concentrated, since that is also where the bourgeoisie keeps up the divisions that uphold oppression concentrated at the highest point. The problem of settlement [*la question de l'établissement*] is resolved through our struggles and not from a petit-bourgeois guilty conscience.

At the factory, they revolt against everything. That's why the student revolt has to bring something as well in its fusion with the worker revolt; we refuse to give up on the revolutionary content of the student struggle and to consider it only a reservoir of future "settlers" [*de futurs "établis"*]. We also refuse to sequester the student revolt in a separate movement, one whose links with the worker revolt are infinitely deferred by a top-down merger of a partial strategy with an overarching one, orchestrated by a few leaders tied to proletarian labor. Examples of the fusion of student revolts in the crucible of the factory include, on the issue of medicine, what was accomplished by Italian *medical* students alongside the workers at Fiat against the hazardousness of the job and against class-based medicine.[30] This could also be done through the critique of bourgeois justice in an effort to establish the principle that "the workers ought to make their own justice." The experience in Meulan, where comrades dealt with the trafficking of migrant workers by attacking the town hall,[31] should have been supported by mass propaganda, but still it points the way. The fight against the hoax surveys, administered by sociology students at Censier along with researchers, developed from organizing a response to the survey on leisure activities that the Renault management wanted to conduct at Billancourt. In the factory, division is the main motto of the bourgeoisie: division between migrants and French workers, between categories, between students and workers, between work, transportation, and leisure, divisions held up through revisionism.

Each of these divisions tends to separate out revolts; to reduce the struggle to the economic level; to justify, for example, the system of degradation of the metro (cattle wagons + advertising = passivity) as a cutting of losses in order to share power with the revisionism inside the factory. Our struggle is aimed at the social division of labor and not at one institution that would itself be the key to it.

We can't reject the social context that the bourgeoisie imposes—whether on students, workers, or other oppressed groups—through the assimilation of all of the oppressed groups into the working class, nor through the coexistence of separate groups that deny their social future in isolation, but only through militant fusion. Revisionism doesn't reproach revolutionaries for being mostly students so much as for being fake students; just as there now exists a large number of fake workers, that is to say, true revolutionaries. Revolutionization challenges all of the social statuses of the different oppressed groups, not through their assimilation to the ideology that revisionism designates under the name "working-class consciousness," but through the fusion of revolts toward the revolution. From now on, the essential task for revolutionaries is to identify the split between the revolutionary side and the bourgeois side. They can't do it as sociologists: they know that Marxism identifies different classes through their position in the struggle and not through the pseudo-objective analysis whose fatal effects we saw in May (each faction's misunderstanding of a student revolt that thwarts all of the patterns).

The very term *proletariat* ought to be reexamined in light of May. The students who fused with the revolutionary workers were a part of the proletariat insofar as the proletariat is essentially the class of those who have only their chains to lose and a world to win. The proletarian point of view is the point of view of the fusion of social groups in the struggle against oppression. The contradictions that remain within the revolutionary camp are secondary contradictions. The French situation of 1970 charges us with the same work of strategic creativity that Mao faced with the peasant problem in China; this grounds our refusal of *out-of-date Leninism*. Leadership of the revolutionary camp doesn't occur through the mode of manipulation; there is no symmetry between the two sides; the crisis of humanity does not come down to the crisis of the revolutionary leadership as the Trotskyists believe.

The leadership of the proletariat in the revolutionary struggle is not the leadership of the working class, as the revisionists and neo-revisionists have described it, over a set of petit-bourgeois and peasant groups. In the time of the cultural revolution, identifying who the enemy is can no longer be done through the inherited framework of preceding revolutions: the divide between revolutionaries and the side of the bourgeoisie extends through certain groups considered up to now to be unified. The side of the bourgeoisie reveals itself in the struggle and includes, for example, the revisionists (despite their label of *worker* so respected by the Trotskyists) or, in the academic departments, the segment of the faculty that refuses to challenge their role of teacher-cop.

Numerous students have nothing to lose but their chains, since they consider from now on their social future (positions associated with bosses, teacher-cops, psy-copogist, copologists, . . .) as a prison. Numerous workers have definitively broken their ties to their work; more and more, young workers refuse to seek their way out by climbing the hierarchy. The imperialist ideology of social climbing is broken for them: they will not agree to practice bootlicking, they don't imagine themselves becoming overseers. The escape from limitations no longer occurs through rising in the institution, but through challenging the institution itself. We want to be neither the oppressed nor the servants of the oppressors. The revolutionary critique of work has permeated the masses: unrest and absenteeism are the norm for young workers. The progressive standardization of jobs (all the assembly lines look alike, and all the offices as well) makes the mobility of labor, the last arm of capital (cf. development of temporary work), a complete delusion. Sabotage and the critique of labor show that in the time of imperialist collapse, revolutionary consciousness means *ruthlessness*. We don't believe that this is only a stage: the working class would make a clean sweep of its revisionist demons just to end up unchanged; the very definition of a working class determined above all by its place in the process of capitalist production is what is being challenged.

Even the revolt of small businesspeople raises the question of their revolutionization: the challenging of a system founded on exchange value came up in May in Nantes or, in certain cases, at the CID when the mutual aid among small shopkeepers destroyed the individualist foundation of their social status.[32] Certainly, the revolutionization of different groups in struggle does not move forward equally, and we aren't able to equate the revolt of truck drivers with that of the small businesspeople, or that of students, or that of factory workers. The student revolutionization has advanced the most in the fusion with worker revolutionization. The point of view of the fusion of revolts demands that we respect the different rhythms of development or else we'll reduce them to parallel antipolice revolts.

The systemization of the critique of the social division of labor, of the critique of the ideology of labor itself, is the task of the moment for revolutionaries. They must pose the question: "What will socialist labor be?" They have to demonstrate clearly through militant work how they break with the alienation that separates the producer from the product, how they break with the ideology of quantitative performance, etc.

The first duty of revolutionaries is to revolutionize themselves in their union with the revolt of the masses. The critique of the family is an unambiguous obligation. In the Chinese cultural revolution, the destruction of the relationship of oppression that subjected wives to their husbands held an important place; in the societies of Western Europe, the very existence of the family unit must be attacked. The family gives training in hierarchy through the subjection of children to parents and of the wife to the husband. It works by absorbing social conflicts whose explosive power puts capitalist society in peril. Thus, the wife will chew out her husband by accusing him of not making enough money, instead of taking on the boss. The liberation of these forces of revolt for which the family plays the role of a dampener (see the positive imagery of the domestic scene in the "popular" theater or cinema) is one of our tasks. The militant who accepts reproducing the familial model in their personal life thereby accepts showing it to the masses as the only model of life possible and imaginable.

The self-punishing ideology of individual sacrifice is not revolutionary. Revolutionaries want to march from victory to victory; they don't think that the revolution rests on the sacrifice of individuals or on their own self-repression, but on the collective transformation of situations. The sad counterfeit Maoism offered by most of the pro-Chinese groups in France has systematically sapped all the vital energy of the personality of Mao himself. The smile of Mao is frozen in enforced optimism in orthodox Marxist-Leninist publications. His eloquence is petrified into a sterile collection of formulas divorced from reality. And yet it was Mao who declared before the conference of party cadres: "Marshal Zhu De and myself have not become fat in a day"; and he added, "Ignorance is a revolutionary virtue: look at me."[33]

The current phase of revolutionization of the masses is the phase of preparation for the revolution, where the forces accumulate to carry out a revolution *to change life*. Despite revolutionary groups being late to understand the reality of the revolt, the generation of May is not yet disenchanted; proposing the centralization of these revolts scattered across all fronts points to attempts at practical organization of life. Building on this organization to pull in 90 percent of the population to the European cultural revolution is the task of the revolutionary Left.

FAIRE LA REVOLUTION, NO. 2, APRIL 1970

....

Fourier,[34] *cultivation of the new culture* [culture de la nouvelle culture]; *in May, his statue was restored at place Clichy by the barricaders of rue Gay-Lussac. The police destroyed it.*[35]

Why another "return to," even a legitimate one, next to the Lacanian return to Freud and the Althusserian return to Marx? We know what that's worth—a kind of bondage. Rediscovering certainties in the midst of falling apart. To ease, to reassure oneself, to dress oneself in orthodoxy. And, cleverly, Revel's triumph: "Isn't imagination just repetition? Isn't revolution just a rerun? The more one listens, the more one feels that way. It is always about returning to something: to Bakunin, to Marx, to Mao . . ."[36]

To each their own ancestor, to each their own nineteenth century—since that's where we always return. Except, Fourier does not appear as a tradition, but as an interruption in the rhetoric of the classroom greats. We can't return to Fourier because we've never been there; he is askew in the political continuities (Marx, Lenin, Trotsky, Mao, initiators of French pseudobolshevism) as well as in the theoretical continuities (the Fourierist resources are confusing and nonscientific compared to the Freudian or Marxist resources).

The following text argues for replacing Fourier in our pantheon. In vain— Fourier isn't going to fill a hole in Marx's system, and the reverse doesn't work either. Avoiding the infrastructure-superstructure closure, and the dialectical temporality that places him slightly before Marx, he is not the missing piece of anything and no one is what he is missing.

Nondialectical, Fourier resists when we try to think him dialectically. Untimely, he is no more assignable to the nineteenth century than Sade is to the eighteenth century. Their relationships are nondialectical, and if there is a cultural tradition here, it hardly lends itself to epistemology, but is purely intuitive, detemporalized, simultaneous like two television sets projecting their clips side by side. Thus neither before nor after, but a constellation.

Repetition and novelty, the old Maoist problem: how to make the old new? May was already caught in it and sought to take up '48, '71, and '17 dialectically.[37] *Champions of the new, modernists, technocrats, and advocates of the ever-true class struggle resentfully watch each other from one side of the battleground, where they want to force the drives to justify themselves with respect to tradition.*

CULTURAL REVOLUTION   31

Indeed, imagination might well be repetition: the repetition of an indefinitely re-producible jouissance does away with stages, the temporal progressions to climb or descend. It's well known Fourier ignored the time of strategy. Whereas the guilty feeling of the "return to" just suggests that we can never live the same joy twice over or more, but can only reinterpret by going back to the source—always and again. We must do and redo Fourier indefinitely.

....

FOURIER

Today we can no longer consider Fourier a "precursor" in the field opened by Marx. The truth is it's the other way around. We must understand that Marx takes his place within the total field opened by Fourier, where Marx explored only one of its aspects, admirably but one-sidedly.

In this way, Marx is marked by an omission, the hiding of an indivisible totality revealed by Fourier that includes in production both the economic type and something else. Something else—that is, what is generally separated from productive forces: life, desire . . . And that is why in Fourier there isn't frequent mention of economic productive forces—though it is there—nor of vertical stratification between infra- and superstructure as in Marx. Simply put, Fourier shows that we need to see production as desire and desire as production.

So, according to Fourier, how are we to understand the essence of production? It's not as commodities, nor the simple inventory of goods or riches, but as the entire movement of passions. A productive *movement* or flux drives history from its origin; it is trapped, deviated, divided, into civilization. And this is why civilization is at odds with economic development just as much as it is with the flight of passions.

The term *flux* must be understood in the sense that Deleuze and Guattari give it, which seems to suit best what Fourier means. With regard to the classifications of civilized institutions, this—or these—flux must be allowed free expression by being put back on the track of "direct growth," whereas flux has only experienced "countergrowth."

Starting with productive flux, Fourier's entire body of work achieves its unity, even with its strange, bizarre cosmogonic theory, which is only the full return to the overlooked connections binding humans to the universe. The desiring production of humans ought to be restored to the nonanthropological context of the desiring cosmic flux . . .

Thus, Fourier's notion of production is not comparable to Marx's. It is much closer to the idea, which has also started to prevail through various and often confusing means, of the necessary harmony of humans with the earth. In Marx, humans dominate Nature; this view remains in the Cartesian lineage. For Fourier, no: humans "produce," of course; they transform things and places, but always in line with the earth, without destroying it or treating it like an object of possession. The link between humans and nature is no longer the same, it is not Cartesian: the desiring productive flux passes between one and the other, and from one to the other. Marx's thought still remains dominated by a metaphysics of the subject. In Fourier, no: there is nothing but opening, and the contradictory, dominating subject fades away and disappears at the meeting point of all the irresolvable contradictions between labor-production and desire-jouissance typical of civilization.

When we say that we must relocate Marx in the field opened by Fourier and not the other way around, it means that we must abandon once and for all the idea of evaluating Fourier's concepts of production within the framework of a purely economic thought, a break that makes the growth of productive forces unintelligible and irrelevant. Of course, that is typical of bourgeois economy; but this idea persists in Marxism,[i] and is not substantially critiqued by him. Everything that concerns the relationship of desire and of production Fourier alone has taught us—and in a revolutionary economy, we will have to recognize this relationship explicitly if we don't want production to run on empty and get caught up again in the dead end of capitalism.

Therefore:

1   Civilization can be understood, according to Fourier, as a cut in the movement (or flux) of passions. A cut of flux, bypass, and loss of energy. By positing a "rationality" that is just an aberration of reason—closing "reason" to the flux that it cannot capture, and diverting reason from the universal energy-giving unity—civilization indiscriminately cuts, fragments, severs.

---

i   Indeed, the rest of the text distinguishes between "Marxism" and the living thought of Marx, still very Fourierist—GH.

Therefore, against civilization, we must:

a   reconsider what has been unlinked from the totality or the unity of its operation. This is a fundamental methodological principle for Fourier: the new achievements of "societal order"[38] should not be understood according to the breaks imposed by civilization; in the realm of production and consumption, what civilization calls "goods" and "profit" do not take into account the considerable number of losses. To understand the notion of "triple profit" that the societal order immediately introduces,[39] we need to perform a reversal that brings this negative into account. This leads to the notion of "negative profit," which consists of "producing without doing anything," from the very fact of association.[40] Savings in fuel, in workforce echoing in "positive profit": restoring forests, springs, climates, etc. Therefore, the "product" is never to be understood as simple product or simple relation of labor force to an object. It involves a liberation and new connections of energy.

b   redistribute what has been cut, and thus separated, from its place. This redistribution is the very object of the *series of passions*, which we can consider a "logic of flux" or a mathematics of continuity (from the point of view of transitions and of the infinitesimal), as well as a mode of connecting the product to productive energy. By demonstrating the autonomous and self-reproducing role of money in civilization, which brings about the absolute split between labor and its product, Fourier articulates the essence of capitalism, exactly as Marx will on this point. Another similarity: competition as essential nature of capital, as obstacle to production and to consumption (considered by him also as productive consumption).

The contradiction between the "socialistic" tendency of Fourier and the principle that maintains "classes" in societal Harmony could be resolved in the following way: the redistribution of the series of passions relies upon the system of classes that is a legacy of civilization. If redistribution sustains this system, it doesn't reproduce it, and, on the contrary, tends to make it socially ineffective by a series of "counterweights." With its own mechanism (of passions), this redistribution inhibits the operation of the civilized social machine, in which money alone, concentrated in the same hands and tending to reproduce itself (in its existence alienated from the product), assures the unconditional social power of capitalists as a class.

Capital (money) entering into the societal economy stops obeying the law of value (in Marxist terminology) since it comes from another form of circulation (in fact the only authentic, passion-based form, the circulation of flux).

2   Remaining on this point, the economic category of "circulation" cannot remain intact once we pass from civilization to societal order; and with the idea of circulation of money, Fourier describes perfectly what will become the basis for Marx's critique of political economy. If the flux of passions are obstructed, there remains in civilization only one sort of circulation, that of money. But this is only a metaphorical and inauthentic circulation. Marx will write (in *Foundations of the Critique of Political Economy* [*Grundrisse*]) that the word *circulation* relies on a false analogy with the circulation of blood, implying that the circulation of money is natural and vital, while the real characteristic of this supposed circulation is that it is alien to the social body and to the product. It separates and concentrates, separates buying from selling: buying without selling in hoarding, selling without buying in speculation, concentration in the game of bankruptcy, etc. Thus monetary circulation can only lead from "commercial anarchy" to "commercial feudalism"; it is truly an obstacle to and not an enhancer of production. The productive possibilities opened in civilization by the discoveries of material movement (the sciences) are subverted and sterilized by this type of circulation, either in their applications to the satisfaction of passions, or in their principle (misunderstanding of the unity of the Universe and of certain forms of energy: the "aromal movement").[41]

We can see how Fourier's thought is far from a simplistic interpretation that would turn its concern into the human arrangement of a world dominated by an (inhuman) technological growth. As with Marx, Fourier stays out of this form of humanism. For Marx, capital hinders productive forces by the principle of competition and the law of value. For Fourier, it is also a question of liberating production, through the implementation and the circulation of both human and material energy. For him, it is not at all a matter of returning to precapitalist or pre-industrial economic forms, even if he insists on agriculture and the household. In civilization, the home is the site where the individual or household act as consumers of a production whose process occurs elsewhere, obeying the law of exchange and of profit; agriculture, divided among families, is subjected to the demands of the market and of commercial competition. It is also the site of the greatest contradiction in terms of waste and fragmentation. In principle, we could probably regard Fourier's interpretation of economic functioning as lacking an essential element because he has not drawn out the law of value in industrial society. In terms of poverty and unemployment, he only *describes* the consequences of the manufacturing industry and of urbanization, but does not grasp the *causes*. And the privilege given to agriculture would be the result of this omission. But if we consider it from another angle, his understanding dodges an overly quick critique: precisely the angle of *liberation* and of *circulation of flux* (energy). For he perfectly describes the process of false circulation in a mercantile economy; and, if he does not exactly locate the source of valorization in industrial society, he articulates the fundamental vice of this society: the independence of labor in relation to its product. And the problem posed by this independence is not only one of the collective ownership of productive forces, nor the elimination of salaried labor. This ownership, even this elimination, only make sense and fit an authentic liberation if labor (productive activity) is reinstated as part of the *total energy of passions*, if it no longer serves as an independent economic category. This central idea is not absent in Marx, but it is not taken as a theme, and it certainly disappears in "Marxism."

On the other hand, for Fourier, restoring labor to the unity of the energy of the passions also means connecting it with the latent energy of the Universe, which is also subverted and blocked by labor fragmented and severed from its product in civilization (= transformed, from activity and satisfaction, into economic and moral category). This is why, in terms of the productive circulation of flux (energy) where Fourier is located, it is the same to say the principle is labor as it is to say that it is satisfaction (or production and jouissance).

3 Finally, this displacement of interest shows how the relationship of humans with Nature can be understood according to Fourier. Nature is the immediately totalizing operative concept that allows for an "overcoming" of classical humanism as well as of naturalism (the fatalism of the development of productive forces demanding an adaptation by changing human passions, which Fourier rejects on princi-

ple). Since he denounces the universal "prostitution" resulting from the process of monetary circulation that governs capitalism (in general, market economy), Marx is bluntly Fourierist on this point. The "value" attributed by humanism to the subjective center of the process (the human being) is their price or the exchange value of their labor power. The subjective reclaiming is the substitution of use for exchange, of "being" for "having." But a production and a society cannot give up exchanges; in their essence, they are exchange: exchange of energy, communication of passions. Here, Fourier fills in advance a place left empty, or amorphous, in Marxism. The generalized circulation of energy or of flux operates at different levels and does not leave intact the sacred notion of the subjective center, individual unit of the "human being": liberation of "aromal" fluid, restoring the course of planetary creations; appearance of new powers for humans, including biological ones; or more directly or more simply— distribution of the individual in groups, enlargement of libidinal energy in *orgies*. It is an exchange without loss, without secret individual reservation, but is in fact productive. It reveals that *the individual is not the full human being*. This doesn't mean that the individual must be absorbed into the group (the pitfall of collectivism) but that it receives from the group additional energy. Energy, desire, are in their essence transindividual.

From this, as Fourier constantly repeats, comes the motivation for the transition to the societal order, a transition that is not purely rational, and is in no way humanist or moral, but is the hope of gain—whose monetary profit is only a provisional aspect, of course, tending to dissolve and disappear in production of material and of passions.

SPEECH MADE WITH RENÉ SCHÉRER AT THE FOURIER
CONFERENCE AT ARC-ET-SENANS, IN SEPTEMBER
1972. A REPORT WRITTEN BY JEAN GORET APPEARED
IN *AUTOGESTION*, APRIL 20 – 21, 1972, ÉDITIONS
ANTHROPOS.

03 After-May Politics of the Self

Start of the school year 1970: end of the theoretical discussion's black-and-white clips.

The movement Vive la révolution (Long Live the Revolution) put out a journal to follow Action, less student oriented, and printed in color. The first edition praised workers' laziness and published the Huey Newton text giving women and homosexuals revolutionary status.[1] The big question was asked: What becomes of our desires in your revolution? To make one's self talk, one must be something of a ventriloquist. For one thing, it will be a concert of selves, quickly tired of only being selves. This regression at least allows a cutting away of revolutionary superiority, the appearance of a politics equal to our desires.

———————

In this article, I make a bit of a mess with a bunch of ideas that I wanted to discuss. Some comrades thought that in it I overlooked the "question of state power" (hey, that's serious.) In short, this isn't an overarching strategy, it's a personal approach to our new attitude. Which concerns all of us.

EVERYDAY LIFE DEPRIVATIZED BY "EVERYTHING"

WORKING IS SUFFERING

"Since Christ's coming, we are delivered not from the evil of suffering but from the evil of suffering uselessly" (Father Charles, *Jesus*, quoted by Vaneigem).[2] Socialism means to be delivered not from the evil of working, but from the evil of working uselessly. No one has yet found the trick to make work seem attractive. We can only try to forget it in part. And so, our lives are made rotten by work: What are you? Where do you work? What time do I wake up? Metro near the job.

On the Left, and even to the left of the Left, we find the solid pillars of the ideology of labor in all those who have always spoken on behalf of those who work, "dignity of workers." The bourgeois say: You must work to make money, to have appliances and cinema. Séguy[3] and many leftists respond: Ugh! It's disgusting, labor is our dignity (that is, our dignity as representatives of the labor of others). Beside those who exploit labor to take money from it, we find those who exploit it ideologically to take power from it. Word thieves.

Two years after May, almost a century after Lafargue and Pouget,[4] some leftists discovered:

1   That they don't want to take power—not them, not this power the bourgeoisie wields;

2   Less easily, that they don't want to make people work toward the building of a socialism of which they would be the grand masters. That sabotage and laziness are on the agenda of the revolution, our revolution in advanced capitalist Western Europe in the twentieth century.

We don't want to work anymore. No more producing washing machines in order to buy them, radios to groom us, objects to eat, consume, stock up, accumulate, prettify with accessories, throw away when there are too many, without ever understanding anything.

Well, all of you ergologists, ergonomists, sociologists, managers, economists of the French "Communist" Party, try again! No need to seek at any cost to plot a continuity between the world we want to build and the one you manage: "Work before just like after the revolution." Like hell! The revolution is a rupture, we won't do it again; as far as we're concerned, there will not be a socialist justice, a socialist university, socialist factories, a socialist family—the same, just painted red.

LIVING THE REVOLUTION

If revolutionaries no longer want to exploit people, they'll have to prove it, even just to themselves. Dutschke and Cohn-Bendit already said it:[5] if the revolutionaries aren't making a revolution, including in their own lives, who will believe in them? What matters isn't necessarily believing in us. The anti-leftist worker out in the sticks will kidnap the boss the following week (see Gavi's book *Workers*).[6] We know that everywhere the people rise up, they have good ideas for fighting, but often some funny overarching ideas. But we also know that the overarching ideas of leftists are often no better: transition from the bourgeoisie to the proletariat while keeping all the trappings, like in a relay race. An iron socialism with a steel dictatorship of a genuine communist party made out of reinforced concrete. We know that revolt is the root of the revolution, we want to support those who skip out on work, those who skip out on the University, those who skip out on the family.

Ah! The family, let's discuss that! But we also know that revolutionaries are no longer in revolt; they no longer know what revolt is, they have learned all too well how to talk about it. As a worker friend said, leftists have this unique feature of never speaking about their background, about their family, but always about other people's. Real vampires. We professional leftists, we the castrati of reason, we the sacrificed—we'll be useful to others in the future—but what future? Leading where?

You think I'm just being provocative! There's real generosity among those who are still long-haired leftists. That may be true, but that generation is already getting old. The few moments of true enthusiasm—a couple of demos, a couple of meetings—mostly get lost in the sclerosis of bespoke factions.

And when there's a fool who draws graffiti in front of me on the chick in the DIM pantyhose posters on the metro walls,[7] I frequently have this reaction: it's too bad that I can't take the risk of being nabbed, since I'm on standby for the revolution; if not, I'd do the same thing. But why would I need to do that? I'm already labeled a revolutionary. I've already earned my stripes.

This is the contradiction we live in: explaining the revolution to people, learning the lessons from it, makes it productive. The professional revolutionary is no less oppressed than anyone else. But the center of life is elsewhere, in compensation. There's no longer any need to rise up; the professional revolutionary already knows that they want the revolution. They've sacrificed the silent moments of their life, the dead time of anything that isn't outreach, demo, photocopying, they've written them off in the revolution's profits and losses.

This is what we no longer want to be. We want to speak from our guts. We want to say what we are, what we feel. We want to feed the revolution with our revolt. No one yet knows what relations will be established between those who have pushed the logic of revolt the furthest and those who anticipated it. We know that those who brawl with the cops every Saturday night could turn out to be racist, that those who sabotage the assembly line could claim that they don't support a woman having sex before marriage. We know that the refusal of "politics" is widespread in leftist France, but that an overarching point of view is necessary for us now as never before. In this phase where we doubt our too simple certainties, our pressed plastic strategies shrink-wrapped and sitting on the shelf, we have a *new attitude* for ourselves: radical (this revolution will not leave anything outside of it), combining freedom of desires and socialization (each of our experiences showing what tomorrow's life can be opens out onto everyone's revolt as well), destroying all the barriers of specialization (we will be poets, militants, musicians, erotic, thirsty to know what the world is in order to transform it, destroyers of the old in order to advance the new).

Our new attitude for rediscovering life also insists that we want to know right away what we aim to build. We want to show that destruction carries construction within it, but not all by itself: we must contribute. Unafraid to experiment, to show that, dealing with family life for example, there already exists something else for a mass of young people: and not only in informal childcare arrangements [*crèches sauvages*]. Something that doesn't resemble compensating indoctrination through a youth movement like the one the French "Communist" Party has built, nor the (limited) direct control of organized leftist groups. Any youth collective is already a living negation of a society where the family model is enforced as natural. Here too an ongoing struggle is being fought: the young prole that flees their family ends their wild adventure with marriage at twenty years old. This also happens—that's our problem too. The family, where internal conflicts work as dampeners to class conflicts (I argue with you because I can't attack the boss, the cop, the social worker . . .); the family that teaches hierarchy (man against woman, parents against children)—*we don't want it anymore.* From this moment, we know that the groups we form (and no false shame, eh? we know how we live) ought to take as their goal not reducing conflicts to interpersonal relationships, but heightening the contradictions in order to transform them into instruments of the struggle against the outside. Groups that don't live in retreat—that false security of the small closed world of our limited desires and our inhibited passions—but in which the thrill of these desires makes the necessities of the struggle more obvious to us.

I want to know that I also fight to lose my miserable and repressed identity, the one associated with my ID card, my social security number, my place in the line, the mystification of my social future (and, accordingly, the radical destruction of the oppressive prophesizing of identity papers is on the agenda). I want to know that it won't stop, that the revolution will not say: it's over, now everyone go home; that it will not end, that we will escape the monstrous prehistory where man is wolf to man under the mask of law and order.

TOUT!, NO. 1, SEPTEMBER 1970[8]

....

Tout! *was thus the—attempted—mainstreaming of a turning point.*

We sawed away at the base of leftism in the name of a "new attitude." Not a new strategy—the marketplace was already cluttered.

What Tout! *said others had doubtlessly already said in a disorganized manner: situationists, surrealists, Lafargue, and various marginal figures of revolutionary thought.[9] But for once, being right didn't mean being powerless. And* Tout! *wasn't just words, it was also a movement.*

Of course, it was no longer a question of sacrificing our true desires to strategy. We could at last say what we had in our hearts, on a massive scale. From its first edition, Tout! *praised worker laziness; it continued by interspersing support for brutal proletarian violence with the discovery of childhood sexuality (the Celma story).[10]*

Above all, its power came from a perpetual struggle: militant struggle certainly, but also a struggle within militancy. Indeed, the editors were not traditional anar-chists; they ignored the continuity of the right course of action for those perpetually downtrodden by history. Tout! *captured its positions on the field of Maoism, the team's starting point. And that gave weight to its rediscoveries.*

A strange Maoism that derived its appeal from being crossed by many currents that were deemed irreconcilable: "respect and listening to the masses" in the Chinese style, individualism of the great French anarchism, communalism [communautarisme] in the American manner, and soon the eruption of sexual liberation movements.

An organized revolutionary effort, yes; however, one that embraced calling everything into question, including its own existence. Tout!, *as its name indicates, hoped to keep the accounts and one day add them all up. Those who made it knew the essence of what it had to say even before the publication of the first issue. "Do it," it said. But do what? When the responses to this question emerged—*MLF, FHAR, *Youth Liberation Front—*Tout! *split up.*

....

HERE AND NOW

First off, we're sick of a few headliners speaking for everyone, of living at the pace of the TV, which makes us dream about what we cannot experience. Sick of all those who speak for others, whether it's political speeches or "works of art." In May, we reclaimed our voice. Each person realized they were a creator: on the posters, on the walls. At Sochaux, frescoes covered May's walls.[11] The public studio of the Beaux-Arts buzzed.[12]

"Do it," say the young Americans who are part of the "Youth Culture,"[13] part of the civilization that the youth built up against pig cops and imperialist advertising. They also say, "Let it go": break on through to the other side of the barrier; learn to distrust money; don't be ashamed of your body, even naked; build your own dreams and tenderness. Don't let them be imposed on you by *Nous deux* and *Elle*.[14] And also: create, not in order to sell, like "artists," but for yourself and for others. "Tune in": let's communicate with the people, know we are a community. We create our life together; we won't each get locked into our own little corner like our fathers did.

"Do it" *now*. Don't keep your dreams for tomorrow. They age poorly. Look what's become of our parents' dreams! Let's not let ourselves be taken in: let's live right now. Let's seize the moment.

Let's break the division dream-reality. "New culture!": it only looks that way from the outside. A way of speaking for journalists and sociologists determined to find something in common with Malraux's Ministry of Cultural Affairs and other profiteers [*affairistes*].[15]

It's not an issue of culture: the surrealist writers were still the stuff of culture, books, libraries, etc. We've all passed from books to life. We don't want to tell jokes: this is brand new in France. After May, it was repressed, it disappeared a little bit.

In the USA, there is a mass phenomenon. In France, it is felt by everyone, but only lived by a few.

"Do it": we don't want to cover up and corset this small beginning, especially by forcing it to wear the characteristics of the American "big brother."

As journal editors, we are not really a movement. We are trying to help the movement: to identify itself, to express itself, and to participate in it. This journal will provide the expressions of this new civilization that is trying to find itself: poems, pop groups, lifestyles, creations of all sorts, workers, students, youth, elderly, women, etc. "Do it": we are going to begin doing it . . . The bourgeois will hear about it.

TOUT!, NO. 2, OCTOBER 1970

....

TALK ABOUT POLITICS

How to discuss politics? As simply as you can, and no longer in the pompous style of the avant-garde. Let's wield the knife from a view that is not based on the rights of tiny factions: Is Geismar a hero? Are the Bengalis as foreign to us as exotic birds?[16] Over the course of some months, we attempted to respond to these questions and many others, always at the basic level called "individual," for lack of a better term.

We got rid of political blackmail, with us or against us; we broke through the walls guarding the divide between sides looking for other investments:

a proletarian hero can be a reactionary figure, the generality of political judgment is based on the exclusion of the particular. This individual of private loves that thinks it is called the self, the trace of an uncontrollable urge that analyzes the frozen world of leftist groups differently.

We made our first steps by speaking differently about what all the leftists discuss. And we went on from there to change the terrain of the discussion, to pass from the Bengalis to the fags.

Alain Geismar, leader of the Gauche prolétarienne [Proletarian Left],[17] faced many condemnations. A certain version of May, made of backward-looking and stiffened heroism, ended in prison.

....

GEISMAR IS GEISMAR

HOW TO DISCUSS POLITICS

On behalf of *France-soir*,[18] let's summarize the radio and TV. According to them, Geismar could have been:

— a brilliant academic, a great researcher

— a brilliant union organizer, a reformer of the University (in the university teacher's union, SNESup)

— a dull father figure

— a brilliant polemical and psychoanalytical writer

— a brilliant television star

What he isn't—still according to them:

— an orator like Cohn-Bendit

— a politician like Sauvageot[19]

— an ex-future president of the republic like Krivine.[20]

Reading his biography in the newspapers, he especially ought to wonder who he is. What's more, we should too. A comrade, that's certain.

But not the "son of the people" (or else the people gave birth to him without knowing it).

Not "the one who showed us the honorable path" (honor, you see, is for me an ex-soldier thing).

Geismar is not Arafat[21] (playing with the resemblances risks suggesting that we've advertised a known name—Arafat's—in order to attract sympathy inspired by the Palestinian resistance).

A revolutionary, that's for sure; a symbol for leftists, no doubt.

But it's not worth telling ourselves stories: Geismar's trial was not the trial of the people, because Geismar is not the people. The people don't yet know themselves, so they don't know those meant to symbolize them.

Leftists know Geismar. I know what he did; he's neither a superman, nor a monster. A militant shaken by May, choosing revolution instead of the gloomy future of the science department.

Let's not be too eager to make more red Thorezes[22] with friends who catch eighteen months in the pen. Let's free Geismar, from prison as well as from the roles we lock him up within.

TOUT!, NO. 3, OCTOBER 1970

....

In the spring of '71, before the Indian intervention, the Bengalis were the fags of the Third World.[23]

....

LONG LIVE FREE BENGAL

I know nothing about what happened in East Bengal,[24] except for what the newspapers have reported. But I need to speak about it. First, because no one seems to be concerned about what it might mean that, under the pretext of a lack of information, the revolutionaries have nothing to say. Second, because it turns out that the Chinese—the same ones from the Cultural Revolution—have supported for years, and continue to support, Marshal Yahya Khan's western Pakistan.[25]

I thought that one of the great vices of leftist politics was beginning to disappear these last months, and then this situation with Pakistan made it violently reemerge. It's the vice consisting in judging whether people are on the side of the revolution according to a set of principles defined a priori, acting as if these people didn't exist and didn't suffer; only judging with respect to the judgment of an authority figure: thus, it sickens me to think that there are revolutionaries who, following what China says, will justify a massacre that they would otherwise condemn. It sickens me because the first political analysis that really helped me in my life was that of the Chinese in the Cultural Revolution.

I said that I don't need very precise information in order to know that I am appalled by China's attitude.[26] I've already heard this argument, "But you don't know the reality, all the information is relayed through intermediaries, etc.," made in response to the Chinese Cultural Revolution; specifically that it couldn't be a true revolution, that we were misinformed . . . [i]

I believe that there is a kind of widespread, impulsive, and immediate feeling that belongs to politics; that one can correct it after, but can't begin by denying it.

Yet, everyone's immediate feeling is that the Chinese support a reactionary government that is committing a genocide of a people in revolt: that it's the Chinese supplying the guns that are used to execute the Maoists among the Bengali people—because they do exist.

I know people will bring up the objection: there are international political reasons for this. But if *we* can't come to accept these reasons, then why would we accept them from the Chinese? The true revolution in Bengal will be as much against the Indian government as against the western Pakistani government[27] . . . How can we allow ourselves to say: as long as the revolution there doesn't clearly comply with established principles, any revolt is doomed, therefore reprehensible—or at least unjustifiable?

I read two outrageous articles in the leftist press: in the *International Idiot*,[28] where there is not a *single word* to condemn Yahya Khan, as busy as they are justifying the Chinese—and in *J'accuse*.[29] From his desk, Glucksmann really wants to acknowledge that there was a popular revolt, but distinction, my dear, distinction! Popular revolt is not popular war! Bengalis, you have not complied, you can go get massacred, you no longer concern me.

---

i And we were, in fact.—GH, May 1973. Here is an example of the disillusionment of Marxist formations, Maoism in particular, which is just another imperial state.—Trans.

Well, this is precisely why Bengal concerns me; because I feel that those who condemn this revolt as not complying are also those who condemn my revolt, as a living being and not a load of principles. Those who determine a revolutionary norm, and who declare all those revolutionaries who don't identify with it as crazy and antisocial.

No, I'm not having these general principles of analysis when they allow justification for whatever particular fact. Revolutionary analysis is universal as long as it starts from the particular, and not when it refuses the particular as abnormal.

We are all Bengalis and we will win!

TOUT!, NO. 13, MAY 1971

....

Summer '71 saw the scandals peak. But the breach of the secrets of bourgeois power left us unmoved. A new "revolutionary apoliticism" was born.

....

WHAT DO WE WANT: TO LIVE!

This year at the beaches, there will be plenty to read about: the abominable Willot brothers,[30] the too elegant Rives-Henrÿs,[31] are on the front pages of the newspapers. The rot spreads throughout each column: How much will they make in the markets? How many little old people have to be evicted in order to pay for a delegate's apartment? Politics are not on vacation. Neither is diplomacy. How many Vietnamese will pay for the Nixon-Mao meeting?

Strangely, you get the feeling that after all it doesn't worry us much. At the end of July in Paris, a revolutionary journal ought to have a field day with all this good (or bad) big political news. It should be all over the front page and beyond.

But what can we say about this that everyone doesn't already know? *Minute* and the *Le canard enchaîné* know better than us how to describe the reign of cash.[32] The "savages" have nothing more to say about the high meetings of the great powers.

In this time when the desire to live, the desire to enjoy, is restricted to a few sunny weeks, why make the grand political analysts perform? Is it that we would prefer not to know what goes on in the heads of these peasants in southern France [*du Midi*] that you might run into on the streets? Is it that it's better not to try to imagine during the relative freedom of vacation what new relationships of love could be established between young people, like in Montpellier during the FLJ festival?[33]

We no longer have to highlight the rot of their France because so many have already realized it. We no longer have to put at the center of our concerns how leftists can exploit the tragedies of the majority, or how to navigate the international diplomatic chessboard. That is no longer our place because we don't identify with the collapsing world of capitalist and imperialist relations anymore.

We are trying now to start out again from our desires lived for themselves, from the desire for autonomy that shatters the political spectacle. A free southern France,[34] for young people who want to live and not just survive; women, homosexuals who want new love relationships; those who want to share everything in communities; these are our still stammering and tentative ideas: stammering because those who produce, those who revolt in their workplaces, only express themselves there very seldom; tentative because we can't say much about the transformation of this immense desire to live into an acting force.

But this is nevertheless a certain idea of France—ours.

．．．

Is it enough to make the private public, to put it on the more or less obscene stage of publishing, in order to escape the double dead end of private/public? To believe this is to act like this article from Actuel, *exposing little secrets, working within the safe zone of guilt trips about cash, sex, home, etc.[35] We fall back on conformity. The alignment of words and actions. A vain attack on sincerity. The moral superiority we chased out the door slips back in through the window. Private life is rotten ground, so worked over by the blade of desire for the authentic, the confining and sterile attempt to speak the truth, to confess or to come clean.*

What pushed us to conduct this survey? To start, the failure to build already within what Deleuze calls in his response "the power of the fake," siding with "do as I say and not as I do." The impossibility of escaping defensive representations so as to distribute private life in another way than being right or wrong; between people who would expand into a constellation of lovers, and not stationed as critics or righters of wrongs, seekers of an exemplary self.

Hence a feeling of uneasiness upon rereading this vain attempt. The push toward transindividuality morphs here, blocked on all sides, gnawing its tail in a bitter battle with flimsy ghosts completely devoid of flesh and blood since it's a hopelessly determined attempt to recenter something that only appears in the hazy margins, where the hunt for truth goes awry.

Thus we flounder in the poisonous swamp of a self-enclosed environment. The survey grapples with the same grayness where communal discussions sink, where words endlessly drive away what they attempt to track down: either the "truth of relations" or something that would have the same framework of regrets and vengeful wallowing. A hunter out to skim the rivers full of glitter, because they can't escape the vicious circle where everyone spins, confining themselves and hell-bent on betting in a meaningless game of poker. Only making limited resources change hands, as opposed to finding new ones.

Tearing apart the "selves" that are proud to run on other gears than blame: there's nothing inspiring in noting that all of these selves boil down to one type, the statistic of leftist careerism. A force that allows itself to get trapped in creating a purgatory of intentions. A force that gets hard for other places than those—too well known, a thousand times rehashed and mended—belonging to a world of ex-militants who have succeeded and who are simultaneously afraid and want to admit it. In order to mix it up with unknown tops and bottoms[36] in intimate material production, we will really have to uproot ourselves from the compost piled up all these years, tear ourselves away from these invasive vines that force us to spin around on ourselves endlessly, in the sweaty nightmare of sociology's judgments.

Bye, bye,[37] ex-militants become designers, writers, publicists, academics, artists: there are many other worlds to explore.

THE GOOD LIFE OF LEFTISTS

We sent a detailed survey about their daily life to about fifty people, leftist leaders and revolutionary intellectuals.

Do these folks live? Is it possible? When they aren't thinking, when they aren't organizing, aren't performing, aren't flaunting themselves, what do they do? Does Sartre change his own sheets? What time does Dany Cohn-Bendit wake up? Questions for concierges, they told us. So what? What does it matter, since these questions obviously get asked and many people wonder about them?

So we wrote up a survey, all the questions people ask, stupid and not stupid: since it's too easy to say, That's stupid, so I won't respond to it. We know your opinions, your ideas, that's not what we're asking you about. Not mainly. Because willingly or not, you end up exploiting people's desire by acting as if it had no importance. How do you live? You say, "But come on, why me? Why my life?" Too bad. You don't have to be out in front, on posters, in photos and in the headlines, if you don't want us to ask you about it. Besides, now that you are there, it's too easy to say that it isn't important, while knowing too well the growing frustration about it for those who read you, watch you, listen to you, or follow you.

Well, more subtly, certain people responded: "But by sending us this survey, aren't you restoring this celebrity cult that you aim to get rid of?" We didn't invent the "stars" of leftism and of the underground.[38] Let people realize by themselves that what they project onto you is the fantasy of their failures, the best of their desires, the lacks in their lives. It's not interesting to know if Krivine can cook or how many times Jean-Edern Hallier has unclogged a sink.[39] Very well, let the people judge, stop playing the game of "I'll show a little, but hide the rest, since you know I'm like everyone else . . ."

Out of the fifty people asked, around fifteen responded, most in order to explain that they didn't want to respond. There were only three complete responses: a long and sincere confession from Gérard Gélas, from the *Chêne noir* theater; a surrealist caper from Henri Lefebvre; and some clear comments from Edgar Morin.[40] All the following quotations were taken from responses to the survey or from the explanations of refusal to respond.

> I did receive the survey. Absolutely no desire to respond to it. I tried to figure out why. I thought beforehand (but only jerks can think such things) that the taste for secrets is petty bourgeois and can only hide something shameful and ridiculous.
>
> (GILLES DELEUZE)

Here is the naïveté we've left behind: today no "leftist" can claim to uphold the wall between ideas and experience.

CLOSED SHUTTERS

Indeed, it would have been interesting to know if there was a big difference between private life and public life, especially if there was something communicable, something to discuss without hang-ups about what takes place behind the closed shutters of apartments.

> I don't have the time; starting a magazine is no small business.
>
> (PHILIPPE GAVI, REVOLUTIONARY JOURNALIST)[41]

So what? Because someone is getting ready to start the daily paper of daily life (the newspaper *Libération*), they don't have the time to talk about their own daily life? There are those as well who "are going to respond right away," but whose responses never arrive.

> I don't want to be a statistic.
>
> (A LONG-STANDING MILITANT)

We are not statistics. And yet, and yet, nevertheless, we had the idea of this survey. Does that come from the old middle-class certainty of being special? We are each unique in our kind, people responded. Not all at once, but over an infinite number of justifications and explanations.

And we can't help but appreciate this refusal to be brought down to a mediocre common law: making money, fucking people whose gender is immediately categorized. But why must the people we ask so often add:

My wife threw out the survey *(and after the survey was sent again, the spouse threw it in the bin a second time)* but I really want to be interviewed. I would have responded to a surrealist survey, but to your survey! Would it be better to respond that I earn ten million or that I live off ten cents? I have no idea. I see clearly your perverse delight in making me talk about cash, *said Jean-Edern Hallier, the most famous of the "leftist" millionaires.*

He responded to us later, in writing, two times in the same envelope. First time:

Dear Jean-François Bizot,[42]

You will find enclosed the response to your collaborators' survey. They insisted that I do it. I did it. Here it is, I'm sending it to you.

Yours,
Jean-Edern Hallier

Second time:

Mister Director,

I let the woman I love throw your interrogation in the trash. My response will seem, I hope, clear enough and political enough to keep me from writing more.

With my best regards,
Mister Director,
Jean-Edern Hallier

This is like the *France-dimanche* of the extreme Left.[43] Come interview me. This survey won't express anyone's personality. It's nasty and troublemaking. Shallow and teasing bullshit. Things are more complicated . . .
(COLETTE MAGNY)[44]

In other words: Long live the tape recorder! Down with the survey! Our voices, our hot and unique voices, that's our truth, our true "selves." Our complex egos, and our ego complexes. So you see how much we make or how many times we jerk off . . .

Except that all of these selves boil down to tiny actions, to tiny worries, and these actions and worries make up a life.

As long as the uniqueness of the self and the statistical constant are seen as opposites, one will follow the other like its shadow: a bunch of tiny selves makes a big whole, and the individual makes up the group in the fantasy of being unique.

> Why don't you cross-examine people in the street, the security guards?
> (COLETTE MAGNY)

And, of course, we can't see why one rather than the other, the security guards rather than the "stars." Nor why one would replace the other, except that the security guards all take part in one oppressive majority, and are all mutually replaceable within a forced way of life. But not the "stars" . . .

> This survey is absurd, not in its intentions—I hate the wall that protects our private lives just as much as you—but because it will tip off the cops. That's all that Marcellin could hope for.[45]
> (DANIEL GUÉRIN)[46]

> What do you do for a living? Undertaker.
> *Where do you get your clothes? At the morgue.*
> (HENRI LEFEBVRE'S RESPONSES)

The joke and Marcellin merge: it's too serious or not serious enough; it's never the time nor the place.

And if, beneath all of this unwillingness, the proof surfaced: there is no mystery, other than the seductive striptease that shifts desire by making it look like intimacy? Shallow and slandered stream, private life's secrets show themselves for what they are: if it is difficult to answer, it's not because the survey was poorly made, nor that there was so much to hide, but because nothing is sadder than the reality of daily life, once it comes down to a self that thinks it's unique. Or else we have to admit that we are made of bits and pieces, of outdated ideas (parents to see, money to make . . .) and scraps of revolutionary will. Not only counting what you try to be, but also the way you are crossed, dissected, carved up, this daily disintegration made up of unwashed dishes, of unmet needs, of guilty hand jobs.

> For years, I undressed without knowing myself; now, if I want to know myself, shouldn't even undress.
> (A FORMER MAOIST MILITANT)

This shouldn't have been seen as an undressing of the self, but as a marking of the impersonal flow of money, of sperm, of clothing. It should have been . . .

> Well, that's surely something else. I like secrets because that's something that we share, like with a lover. I like secrets because they don't keep everyone from knowing everything about everyone else, each about the other, but they create a condition where we can no longer tell the true from the false, and this power of the false finally emerges. I don't like surveys because . . . the same appeal to the power of truth reigns in them.
>
> (GILLES DELEUZE)

There is no lovers' understanding among those who lay claim to May. They all still need the ideology of truth like the bourgeois always need gold to establish trust in their means of exchange, their currencies. In the same way, they can only exchange the pretense of truth, because they don't believe in each other enough to resolve the false issue of their "truth" in the interest of [*au profit de*] scheming together about important issues like food, clothing, touch, space, or money.

> I don't have an outstanding life. You don't brag about fifteen to sixteen hours of work per day, you want that to change. My only happiness is to be able to use all the time, this full time, to try to change the scenery. I explain myself all the time, I question myself nonstop and I try to answer and if it seems interesting to me, I publish it. Sure, it's not a life. To live otherwise—job, hobbies—is worse. Either way, you don't enjoy talking about it, that's pathetic and sickening. We are all prisoners. I am a jailbird. I write on the walls. I try to write to the other cons. But if it's in order to say how many cockroaches I found this morning or how many crusts of bread I stashed under my mattress, I don't have the guts to answer. Just the work of this little burst. PS: I have an escape plan.
>
> (GÉBÉ)[47]

EVERYBODY, HE WORKS . . .

Now let's go another way. Let's conspire about these details without worrying about who answered or why they didn't answer. Your profession? Who of us has a "profession"? But also: is it because we don't want one, is it because we don't know what it is, is it because we don't want to know?

What's your profession? Theater as "profession," that doesn't interest me. I don't like holding corpses in my arms; yet, the profession of theater stinks especially today: bad smells of self-denial, of trade-offs, of universities, where all of that is molded. Well, the Chêne Noir theater is a profession: a living thing . . .
(GÉLAS)

As a rule, there are no longer professions. No more hourly jobs either. *I work fifteen or sixteen hours,* Gébé said. And Gélas states: *Right now, from four in the afternoon to three or four in the morning. But when we leave the theater, everything keeps going. So, an hourly job like that? Twenty-four hours in the day and the hours of sleep are not the last to be counted.*

That's strange! No one admits to having a profession, yet they've been doing the same things for ages. Clémenti or Kalfon don't feel they are "actors."[48] Deleuze or Lefebvre don't see themselves as profs, but each continues to do what he does. The times and places no longer exist, but it's full time, in a fixed location. The profs aren't actors, the actors aren't profs. What does this mean? The shameful leftist social climb? That's somewhat obvious. To be a leftist is also a way to be different, to stick your nose out of professional drabness. That doesn't always mean getting paid: Gélas makes eight hundred francs a month,[49] some former militant journalist works as a truck driver, those at *Libération* will be paid like security guards. And when there is pay, it's not necessarily disposable income: there are some for whom the way of life just lets them get famous: Sartre lives like an ex-student in a dorm-style studio.[50]

GOSSIP, GOSSIP

Let's reclaim gossip, for lack of any other possible communication. There are many leftist "stars" who live like everyone else. But there is also the opposite: those who, packed with cash, try to purge it by investing in newspapers and movements. And then there are all the comfortable spots, all those situations that allow moneymaking to coincide with doing what you want to do.

Researcher at CNRS for twenty-three years. Pretty strong overlap between my livelihood and what interests me, freedom.
(EDGAR MORIN)[51]

Between four and five thousand francs monthly,[52] no complaints, on the contrary: let's organize in order to have enough to live off of and to sustain what we like—it's often possible for a few university students. But that could also be organized without being exclusive: women in the MLF are fashion designers,[53] some militants are lecturers, some fags are dissident journalists. The only thing we could change here is not to demand everyone quit or blame themselves for constant "recuperation." Our problem lies somewhere else: how can we generalize "recuperation," sink the boat by overloading it, instead of emptying it in order to uphold "purity"? It's often uptight and shameful leftists themselves who argue for the elitist character of these jobs and in this way unconsciously defend their status. So what? Anyone is capable of being a designer; anything goes in journalism today; pirating university degrees could be organized on a grand scale. Everyone gets a PhD; it's not impossible.

HOUSED, FED, WHITEWASHED

Clothing, food—a put-on disregard hides many concerns. To begin with, because protective clothing and a nutritious bite still smack of mom and dad.

> Where do you buy your clothes? Most often, I don't know since it's my mother that buys the few clothes I have. For example, she knitted all my sweaters. My mother has simple taste.
> (GÉLAS)

Where does Krivine buy clothes? Alas, we were unable to get a response. Of course, flea markets, chance, and what have you, most often provide clothes. "No personal comments, it's impolite," Alice would say.[54] We would gladly believe that—excepting fags, women, and some others—the leftist is born totally dressed and that their clothes renew themselves while being worn through some mysterious self-producing process. In the same way, food must fall right into their mouth, without holding them up for a minute from continuing their work as revolutionary informant. They shit, no doubt, but they write down on the toilet paper whatever they are thinking about while they do. A real body without organs, a giant awkward baby fed and mended by caring hands. Hence the importance of the restaurant: food comes and goes without having to ask where it came from, which avoids arguments with the MLF. Indeed, the leftist leaders[55] and stars most often eat badly. Noodles and omelets rule as uncontested masters in kitchens scaled down to necessities, to the idea of food more than its flavorful reality. Or else, chowing down becomes the symbol of a potlatch condoned by overburdened schedules and the awaiting Great Work. No, we don't wake up early, for the "full-time" schedule (actually most often made up of "lost time," of perpetually missed meetings, of continually botched tasks . . .) surely shifts in relation to the sun, since nothing is ever finished on time, but also nothing can wait. In militant timekeeping, many have held onto the double bind of false precision and real loss. Neurotic time, perpetually stuck between the future of the next appointment or next meeting and the past spilling over from the last one . . . Time without present, time that is not productive except by chance or by fluke. And for the others, the dark ones, the nobodies, there is always waiting time . . .

ACQUAINTANCES AND STRANGERS

Do you take in strangers? If I'm not home, no. Too much theft. After all, you have the right to hold onto your books or a comforter, or jewelry or musical instruments, or even to the key to your bedroom, or to an old bit of wood. . . . Well, every time, they take off with them! I respect guys who do holdups, even though it doesn't seem useful or effective to steal from the poor, since they have nothing and this nothing is necessarily loaded with memories and emotions. But to steal from the poor people whose homes you sleep in, no way . . .

(GÉLAS)

To be or not to be a cop, to put boundaries on a self that stretches as long as the apartment walls or to let everything pass through you. Here's the key to the whole deal with private life. It always begins like this: whose home is this? Indeed, we all live in a (relative) breakdown of the idea of owning property. Actually, it's rather a "thinning out": the network of "home" gets messy, overlaps, is not necessarily linked to ownership, nor even to the location of the places. There are those who own (more), those who rent, those who have borrowed an apartment, those who stay as guests with the borrowers . . . But the boundary of "home" hasn't vanished anywhere, even if it has pulled away or wandered more or less extensively within a group of friends and friends of friends . . . As for the acquaintance: within five years, why would it be different? The family: of course, it's always there. Therapy: those who go (numerous these days) don't speak of it, those who don't go respond:

> In therapy? I don't like cops and we don't need doctors, we need revolution.
> (GÉLAS)

It's okay if typical family relations are, as Edgar Morin responds, "neither the worst nor the best." Once a week, have dinner with family. Of course. There are even those who like their parents:

> What is your relationship with your parents like? Good, since they are good. Sometimes, you hear liberal intellectuals or people like that say their parents are good. But then, it's because these parents understand a bunch of things about a bunch of topics—know an awful lot. Mine, they don't understand anything about anything, and they are not intellectuals. So, why do I say they are good? Because I love them.
> (GÉLAS)

And then, and then . . . And then Politics and Sex, like the ass and the ox, surround our little daily nativity scene.[56] By the way, some gossip: Edgar Morin has had *one* homosexual relationship. And then the platitudes: masturbation vanishes with the meeting of the Other (geez, Louise):

> Jerking off:[57] during my adolescence, like everyone else probably. As soon as I met others, it went away. If I was in prison, or a sailor on a ship, or a cosmonaut, then I would probably masturbate or even better fondle myself. But that's not the case. That said, you can really fondle each other in a couple: not in order to overcome taboos, but because that could be enjoyable. Now, when we make love, we are asked, Do you suck, do you jerk off, do you fondle each other, do you fuck in the ass from behind, do you fuck in the ass from the front, do you get fucked in the ass? And so on. No, when we make love, as I've already said, we love each other.
> (GÉLAS)

It's so convenient. Love. Love is like Revolution, it means everything without ultimately spelling it out.

Such as these, in their own words:

Yes, now I'm doing architecture. I work so much. I have always wanted to do things with architecture. Besides, what matters is philosophy. I reread Hegel, Montaigne, Molière. The great thought, the Eternal. Anti-Oedipus? A fraud. Psychoanalysis, like Jewish thought, is a question. When it becomes an assertion, it is fascist. *(This is a former leftist leader, an architect).*

A year ago, I could have shot myself. Now, things are better. My kid? I see him three times a week. I live with friends. Sexually, I am okay.

Yes, what I want to do is architecture. Redo the design of Paris. Build with stone and concrete, durable material. The city is livable. These ecological delusions, the whole story of "dying totally alone," it's a myth. With ten years in the bag and ten more years to come of being a militant: the present is nothing, we've had it for ten years. A union of the Left? I don't vote for people that will put me in prison.

Politics, profession, child. An *I* that's okay, always stable. I guess that's life!

THEIR CYNICISM AND OUR MORALISM

Is it shameful to do architecture? After all that has been experienced, over-turned, undergone, built, we shouldn't — sorry, we can't — return to the gloomy and hopeless cliché "That's life." Long-lasting belief that we have always been this way, that humans are hypocritical and eternally thirsty for money, it's just nice not to die. That's not enough to set us in motion, and when we come to a standstill, we die. We shouldn't be afraid to say what we want to do under the pretext that it is bourgeois. Capitalists are cynical, they set aside the guilty conscience for us, because they need our guilty conscience to ensure their cynicism. The vision of leftist daily life is made up of too many prohibitions, of "you will not do that, won't want money, will free yourself from family," etc. What is too often left for us is moralizing, blame aimed at the happy bourgeois, doubled with the guilty conscience of too often wanting to live, or even actually living, like them. Moralism went over to the leftist side with its parade of inescapable lies and deals. Is paying thirty francs a person in a restaurant allowed? Is it forbidden to want your girlfriend or boyfriend not to sleep with anyone other than you? Can I do what my neighbor doesn't do, or at least what they say they don't do?

We can't believe that a new life can emerge from a game of prohibitions and transgressions. We don't need to live like we claim one ought to live (Do as I say, not as I do), but rather to understand better, to scheme better, to connect our desires better. We don't know the new life yet. Making it fit what we believe it should be turns us into new Jesuits or new Puritans, while we should be the new libertines. Libertines—not "partiers," but those atheists and explorers of jouissance that heralded the Revolution in the eighteenth century. But they didn't second-guess themselves.

ACTUEL, NO. 29, MARCH 1973

04 Youth Culture / Pop High

Flashback.[1] Let's return to the after-May self, a still-empty shelter that a reality without principle will quickly overwhelm.

"Drugs," pop. The end of militant self-control. We let ourselves be overrun, trampled. Maybe not the deep massage we had thought, but who cares? And who cares if the vital flux comes through worried explanations?

Creation, communication: the two master words of the new pop humanism. Today we would say, production, circulation of flux. Not that these words are irrelevant: they give shape to the sentimental and more or less sexless mess of pop festivals. But most importantly, they expand the vocal range where desire can try to sing.

Militant discourse stops at music, the coherence of projects stops at getting high. A body awakens, stirs, stretches; in writing, at least, the penis is only slightly erect, but it's a body that is otherwise disposed born from the ashes of the movement.

At the end of 1970, de Gaulle died of old age, Janis Joplin and Jimi Hendrix died of overdoses. At least that's what the newspapers reported: the truth—known later—was more complex. But the desire for dramatizing took over these deaths in order stand them up against the old idol who finally croaked.

Black and white, stoner and alcoholic, we've built them a pageant float, ceremony of a new culture finally reclaimed. A late discovery: it's less about convincing with texts (even though the hydra of messianic zeal reappears here at the end) than conveying the intensity.

The old yet rehabilitated heroism says drugs are a bit like death: fortunately, a new rhythm emerges in the same phrase, the rhythm of a livelier and redder blood; colors come to the pale face of the new self, and its nostrils throb with the fumes of music.

Okay,[2] pop is never more than the pacified and dulled weakening of rock, whose revival killed most psychedelic opportunities. End of the pop festivals: from Wight, which was like a concentration camp with double walls of sheet metal and police dogs, to the "tragic" Altamont, rosewater turns into sulfur.[3] Pink Floyd is replaced by the Stones. Jim Morrison completes the legendary trinity of dead drug users. Rock 'n' roll suicide.[4]

Behind the ideology of creativity, these two deaths are pretty much just that.

....

THEY DIDN'T DIE OF OLD AGE

In our view, *the news* means *what concerns us*. So, de Gaulle's death, please: that only concerns us insofar as it compels us to respect the concert of wailing.

Deaths for deaths, we have ours: we won't forget the 144 of Saint-Laurent-du-Pont.[5] *Hara-Kiri Hebdo* was banned because it dared to run the headline "Tragic Ball in Colombey: 1 Dead."[6] It was unacceptable because it made the comparison out loud.

Do you remember Jimi Hendrix, Janis Joplin? I learned of their deaths at the print shop. The typographer with long hair and flowery shirt who told me about them wouldn't have seemed surprised except that they made the front page of the newspapers. So what? That's as good as Nasser,[7] Mauriac,[8] or de Gaulle.

The bourgeois die because they are old. We die because we are choked.

Apparently Jimi Hendrix had asked people to laugh during his burial, to sing and dance all over. It really sucks to have to write about the dead: their burials happened like all burials and all the articles about their deaths looked like vampire bites. He died like he killed his guitars, from an excess of rhythm. She died like she was trampling an unfulfilled life in a rage. Not of old age.

It seems Jimi Hendrix and Janis Joplin were being treated with apomorphine. Read Burroughs's book to know more about it. It's a treatment for people using heroin, and the doctor who invented it had his license revoked.[9] Nobody really knows the treatment, no doctor is willing to explain it.

It is so much simpler and more moral to treat heroin users through abstinence. Much more painful too, but they asked for it. The newspapers didn't mention that when people take sleeping pills with apomorphine, they die from it. Thus, suicide if you like: they died assassinated by medical obscurantism, because the conditions of treatment aren't specified anywhere.

CREATING WITHOUT OPPRESSING

According to the newspapers, de Gaulle was a shaper of history: "Even if we don't agree, we respect the great dead."

According to Reuters (ten lines for a death), "Hendrix was famous for his frenzied manner while playing . . . His music was deafening and tuneless."

A frightening medieval obscurantism. Of all the pop musicians, Hendrix was probably the one who knew best what the guitar could do. In my view, that's more important than knowing how to write like Machiavelli or to govern like Caesar.

He even dominated the guitar so well that he was the only person able to destroy it. Able to walk out when he was being booed. Combine the most far-reaching revolt with the most absolute mastery of musical expression; the experimentation with an instrument's possibilities (his first group was called Experience)[10] could lead all the way to its destruction. Jimi Hendrix didn't oppress the audience: you've all seen Monterey Pop (if you haven't, go watch it).[11] Coming in pretty high, Jimi Hendrix destroyed his instrument, broke his amps; Janis cried, her voice broken, and walked offstage. In this way they showed that they gave voice to all those who can act like them, to all of the potential creations that the festival stage stifled.

The people who have been to the pop festivals or to a Sun Ra concert know: if you beat on tin cans to make rhythm, what you make will be pretty bad.

This is the dilemma the pop movement suffers from right now. It is pandering to say that people spontaneously create anything but extremely basic rhythms. When the leftist snobs of Paris condemn pop in the name of free jazz, they start from this acknowledged observation: musically, free jazz is infinitely richer. But they also know that this very richness is oppressive.

Jimi Hendrix was Black, one of the rare Black people in pop.[12] As you know, pop is more of a white thing. In France, the in thing is to take only free jazz seriously, since it is Black music. In Harlem, who knows free jazz? But who doesn't know Jimi Hendrix?[13]

At the time of his death, he got ten pages in every American paper. Pop is the people's music, and Jimi Hendrix was the main Black pop musician. Perfection and accessibility can meet when challenging the musical form is written into the music itself.

You've all seen *Woodstock* (if you haven't, come in just at the end for Jimi Hendrix's set). An expert in destroying musical forms from the inside, Jimi performed the most wonderful kind of subversion an American soul can imagine, of "The Star-Spangled Banner," the American national anthem, sung at the beginning of the day by little Americans at school and at the end of all the baseball games by all the good Americans.[14]

The national anthem pulverized, out of tune, backward, sublimated, transformed in the hands of this Black demon. American leftists have already hijacked [*détourner*][15] the national flag by returning to the people the original flag of revolt against England. If you were surprised to see "Radicals" hanging the American emblem, look closer: thirteen stars, thirteen States leading the fight against English imperialism in the eighteenth century.[16]

Jimi Hendrix did the same thing with "The Star-Spangled Banner" that Aretha Franklin did at the Chicago Democratic Convention demonstrations, though without words.[17] He showed that the most well-known tune for all Americans also had the most potential for subversion, that the tune that echoes in each person's head can be emptied of its imperialist content, that this tune belongs to no one, that no rhythm belongs to the bourgeoisie.

After Otis Redding's death in 1968, Black liberation pop saw itself in Jimi Hendrix. But he maintained a surprising distance with his music, his faraway and distorted voice didn't stoop to explain itself to the audience; as opposed to so many others (Mick Jagger included), Jimi Hendrix didn't speak more than he sang.

Janis Joplin, furious little girl, screaming and crying (listen to "Ball and Chain"), doing with her voice what Hendrix did with his guitar. "Cosmic Blues," whose orchestration, still dictated by the big record companies, can't hide its violence—she made it after breaking up with her first group,

Big Brother and the Holding Company. Listen a bit to Joan Baez's sweetened treacle, compare to Janis Joplin's screams of desperation, and you will see that revolt is not reserved only for Black people.

It's really too stupid. Two children of the blues, who boiled down the coolest parts of pop, smashed the gates.[18]

Their deaths are not more illustrative than that of a young man who set himself on fire because he had long hair. They are not more illustrative, but they focus and identify what all living beings must fight against: the stifling of a system that only gives creativity the choice of self-destruction.

CREATE OR CROAK

In France right now, all of the relationships between rebels and musical expression come down to a choice: prefer to listen to creators with black skin because that induces more guilt, or express yourself with ti-ti-tititi-titititi-titi.[19] This is what we want to escape today, the vicious circle, identification-poverty. Our misery is the material for musical creation; we won't escape by copying American pop, because pop can't be copied. In the United States, talking about pop has a meaning: young people form as many bands as there are universities or communes. What is pop(ular) there is elitist here. In Italy, the revolution has virtually built itself against pop (go talk with a worker at Fiat about Jimi Hendrix). In England, they make pop like a counterrevolutionary tranquilizer (go to sleep to the sound of the Beatles). In France, there is a group of comrades who founded the Pop Liberation and Intervention Force.[20] They try to tackle this absence of French pop music head on. They explain that the tactic of record shops right now is to bottle up recordings of French pop groups, because everyone feels that the explosion will come, that they must be ready to exploit it commercially.

A high-speed race has begun between revolutionaries and recuperators. We saw it at Wight: the young French people shaped by May will not make pop like the English, they want a music of struggle, not of compensation. The government has understood that any pop fest in France is fraught with possible explosions: the cops' reactions at the Sun Ra concert at Les Halles proved it.[21] Thus, in the French cultural misery, in the fear of death that reigns, reigns in our sad after-May, anything that approaches the creation of authentic pop will bring back a part of the hope taken away by the professional revolutionaries. After-May's angst is our desire to create and not simply challenge. It remains to be seen if the bourgeois will dive quicker than us into the exploitation of this desire.

Create or croak: it's up to us to choose.

L'IDIOT LIBERTÉ, NO. 1, JANUARY 1971

....

At the beginning of 1971, bourgeois and leftists met at the crossroads of "drug problems." A law passed in January authorized night searches of houses for drugs. Tout! *is the only important leftist journal to tackle the issue honestly, though not without internal debate.*

The article was seen as multiple violations. Violation of the new law—it forbids glorifying drugs, and the text gets Tout! *an indictment. Violation of the law of medical knowledge, the only authority allowed to talk about drugs. Violation of the unwritten law of revolutionaries: a subject not to be tackled, just as policed as the "shit"[22] itself.*

The pleasure of a "joint"[23] thus has the flavor of transgression. And so another law to break gets restored within the new normality. Drugs, a poorly sealed concept,[24] leak out between harmless hash and poisonous heroin. As a result a new type of "drug" is formed: the whites *(heroin, cocaine, morphine, etc.) And new excluded people: junkies. One shot and it's over: the myth works well. And just as the* FHAR *at its beginning rejected pederasts and trans people[25] for being outside of the homosexual norm, heroin users have no right to the liberatory label . . .*

Thus the new body in revolt allows itself to be reshaped through handling. The sad heroes of Crumb and Shelton replace the silly pacifists of Woodstock.[26] This body collapses into a hairy heap of ice cream eaters. Or else the young and rich Americans, concerned with their health and gracelessly living the high life, knowing that kef only kills undernourished people, can make up for vitamins lost during a "trip" without risks or danger.

———————

"Drugs," like "sex," words that fill the mouth and empty the head, stupid nicknames for desire. There is hardly anything to say about dope,[27] hardly anything to know about the issue, unless of course it's on the side of chemistry and physiology. In that regard, users just like doctors employ a vague institutionalist psychology: the only certain thing, ultimately, is that dope dissolves all of the requirements of working time for a body with an increasing appetite and oblivious to harmful effects.

The reassuring talk of stoners: for hash or kef, we invent Third World popular traditions, deep Baudelairean literary roots.[28] A respectability to add to the ultimate justification: it's harmless, let's legalize it. This is the approach of this article, with its simple opposition between physical harmlessness and social harmfulness.

There also remain real social consequences in the phenomenon: not a word in this text about the "deal,"[29] buying or selling the raw materials. Drugs show up on the table all by themselves, just like the family meal. For even more than the junkie—and this overlaps—the dealer is part of the world of those condemned by the liberating puff. Scorned for doing business with the new culture's soul, the dealer represents the voluntarily made loss in the most unstable edge of hallucinogenic youth. After all, they are paid, willingly taking on the risks in place of the buyers in the sweepstakes of the war against taxes.

Decentralized business: it's made up of a variety of parallel connections between producers and consumers. Anyone can someday bring back a bit of "it." The centralized-hierarchical system of "hard" drugs (big trafficker, distributor, little dealer, consumer) is rarer in the circulation of dope, where the separation of jobs is less distinct.

With the dealer, the social tissue of a real marginality emerges, with its own connections, stuck to the bottom of the social boat like parasite shellfish, slowing down its course.

DOPE: SO DOPE!

Lately, a process with several different moments has unfolded:[30] it began with all the fuss about what happened in Bandol,[31] then continued with the vote—in secret, by the way—on the law that even the magistrates protested; it was all finished up with a series of articles in the big newspapers that came to justify the law just in time. In particular, a few days after the vote *Le Monde* published a series of four articles titled "Drugs: From Anxiety to Slavery." The author was a certain Escoffier-Lambiotte.[32] You know her already, she is the female Muldworf[33] of *Le Monde* who assailed abortion a few years ago. She used the most beautiful words to defend the West threatened by the hallucinogenic tidal wave. A coincidence? Yeah right! *Le Monde* advertised these articles over a number of days.

It starts in the usual way: "Drugs" includes everything from hashish to heroin. It's been years since liberal doctors a little more honest than their colleagues fought for people to stop covering everything and anything with this completely ideological term. Escoffier-Lambiotte has none of this consideration. The only problem with these articles is the explanation and justification of punishment. Punish what? She doesn't even really know. Punish deviancy and "abnormal" behavior by finding their common material denominator, "drugs." Once we accept the phenomenon of drugs as fundamentally punishable, we can get away with saying—and she gets away with it, at the end of her text: "Is it society's fault or rather the youth's fault?"—which only works toward making us accept that there is inherently fault.

Some American doctors have made a plea for the legalization of marijuana. "An uninformed pandering," Lambiotte labels this . . .

And Escoffier sneers at the English Nobel prize winner Francis Crick, who demonstrated the harmless characteristics of marijuana![34]

Here are the disorders caused by marijuana according to the same Escoffiery:[35] "Memory impairment." What memory? If it's in order to remember when work starts . . . Anyway, if one forgets certain things after having smoked marijuana, everyone knows that it only lasts a few hours. What would they say happens after a true French bender! But for Lambiotte, memory is a thing that runs quite indifferently to what it has to remember.

"Impaired judgment." What is impaired judgment? Is it when people don't think like you?

"At high doses, heightening of sensory perceptions"; "all of these disorders" . . . Why is it a disorder? Couldn't "heightening of sensory perceptions" actually be a priori an asset?

It's all like that. In the table that she reprints (*Le Monde*, January 13, 1971), we read the heading "danger" across from different "drugs":

Indian cannabis: "disorders of judgment, distorted perception, acute psychosis."

Opium: "physiological enslavement, sexual disorders, physical and mental decline."

Well, that's clear-cut, exact and scientific. "Sexual disorders"—and what about your own sexuality, dummy?

Note, no one said that everything she files under the name "drugs" is harmless. And for a reason: her table goes from opium to gasoline, by way of heroin, LSD, barbiturates, sleeping pills, ether, toluene![36]

Well, one table for another; here's ours:

NAME	SCIENTIFIC USAGE	DANGERS
Ricard[1]	None	Bailout of the PCF[2]
DDT	Several	At high dosages, genocide (Vietnam)
		By teaspoon, acute psychosis
Fiberglass	Sometimes	Absorbed in pellets, causes diarrhea
Tar	Regulator of the migrant population	By injection, bad for circulation[3]
TNT	Boom	Immediate and total decline, sudden death
Exhaust gas	Experiments on rats	Breathed at a high dosage, burning of the lungs
Television	None	Stupor, dependency, disorders of judgment
Horse races[4]	None	Psychotic episodes close to the finish lines

1. Ricard is a brand known for its pastis, an anise-flavored aperitif.

2. PCF stands for the French Communist Party.

3. The French *circulation* can also have the meaning of "traffic" or "traveling."

4. The French term here is *tiercé*, or "trifecta," meaning a bet placed on the first three horses finishing a race. Betting on horse races is an activity that has a (negative) working-class association, taking place in cheap bars in less wealthy neighborhoods.

ABUSE OF POWER

It is an outrage that doctors legislate our sexuality or what they call "drugs." We do not recognize Muldworf's or Lambette-Escoffior's capacity to do so. Their only criterion—the only basis of their reasoning—is the classification of "normal" and "abnormal," of the unusual and the typical, of what is done and what is not done. The rest of their talk is only ideological dressing aiming to show the law of society in a scientific light.

Mind you, it's rather reassuring to know that there are three hundred million people for whom it's as normal as a cigarette. But constantly on crusade, Escoffier-Lambiotte refuses to let Arabs and others smoke in peace. She wants to legislate that too. They don't know it, but that's bad for them. They've done it for thousands of years, it's one of the foundations of their society, their way of socializing, of talking with each other. But they don't know that their judgment is impaired! Let's fix them, let's fix them, for heaven's sake!

But no pity for young Europeans. It's one thing for the "poor" populations (the world is made up of the coexistence of the poor and the super-rich, without being able to make the tiniest connection between these two phenomena)—but, for the wealthy children!

At the beginning of January, there was a fairly interesting letter in *Charlie Hebdo* that explained the social usage of kef in Morocco. How the guys laugh at the official word that condemns the harms of kef (whose commerce brings nothing to the state). How within popular sociability, it is a part of people's friendly relations.

The guy who wrote it had a kind of naively naturalist point of view: he thought that what God gives us is good, plants, hashish, kef, marijuana, and what is artificial is bad (heroin or LSD). Actually, that's not the problem.

DRUGS AND THE DRUG PROBLEM

First off, "drugs" are not a pharmaceutical category, but a social need.

Put simply, let's say that it's true that kef, marijuana, or hashish are pretty much harmless physiologically. As harmless as tobacco, at any rate. Of course, in small doses, more harmless than many other products: the American doctors' report to Congress makes clear that it was impossible to discover the deadly dose, that there didn't seem to be one.

Heroin is a poison, but, according to some, wine contains the same toxic ingredients, albeit at a much weaker dose.

LSD is a difficult experiment that American youth have conducted on a mass scale; we must handle it with caution.

Indeed, mainly because, under the current conditions of repression and amateurism, the making of LSD mixes in amphetamines, or even strychnine, which are highly toxic chemicals.

But they don't make claims for the socially harmless characteristics of hashish or marijuana. On the contrary, they think they are dangerous for our societies, weakening our minds. Meanwhile, heroin is not socially dangerous, since for dozens of years, traffickers have made it in Marseille under the complacent eyes of the cops.

Yes, cops use heroin as leverage, while the bourgeois, by systematically making the equation of heroin and hashish, lead those who can't find one right to the other.

The heroin consumer, first of all, is a consumer; they generally do it alone. It doesn't inspire you to speak or move, but instead, to withdraw into your own corner. And then, it doesn't change much in the mind: it's kind of a dangerous painkiller. It makes you forget; it gives you the sweats; eventually, it creates a real dependency. Heroin traffickers are part of the "old money" underworld, since the bourgeois have had their heroin users for a long time.

It's true that now there are more of them among the youth. It's true that it's not required to go from hashish to heroin, but it happens. Young Americans in Berkeley proposed—and already began—to care for heroin users by helping them use harmless substitute drugs: methadone, for example.[i]

Escoffier-Lambiotte finds that scandalous, because it amounts to switching one drug for another. They should use the old method, as they did with crazy people: tie them to their bed until it passes or they die from it.

But with hashish, kef, marijuana, you don't smoke alone: young Americans and Arabs use it in a collective social way. A circle where you can discuss more freely.

TRANSGRESSION . . .

Escoffier dives right into regression; obscurantism is the program. With regards to drugs, "dependency" can be "physical or psychological." That is: if you sometimes smoke hashish because you want to, you are "dependent"

---

i   In '71, we said this about methadone. It seems that it's false, which doesn't mean that medicine can't go further in this direction. —GH note from 1974.

on par with the heroin user who shoots up twice a day in order not to die. Come on now!

A different kind of "scientific" precision: "There are 30 million alcoholics, but 300 million cannabis smokers and 400 million opium smokers."

Strange, isn't it? Here's why: an "alcoholic" is someone who is completely destroyed and who drinks nonstop. A "drug user" is someone who smokes hashish once in a while like you drink a glass of wine.

Likewise, you never take LSD alone. Young Americans treat it a bit like an "acid test":[37] you say everything you have on your mind. Things you've repressed show up. Actually, doctors use LSD exactly for that. But just simply looking, seeing what's there under the skull, even if it's from a "scientific" point of view—the bourgeoisie will repress it more and more. It's the unknown, the reign of relativity: at a time of ideological breakdown, it's bad for them.

So, "drugs"? Nope.

Everything separates the fifty-year-old heroin user, pudgy and full of cash, who gets his fix on the sly, and the young people who meet up to discuss and smoke: an entire culture, an entire view of life, an entire relationship to the collective, an entire understanding of transgressing taboos. Notably, it's true that the smoker finds it even stupider to go work afterward ("impaired judgement").

If young people smoke and if most of the time after smoking, they don't want to do anything, it's because the main freedom that they've been able to wrest from the system, at least subjectively, is to do nothing. In a society based on respect for labor, it's a transgression. No, getting high doesn't make you either smarter or stupider. It all depends on how it happens. The typical "drug users" who invite punishment can't overcome the stage of passivity. They accept the image of the drug user. But we can certainly talk and act on hallucinogens. Just differently, that's all. A new dimension appears for everything you do. While getting high leads the American army in Vietnam to decadence, it is also present at the heart of the victorious struggle of the Laotian and other guerrilla fighters. Young Americans who smoke are not ashamed of it. They don't hide, at least when there are no cops. You only have to see a pop festival. This is a collective transgression.

What does it transgress?

More than the law as such (the cops), it transgresses the prohibition placed on any way of transcending the "self" that society forces on us. We don't have the right to know what would happen in our heads if certain walls fell down. Everything that is not exposed (in the social sense of the term, "normal") is forbidden: it's true that the effect of hashish—at least what they believe the effect to be—is "no longer knowing what we are doing." This doesn't mean we do whatever we want! But imagine if we discovered a meaning for this "whatever we want"!

We can't get away with having two behaviors in our head: when the effect of hash makes us wild—and that occasionally happens—it's because we want to take a step back from the "normal"; and if we take too far of a step back, we might go mad. Liberation of fantasies, of the unused 90 percent of the brain? Difficult to say. In any case, this is how the youth lives.

Well, a few words about the police view of drugs for those who think that the bourgeoisie is interested in their expansion, or even encourage it. Besides being factually false (see the whole handling of the "antidrug committee" founded by the son of Boulin, minister of health,[38] or the ideological role of the antidrug fight in the UDR,[39] all the parliament members united by the fear of hashish), it has the drawback of placing revolutionaries and bourgeois on the same side regarding this issue. The bourgeoisie says: "They take drugs because society doesn't give them a chance." Militants add: "Because they have not yet found their role in the revolution." In the two cases, it's understood as a deviant behavior with respect to the norm. As if the content of the revolution was above all the removal of everything that hasn't already been deemed revolutionary. That doesn't work for me. Getting high is not our revolution, but the revolution is not our high, insofar as the revolution "would suppress" getting high and replace it, as it would replace all of life's processes. The revolution is not what allows us to replace life.

. . . AND ACKNOWLEDGMENT

Indeed, the bourgeoisie is scared to death of "drugs," because it automatically thinks of the American situation: millions of young people bound together, unified by a common transgression. It thinks that if the youth get high, they will leave their jobs and social environment by the millions, as in the USA. But just because they're afraid, it doesn't mean the others are right. Put simply, it's true that the widespread emergence of hashish in France is a double event: on the one hand, a certain number of militants, people for whom the revolution was a daily activity, ran away from an impossible May. But it is more important to note that, for many of the youth, mainly for those who just glimpsed May, for those who are isolated in their region (see the number of arrests for drugs in the remote villages), the discovery of hash is above all a way to meet up, to become united. An expression of the desire for immediacy, to change right away, an inward prolongation of what May glimpsed. Even for militants: they often experience it, but perhaps it's a rationalization after the fact, like a way of better knowing the enemy that is in each of us. The young workers who have discovered kef in contact with migrant workers refuse a lifestyle where they were classified as Western. They have chosen what has been presented to them as the most debased, as what belongs to an "inferior civilization." In this way, they show the distance they take from the bourgeois way of life. Thus, if there is escape for some, there is also discovery of something else for many others. We can't say to the youth without blushing: "Repress your desire to smash[40] the system in you, in the name of the revolutionary that you could be."

TOUT!, NO. 8, FEBRUARY 1971

....

In December 1971, Pompidou gave an important speech on the glory of French families. For once, beyond the vicissitudes of daily politics, the president attempted to fill the system's ideological hole. We too, he stated, have a long-term political idea, a conception of humans; the family remains the unchangeable lynchpin of human solidarity against dehumanization, the rule of the machine, the rise of violence: it fully satisfies the needs that the pop trend expresses in its own way, the "desire to join together."

Short-lived, slick attempt: dumping family values onto the new pop humanism. Yet it's true that "Woodstock Nation" is susceptible to the mommy-daddy virus. A Louis XVIII ready to welcome new romantics.[41] Actually, the paunchy ruler won't be able to learn anything from the communitarian outbreak. The two civilizations will remain in a face-off—after all, we're not Dutch.

Tout! was the only journal in the press of its kind to engage in the antifamily crusade, placed among the numerous tasks of destruction. "Families, I hate you"[42]—the rant thus gives even more importance to its adversary, especially since the communes formed during the same time remained largely family oriented. Beyond the "family" unit, the exploration of a body different than the one molded by Oedipus can kick off.

When the dust settles from the fight against families, we will find the penis finally erect.

POMPIDOU, WE WILL NOT BE YOUR FAMILIES!

Le Monde thinks that Pompidou gives a humane tone to the head of state. Sure! Values are crumbling: they take the tune up again in the old key and desperately try to breathe a little soul into a stuck society.

Pompidou takes after Guizot (Louis Philippe, remember)[43] and Malraux. He really understands that we have all had enough of being separated, enough of a civilization that places all interpersonal relationships under the banner of money and competition, enough of being alone in cars, boxes, public housing, watching TV. It's so bad that they can no longer hide it from anyone: everything around us is so dehumanizing, they just add more and more layers of varnish to a cracking wall.

Pompidou has Leonard Cohen and Joan Baez in his record collection. He understands that everyone, delinquents, pop fans, are driven by this old and grand instinct to "join together" (this is the president's style). So, long live confusion!

Lacking new ideological gimmicks, even temporary ones, they try to rediscover "nature" in the most fossilized parts of bourgeois society; they will try to funnel into it the great need for reproduction, communication, and creative responsibility: in order to do so, they are beginning to persuade people who couldn't get themselves back on track by handing out bonuses to the working population.

PÉTAIN'S RETURN

The old Pétainist slogan, Work, Family, Fatherland, remains the basis of bourgeois thinking.[44] The family "is best suited to resist weakening because it is based on nature, on the law of the species" (Pompidou).

And it is not only Pompidou who defends these ideas. On the "Left," the CGT and the Union of French Women[45] responded to the president's speech, We are the French family.[46] Watch Muldworf, the PCF's ideologue on the matter, reconnect with the "natural family." They are perhaps even more sincere. Pompidou poses as defender of the family. Pretty funny, right? Marchais makes a much better father figure.[47]

Papa Pompidou, do you even know what a family is? You know what it's like for kids to be subjected to their parents, their interrogation when you come home late with a report card when you are twelve years old? You know what it's like for a woman to spend her days stuck between cooking and doing laundry? You know what a family dinner is like where the father reads the newspaper and the mother serves the kids who gobble it down as fast as possible in order to escape?

"Each person finds [in the family] the possibility of being both themselves and part of a group." Yeah right! "He knows that the resources are commonly shared and divided according to each person's needs . . ." What about kids in the country, who are made to work like beasts, the true proletariat of farming families? And the selling of kids to factories?

And then when you are sixteen and want to fuck, what do you share in common with your family? You hide out . . .

Ah, if only we could neuter children for ten years! You know that there are families that fight every night? That most families are a daily hell, the father who yells at his kids because he can't yell at his boss. And you want to reestablish parental authority, or rather make kids learn to obey, right? Is that it? Make women learn to stay in their place? Make men live by crushing their loved ones, to get revenge for being crushed elsewhere?

ALL BROTHERS

Yes, we are thirsty for understanding, for solidarity, like you say. But we feel this thirst against our families, those of daily routine, those of "the normal group," of coercion or of chauvinistic pride, those that have crushed our childhood dreams or censored our adolescent ideas.

We don't want to share oppression in common, we want to share freedom. The freedom to control our bodies and our minds without compulsory worship or recognition; we no longer want to be born as private property.

A home, yes, we want that; to be together also. Your family smells stuffy for those who don't have the means to afford windows on life; your family is already dying and won't resist the building of new social relationships, even embryonic ones, even at the heart of the rotting capitalist society.

Your families are falling apart, and as a great bearded man might say, "Don't accuse us of having destroyed them, it's you, it's your individualist system based on competition and private property that destroyed them."

You need millions of healthy babies because steady production and steady consumption is better than nothing (but we'll leave demographics to the despicable Debré).[48] You no longer believe in the family, but you know that it could still keep people under control.

A France with one hundred million French people, a project dear to de Gaulle. One hundred million to exploit and to chew up in the name of "consumption," what a leap in profit, and also, what stability! And that would make those pathetic migrants less visible, no more need for importing. A golden dead-end for the need to make love: ideologically and materially, even more families could mean fewer cops; that is, bring censorship back home, tenderer and sometimes even friendlier: "I couldn't really do that to mama . . ." While they keep citizens in line, look who keeps their children in line, it's their job, masters according to God, they'll be proud of it . . .

Count on it, count on us . . .

Pompidou is old, his families have only taught us one thing: insurrection! We have found a hope *against* them.

Even if it isn't so easy to get out, when you are isolated. We will no longer try to do better than our parents; and yet, we already know that we will love *our next family* more than you; *it will have fifty million people just to start with.*

TOUT!, NO. 5, DECEMBER 1970

05 Fags

Twelfth issue of Tout! *Finally the clock strikes twelve for sexual liberation. The desiring body arises and walks, to the astonishment of militants and those who had thrown sex into the battle without really knowing what they were doing. This twelfth issue, which officially announced the Homosexual Revolutionary Action Front (FHAR) and supported the MLF (Women's Liberation Front), had the highest sales of the journal and of leftist voices in the era. Soon after, it was seized by the police for "offence to public decency."*

    Break with the raunchiness belonging to Reichian sexual liberation.[1] Break also with the sexual conformity dominating the youth, which sees heterosexual coitus, man on top, as the natural and highest form of the revolution in morals.

    However the new slogans still uncover an egoistic body, less liberated than devoted to liberalism. "Our body belongs to us," "freedom of our bodies," the leading article stated. It's liberalism, since they claim to return each person to a fundamental freedom to use their body however it suits them, humanism of a sexual habeas corpus that leaves out the richest aspects of social sexualization. At the most, it's a declaration of the rights of the body, an "'89" of sex.[2]

    Quickly enough the dross of this ideology became apparent. After the claim of a personal sexual responsibility, the new statuses congeal in the joyless affirmation of categories well ensconced in their separate autonomous zones: fags, women. Overlooked was the emergence of unclassified groups without rights based in the "liberation movements" steeped in liberal psychology: there were hardly trans people in the FHAR, even fewer in the MLF.

    *Above all, since they were rigid about the argument that "our body belongs to us," they missed out on a break with the conversation about sex that would have had major implications; a break already present in Sade and Fourier (*The New World of Love*):[3] evidence of the nonanthropomorphic character of sexuality. In demanding the assignment of gender to the free and conscious person, they perpetuate an old deception. Our bodies, belonging to us—how sad! Each person's body "belongs to all who want to enjoy it" would already be a more satisfying statement.*

Dangers of a sexual ideology hardly escaped from the personalist limbo: the FHAR ignored the pederast lovers of children, a nuisance since they live out their passions beyond the rigged question of childhood "consent." *Wrapped in the new sexual liberation, high school students, fodder for the newly opened battlefront, take pride in their fake free will, which pushes them to experience their "natural tastes" among themselves. The refusal of heterodox desire, like that of an adult toward a child, to take an example that is fundamentally transversal, may be referred back to the so-called freedom of choice.*[i] *The hell of categorical imprisonment is paved with good liberating intentions.*

Fortunately, save for some "sexologists" with faces like priests, no one in France will rise to the bait of reintegration into the dominant morality.

....

OUR BODIES BELONG TO US

This issue bears witness to what are called, contemptuously, shamefully, or medically, *sexual questions*. But aren't these questions that our body poses every day at the center of life?

Revolutionaries who refuse to recognize this fact, to see its implications and their relevance, have the same attitude as those who during the Dreyfus affair claimed to represent the working class and the revolution, stating that "it was the bourgeois' business and did not interest the proletariat."[5]

So, fags and dykes, women, incarcerated people, people who have had abortions,[6] antisocial people, the mad . . .

We have not spoken for them, they have spoken . . . and as a result of their desire and of their oppression, they demand the power to do what they want with their bodies.

The MLF first consciously translated this demand to express desires freely, to exist as one is; and this emergence made a break in our approach, our understanding, and our ability to make a revolution. They demonstrated the extent of their oppression in all aspects of life, and thus, all possibilities for subversion. A campaign like the one for abortion attacks the entirety of the bourgeoisie around the concept of life, and at the same time,

---

i   See on this theme René Schérer, *Émile perverti* (Paris: Robert Laffont, 1974)—GH.

it is a practical fight against laws and power. This campaign also shows us the limits of the people on the Left: they accept the battle against the laws, but for them it was ultimately a way to reestablish harmony within the couple or the family, seriously undermined at this time, and thus to conceal this demand that has already emerged on a massive scale:

Free use of our bodies.

Since childhood, we have been made ashamed of our bodies. First, they prevent us from jerking off, on outlandish medical grounds; they prevent us from putting our elbows on the table, they force us never to be naked. They shamed us for our bodies because they express our desires, even when we don't dare to speak them. They told us: submit your body; wear ties, underwear, and bras; give a military salute; don't lie on the grass; don't sit at your boss's desk; stay seated in class . . .

TOUT!, NO. 12, APRIL 1971

....

Issue 12 of Tout! *contained two calls that made the* FHAR *go public.*[7]

....

FOR THOSE WHO THINK THEY'RE "NORMAL"

You don't see yourselves as oppressors. You fuck like everyone else, it's not your fault if there are sick people or criminals. You say you can't help it that you are tolerant. Your society—since if you fuck like everyone else, it's really yours—treats us like a social plague for the State, an object of contempt for real men, a topic of fear for housewives. The same words that are used to refer to us are your worst insults.

Have you ever thought about what we feel when you say these words one after the other: "bastard, scum, fairy, fag"? When you call a woman "dirty dyke"?

You protect your daughters and your sons from our presence as if we were plague-ridden.

You are each responsible for the horrible disfigurement that you have inflicted on us by blaming us for our desire.

You who want the revolution, you have wanted to force your repression on us. You fought for the Blacks and you called the cops cocksuckers, as if there were no worse insult.

You, worshippers of the proletariat, have boosted as hard as you could the preservation of the manly image of the worker, you have said that the revolution will be made by a surly, male proletariat, deep voiced, buff, flexing his muscles.

Do you know what it's like for a young worker to be homosexual in secret? Do you know—you who believe in the educational quality of the factory—what he endures when work buddies treat him like a faggot?

We know, because we know each other, because we alone can know it. Along with women, we are the moral doormat you use to wipe off your conscience.

We say here that we have had enough, that you will no longer beat us up, because we will defend ourselves, we will chase your racism against us right down to language.[8]

We'll go even further: we won't be satisfied with defending ourselves, we are going to attack.

We are not against "normal people," but against "normal" society. You ask, "What can we do for you?" You can't do anything for us as long as you each remain the representative of normal society, as long as you refuse to see within yourselves all the secret desires you have repressed.

You can't do anything for us as long as you do nothing for yourselves.

TOUT!, NO. 12, APRIL 1971

....

FOR THOSE WHO ARE LIKE US

You don't dare say it, perhaps you don't even dare say it to yourselves.

We were like you a few months ago.

Our Front will be what all of us make of it. We want to destroy the family and this society because they have always oppressed us. For us, homosexuality is not a way to tear down society; it is first of all our situation, and society forces us to fight.

We don't make the distinction among ourselves. We know that homosexual men and women live different oppressions. Men betray male society; homosexual women are also oppressed as women.

Homosexual men benefit as men from advantages that women don't have. But feminine homosexuality is perhaps less shocking for men, who have used it as entertainment.

We must address the contradictions that exist between us.

We want to find out how our alliance with the MLF can be made without submitting to heterosexual ideology.

To find this out, we need you.

Repression exists at all levels. We have suffered the brainwashing of hetero propaganda since childhood. Its aim is to root out our sexuality and to return us to the *natural* fold of the sacred family, the breeding ground of cannon fodder and of capitalist and Stalino-socialist surplus value.

We continue to live this repression daily while risking blacklisting, prison, bans, slurs, dangers, smirks, pitying looks. We will reclaim our status as social plague up until the total destruction of all imperialism.

Down with the cash society of hetero-cops!

Down with sexuality reduced to the procreative family and to active-passive roles!

Let's stop hiding in the shadows!

For self-defense groups who will oppose the sexual racism of hetero-cops with force.

For a homosexual front that will have as its task storming and destroying "sexual fascist normalcy."

TOUT!, NO. 12, APRIL 1971

....

One individual scratched the militant disk with the help of a few psychological tricks. This individual, this fag, flipped a hidden switch with an unintentional act, powered up a saw to cut the real otherwise: acting like a queen among militants, or acting like a militant in a pack of queens were its first effects.

Some homosexuals refuse the game of origins (where does your problem come from?) that mass psychoanalysis—the kind practiced by social workers—wants to force them to play. If there are no results, something tells us desire is an orphan. A refusal to trace back to causes, to beginnings, to the timeless and icy argument over "whose fault is it?"

We don't know where it comes from, and it no longer interests us to find out, but we know all too well what we are. And as for all of this handing out of fag pamphlets, who speaks with the warm and unsettling voice of the desire so dear to Genet?[9] Is it the preacher of liberated homosexuality, or the young prole whose cock was probably beautiful?

The bullshit pride of being one, which gives up the chance of taking quite literally a statement shaped like an erection.

And for what? In order to strengthen a "view of the world," guiding respectable interpretations. Behold the fruit of this pompous stiffening: the thinning of the web of social-desiring relations, the removal of all the nonconforming calls of desire. No more drugs, no more preaching.

....

WHERE IS MY CHROMOSOME?

Quite recently, while reading *Le nouvel observateur*, I learned that they had discovered the cause of homosexuality: it would appear that we have one chromosome more or fewer, I don't remember, probably fewer. Don't be cruel to homosexuals, it's not their fault. After all, this explanation is way better than the one that made the rounds in leftist circles up to now: "We must not punish homosexuality, except of course in the case of relationships with minors," (minors tell you to piss off; I was one, you know), "and homosexuality will disappear by itself when heterosexual relationships are liberated. It's the fault of their surroundings, it's not their fault."[10]

It's true that we don't choose to become homosexual; anyway, I don't have the feeling of having chosen. One fine day, in high school, my little classmates treated me like a faggot—I didn't know what that meant, but I was somewhat proud of it because I felt like they envied me. It was when my mother cornered me in the hallway to ask, "But at least you're not homosexual?" that I became ashamed of it.

We are not products, and those who believe they are helping us by saying, "They didn't ask for it," only knock us down. Who cares what made us this way: we are not results, but people.

We see ourselves first through others. I've experienced this feeling all over again lately, after having had a few FHAR meetings. I live in what is known as a commune, and I am always with militant friends. These days people in the commune, just like militants, think, "I'm showing off." A bit of underlying exhibitionism wouldn't surprise us. And when I kiss another guy in front of friends I always feel like they do all they can in order not to be uncomfortable—which only accentuates the discomfort.

We don't choose to be homosexual, but we end up with a label stuck on our backs with people who laugh at some of our inflections. We don't choose to become homosexual but we choose to remain homosexual, and that happens very early. A certain sense of betrayal, hiding something from your parents, and kind of from everyone, which is both repulsive and delightful: when two guys find themselves in front of others, they share a stronger connection than anything that could bind together "normal people." But in this pleasure of secret complicity there is both something radical (the feeling of escaping on one side everything that allows people to judge you) and at the same time a kind of masochistic pleasure that I'm bored of. And then I also found that there was no use staying masked [d'avancer masqué];[11] it was pointless to act as if it weren't so, everyone always knew, as they say.[12] With this little game we become at best someone that the "normal" people with progressive ideas can burden with their protection, like a kind of eccentric whose flamboyance is accepted with a more or less forced smile.

One of the things that has most frustrated me is that when guys know that you are homosexual, they always think that you want to sleep with them—as if a homosexual didn't have the right to choose, or as if any old cock were good enough for them. That happened again recently: we went to pass out flyers for the FHAR at the entrance of a nightclub where the young proles go to dance on Saturday night, and sure enough: "I have a nice cock, eh, is that what you want?"

We see why "normal" guys don't say homosexual, but faggot or queer. Whoever takes it in the ass obviously can't fuck anyone else—is necessarily feminine.

There is another myth that dies hard: homosexuals don't like women. It's true that we have often ended up putting in our head what people say about us; for a long time, I've had phony relationships with women, whether they have taken me for an especially challenging male, or they have wanted to "cure" me, or finally quite simply I've reproduced with them the relations of oppression in a form of imitation of other males, to act as manly as my neighbor. What has happened recently has pretty much changed the relationships between us: mainly because we have discovered that wherever women were fighting against oppression by men, they opened the way for us. There is something a bit paradoxical, but which I have been able to verify, in the fact that we simultaneously desire men and despise manliness. Manliness always seems to ring false to us because we know that it covers up cowardice concerning its own desires. All homosexuals have had the experience: how many seemingly super-manly men will end up taking it with the secret pleasure of finally being turned into an object of desire. That's where we trouble them, since we make their desire to be objects quite clear at last, to be possessed even if they fuck us.

"Normal" people—or more precisely, normal society—have imposed the image of women on homosexuals. This image that they've built in order to oppress women better, they've also forced on us: hypersensitivity, jealousy, shallowness, etc. But unlike women, our weakness also makes up our power. Because we are also men—or at the very least we ought to be. We are proud of our betrayal. I had a friend who really acted like a "faggot," and I spent years kicking him under the table to stop him from playing the "queen." I believed I was already quite liberated, but I thought that in order for homosexuals to be accepted by revolutionaries they would have to reject the feminine image that "normal" society attached to them. What I've found since is that the contempt for "queens" was above all a way to divide us, to sort out the good and the bad homosexuals; and I also found that only by making shame more shameful can we progress.

We reclaim our "femininity," the very kind that women reject, at the same time we declare that these roles have no meaning. Among us, in our meetings, we are trying to end the petty relationships of exclusiveness and jealousy, of gossip, that have been forced on homosexuals: we try to be as open and direct as possible among ourselves, and we probably are, far more than whatever group of "normal" people are among themselves.

When we went to hand out flyers in homosexual clubs, we were struck right away by our own fear; we were all dead scared in front of the door, with our bundle of flyers. Much more fear no doubt than for a typical militant action, even a more violent one.

But when we begin to realize that we are a community, even those guys

I hated, those office employees who hang out at the clubs for queens, it seems much more important to me that they are with me.

To the outside world, we reclaim our femininity because we know that they prohibit it and it shocks. Nothing more delightful than the panicked face of a friend who watches me drop expressions or gestures that in his eyes are the kind a fairy makes.

Why this worry? Because the domination of males is based on the idea that when you have certain bodily characteristics (a cock), you are stronger, smarter, etc. We, who are physically men (even though some people still believe in hidden abnormalities), are socially and psychologically women:[13] we thus call into question the very basis of male domination. What gives our situation a radical character is that we have already in practice overcome the social roles of men and women and also—for the "normals" who are reading me—the guy who acts like a queen is not always the guy who gets fucked.

We are richer in establishing inventions and freedom than "normal" people could ever be.

That is why we say that we are proud to be homosexual: of course, there are still super-revolutionaries who lecture you in order to explain that one should not privilege homosexuality over heterosexuality, that you mustn't do reverse racism, that the future belongs to bisexuality, or even to pan-sexuality—being able to express all the sexual desires imaginable. Perhaps that will be true one day. No doubt it's our aim, although I am not sure that desire is at heart undifferentiated. In the meantime, those who speak this way only offer me one path: sleep with girls to demonstrate my complete liberation. But it just so happens:

1   That these days, girls are, correctly, fed up with being objects that you fuck. What the girlfriends of the FHAR have told us is that for them bisexuality would be to submit themselves all over again to men, who have always considered feminine homosexuality as an add-on, a show, and a nice preparation for their own pleasure in coitus.

2   That personally, I would have the feeling of going backward instead of further liberating myself.

The high schoolers' movement, for example, which carries so much hope otherwise, where each person tries to be the most liberated possible, is still stuck reproducing Situationist-type cartoons on the topic, "long live the orgasm," where by chance a guy fucks a fine chick—on her back of course—(I think it's in "Crève salope").[14]

Sure, we're cool with sexual freedom as much as you want, but we will begin by saying what we have in our minds. That's how we are the most alarming, when we say, like the American Martha Shelley,[15] "We will be normal when you are all homosexuals." We will only allow ourselves to be challenged when we have awoken the sleeping homosexual in each of you.

TOUT!, NO. 12, APRIL 1971

....

And here it is, the restrictive framework of the homosexual thirsty for respectability, at the height of his totalitarian madness. "Toward a homosexual view of the world," not a word that didn't piss someone off. A general system for expressing any event, like the good old philosophy in the manner of Dilthey, of Weltanschauung like in the days of textbooks—and homosexual, on top of that, meaning permanently self-sufficient.[16]

Clear boundaries cheerfully demanded. Let's be among our own in order to bring the outside to us. The liberal flattening out of the game of drives: love is dedicated to equality, which joins with personal liberty as the pillar of the republic of sexes.[ii] What's missing from the three-part motto of the sexual Estates General is fraternity: it comes to take the place of fucking in relationships between fags and lesbians.

In the new Jacobin club of fags, admission is subject to "passing through fully accepted homosexuality." The world should find a center, a direction: but that won't happen, fag, your respectability has gone to shit.

---

ii   Moreover, current sexology makes grand use of all this sexual republicanism, largely foreign to the vitality of the drives (see the themes of someone like Meignant)—GH. Michel Meignant (1936 –) is a French psychoanalyst and sexologist of whom Hocquenghem was critical—Trans.

TOWARD A HOMOSEXUAL VIEW
OF THE WORLD

"Love is not looking each other in the face, it's looking together in the same direction" (Saint-Exupéry).[17] Which supposes that we are one behind the other (token fag, ha ha!) but not necessarily one inside the other. Homosexual power? Revolutionary organization? There are plenty of friends who wonder what the FHAR is. We've had two months of actual existence, and now it's anyone's game to put together a "manifesto," a "minimal political base," etc.

To such an extent that one group has named itself "Political Committee" and has spawned a short masterpiece of revolutionary banality, forgotten as soon as it was read.

And at twilight, at a General Assembly held at a university residence hall, we heard a contest of spoken leftism, measured by the clap-o-meter, on the theme "If bourgeois homosexuals believe they can come here, they're mistaken." Statement without effect, besides. Apparently no one felt targeted.

So? We are eight hundred, without any direction, without a base?

That's right. What makes the FHAR, and which no political base would be able to sum up, is an implicit agreement, tested through small group meetings rather than General Assemblies—one manner of speaking among ourselves, another for speaking to others—something that can't be trapped in any formula, because it is political and vital at the same time, what has been awkwardly called: "discussion club . . . ," "cruising spot," "political splinter group" . . . It's all of that, and something else.

And sloppy general assemblies; little groups that are half orgy, half psychodrama; queers and leftists.

And a major problem with women.

I think that we will not write a manifesto, since the fucking GAs are constituent: at eight hundred, we can only centralize information. We have all the time: we don't have, like leftist groups, the anxiety of splits, the fear of the death of the group.

We are not a group, but a movement. Let's ditch the label: the FHAR belongs to no one, it is no one. It is nothing but homosexuality in action.

All the conscious homosexuals are the FHAR: every discussion among two or three people is the FHAR. Jealousy, cruising, makeup, love—that's the FHAR, like the demo on May 1 or *Tout!*, issue 12.[18]

The doubts, the setbacks, that's also the FHAR.

I have the feeling that in the FHAR, nothing gets lost: usually, having multiple emotional relations weakens each one of them. Not for the FHAR, I think.

Yes, we are a nebula of feelings and action. And I don't agree with the hasty clarifications; with this race toward identification: knowing what we are, situating ourselves in relation to leftists. We no longer need daddy, even in the form of a political base.

When we write that we are against American imperialism, for the workers at Renault, against the bourgeoisie, what's the point? To soothe those among us who are ex-leftists?

"We are more than just homosexuals, because we want the revolution," "We ought to adopt a general stance on class struggle." That is what some of us say—not necessarily those who have been in leftist groups, by the way: just those who are still dazzled with the idea of politics.

Well! I think that we don't need any other starting point than our conscious homosexuality; that we fool ourselves if we believe that a conscious homosexual is a homosexual like any another, just dressed up as a revolutionary.

Let me explain: I believe that homosexuality lived in a conscious way is more than a form of oppressed sexuality; it is not only a way of envisioning emotional relationships; it consists of more than a position toward the family and heterosexuality.

We are not revolutionaries who specialize in the sexual problem.

I think that conscious homosexuals have a way of envisioning the whole world, politics included, that is unique to them. It is precisely because they live by embracing the most *particular* situation that what they think has *universal* value; that is why we don't need revolutionary *generalizations*, abstractions repeated half-heartedly.

I even believe that the homosexual vision of the world is, right now, the most radical way there is to speak about *everything* and act on *everything*. It's this vision of the world that makes us, facing any event, daily or political, all react together, without needing to plan ahead of time. And without a political base.

I am going to try to say how I see this homosexual view of the world: that doesn't mean that I believe it is possible to sum it up in *one* manifesto—on the contrary. Firstly, we homosexuals refuse *all* the roles: because it is the very idea of Role that disgusts us. We don't want to be men or women—and our trans comrades can explain that best. We know that society is afraid of everything that comes from the deepest parts of ourselves, because it needs to *classify* in order to rule. Identify in order to oppress. This is what makes us know how to clock people, despite our alienations. Our inconsistency, our unsteadiness, frightens the bourgeois. We will never be able to freeze ourselves, even in the position of the proletarian revolutionary: we have suffered the role of man that they have forced on us in the flesh. From now on, every role disgusts us, boss just as much as slave. Secondly, we feel a sense of *betrayal*. Between ourselves, homosexual men, and women, this difference remains: we have betrayed the side of the oppressors, the males. Betrayal, we're experts in it. Because we know from now on that we can only betray whatever freezes us and becomes oppressive? At any time, we can take a critical glance at ourselves, because we don't really know well what "ourselves" is. They told us we were men, and we were treated like women; yes, to our enemies we are traitors, sneaky, dishonest: yes, in any social situation, at any moment, we let men down, we are snitches and we are proud of it.

More than any other, the very idea of *normality* has oppressed us. They have explained to us that it is *normal* to fuck women; well, we understood. What is normal is the same as what oppresses us. All normality pisses us off, even revolutionary normality. We know well that a "normal" revolution excludes us. But we understand that the real revolution excludes normality.

Finally, we have developed a heightened sensitivity to relationships of *power*. What we call "male domination"[19] doesn't end with the manly man, proud of his big dick. We know how to detect intellectual male domination, a kind of confidence in stating his ideas. Pseudorevolutionary male domination that wants to topple everything except itself. Where others take pronouncements as currency, we sense deceit and attack. Among ourselves, a network of power relations endlessly weaves and undoes itself, as quickly destroyed as built.

All of this allows us to experience every issue according to our truth: I could say why I feel myself on the side of a free Bengal based solely on my homosexual vision of the world: because revolutionary "normality" excluded the Bengalis from the side of the true revolution: that of the genuine people's war, standard-type normalized Maoist criteria.

Living our homosexuality therefore doesn't end with sleeping with guys. It only begins there. Our view of the world is: "Love between us, war against the others," with it being understood that this "between us" is endlessly expandable, that the aim of this war is to spread it.

No real love without equality: the world is thirsty for love, but we know that the love heterosexuals offer is used to hide the domination of women by men. That is why homosexual love is currently the only love that aims at equality because, being marginalized, it has no *social use*; because power struggles are not initially imposed by society; because here the roles man/woman, fucked/fucker, master/slave are unstable and reversible at every turn.

This is what we defend under the name "Homosexuality." That is why we say, "We will be normal when you all become homosexuals": we don't want a homosexuality that would be accepted alongside heterosexuality. Because in our societies, heterosexuality is the rule, the norm, and you can't make the norm coexist with the abnormal. There is always a struggle between them.

We want the end of heterosexuality—in the sense that heterosexuality is at this moment inevitably a relationship of oppression.

This is not a sexual issue. It is above all an emotional issue.

The relationship of penetration of the woman by the man has been given such value by the Judeo-Christian-capitalist system that no heterosexual, however liberated they are, can pass it up. If he doesn't fuck his woman, he feels frustrated.

There are many who say: our aim is not to establish a single sexuality, homosexuality. We are for bisexuality, for sexual and emotional freedom. They also say: what counts is a true love relationship, between everyone, men and women or men and men or women and women.

But there is no egalitarian love without struggle because all of society turns love into a way to uphold inequality.

And the practical form of this struggle—we can't avoid it—is the passage through homosexuality.

The passage through *fully* accepted homosexuality: I believe that those who say "but my tastes are bisexual, I want to be able to love everyone" want to do without this passage through the moment where sexuality and feelings totally escape the dominant model. In short, as Margaret would say,[20] I don't readily believe in bisexuality, because it inherently derives from the prevailing form of emotional relations, heterosexuality. It replicates the relations of oppression.

I could only believe in bisexuality derived from homosexuality—that is to say, once the homosexual struggle has effectively destroyed all sexual norms.

On that day, even the words *homosexuality*, *heterosexuality* will lose their meaning.

Not before.

So, until that day, I will never be able to like heterosexuals as I like homosexuals. Because they will keep oppressing me. All those who dream of love without struggle against the dominant form of love give themselves up. Like many of the American hippies: by insisting on establishing true connection among all beings right away, they have hidden the struggle, including among themselves.

"Woodstock nation," the youth world of the pop festivals, has taught us something: that the class struggle was also a struggle for the expression of desire, for communication, and not simply an economic and political struggle.

But it tends to hide something from us: that we can only truly communicate by being equal. Which is specifically impossible as long as heterosexuality, even "liberated," remains the norm of the world of youth. There is no real love if sexuality is repressed: everyone agrees on that.

But then, don't we repress hetero love, like the heteros repress homosexual love? I don't think so!

For example, the relationships that homosexual men and women have in the FHAR. These relationships are, I think, true love relationships. And yet, we don't fuck each other.

Well, it is precisely *because* we don't fuck each other that they are true love relationships.

Sexuality is not at all *repressed* in my relations with a lesbian, while it is in my relations with another woman, who still more or less thinks that I am going to sleep with her . . .

Sexuality is not repressed, but on both sides the relationship of penetration[iii] is *consciously* refused.

What helps shape our understanding, our *egalitarian* love with lesbians, is that like them we refuse to perform the relationship of penetration among ourselves.

---

iii By "relation of penetration," I mean here the heterosexual relation: the bearer of the dominating phallus penetrating the submissive vagina, the whole thing tied socially to reproduction (even if it is for the most part avoided by the pill).

Nothing to do, obviously, with sodomy as a reversible homosexual practice, even if it mimics at times the heterosexual relation of penetration—GH.

We don't *repress* anything: we *refuse* together, from a common understanding, the dominant sexual form.

This understanding is a true love because it is based on an authentic *desire*: the desire to escape the normal.

It is love even in a libidinal form: we love kissing each other, we think we are beautiful.

Only the bourgeois think that true love finds its reality in pushing a cock into a vagina.

There are thirty-six thousand other forms of love. Even more: this form, cock in vagina, is exactly the kind that prevents true love right now.

Every emotional relationship has its sexual expression: but this sexual expression is not necessarily penetration—on the contrary.

TEXT DISTRIBUTED BY THE FHAR IN JUNE 1971;

REPRINTED IN *REPORT AGAINST NORMALITY* (PARIS:

ÉDITIONS CHAMP LIBRE, 1971)

....

After the FHAR, these homosexual militants became media spokespeople, for better or worse. A quickly tiresome experience, a tedious performance, as this interview shows.

....

"IT'S YOU WHO MUST BE CURED"

THE OFFICIAL "HOMO"

— I started from a totally personal experience. First, I'd had enough of hearing this: since you are homosexuals, we consider you to be really great guys, because you've come out. We then become public representatives of homosexuality. Not only will the people no longer blame you for being one. On the contrary! They will congratulate you. A little like they would sing the praises of an Algerian who became a political leader. Or else you are one of those who, as they say, can't accept themselves.

But they themselves believe a bit naively that their real goal is to come out as homosexuals . . .

— Why not?

— Once society recognizes you as a homosexual, you're well on your way! You are merely more trapped. Society is quite happy to make you play this part. Ultimately, it will even use you as a specialist in homosexuality. Outcome: no more personal life. As for me, every day I meet twenty guys whose stare tells me that they know they're speaking to the representative of homosexuality . . . revolutionary homosexuality, of course! Well, that's got high value! You're a card-carrying leftist! That's why homosexuality ought to be destroyed. Obviously I'm speaking about this separate category of fags.

Homosexuality, as a separate category, is a quite strong and cunning way of cutting individuals down to something trivial. It's so convenient! When homosexuals come out in a newspaper or any setting whatsoever, all of the group's homosexual fantasies converge on them, they are expelled from the others' ego, that is to say from the heteros that see them. And when you accept playing this part, calling yourself a revolutionary faggot, the "normal people," all while recognizing the value of your homosexuality, make theirs vanish. You thus perform a great service to heteros.

A FORCED CHOICE

— After all, not everyone is homosexual!

— Actually everything happens in the following way (and psychoanalysts don't hide it): in the beginning, children are polymorphously perverse. They are capable of taking pleasure from all the parts of their bodies and from any object. Perverse, but in a technical sense: Freud makes clear that the word does not have a moral meaning. In a second phase, the subject's sexual identity takes shape. The ego, the personality emerges through the relation to the mother, narcissism, etc. And, as if by chance, the subject, at a certain moment, finds itself before an absurd choice (at the level of desire, it makes no sense), a bit like Hercules between vice and virtue. The subject wonders deep down: am I homo- or heterosexual?

— As Stekel says,[21] it's the whole tragedy of Western Christianity, right? With only one God to love, are you homo- or heterosexual?

— Yes. But they don't tell you that if you want, you can be homosexual or heterosexual. They force you to choose heterosexuality, that should go without saying. If you don't stop yourself in time from jerking off your little friend (which all the heteros have done at some moment in their life), if you continue on this infantile path, you will pay the price for it: homosexuality will be your fate. From time immemorial, you were doomed to that. So you were, as they said, a homosexual!

— In your book,[22] you make a very interesting comment about the form that the repression of homosexuality takes today. You say something like, for normal people, homosexuality is kids' behavior, it's infrasexual.

— Take the *Simon Report*.[23] There is something amazing about this book. They asked people: at what age did you have your first complete sexual relationship? The average response was: nineteen years old. This was for men. Clearly, for each of these subjects, homosexual relations—masturbation alone or with little friends—don't count. The first sexual relationship, for them, is the fling with a chick, getting engaged. What must we conclude? People responded honestly to the survey, at least I want to believe so. They have thus *blocked* a whole part of their sexual life in their head. It's absurd . . . According to Kinsey's surveys, it's between thirteen and nineteen years old that men have the greatest sexual potency.

GUILTY SOCIAL CONSCIENCE

— What is the origin of *homosexuality* as a separate category?

— The appearance of this separate category, which allows us to think of deviancy on a sexual level (the condemnation of homosexuals is not primarily the repression of sexual relationships between men, it's the deviation with respect to the permissible sexual norm), it's kind of the product of one of humanity's obsessions. You can compare it to the Oedipus complex. Up through the nineteenth century, we lived within the obsession of the murder of the father. It was a ghost that haunted the history of societies. But this wasn't understood before the beginning of this century. Freud was the first to discover that our emotions, our love, our familial relations are based on the desire to kill the father. No one had realized that, had felt that before. At the same time, this discovery really altered all of past history: we saw it in a new light. In the same way, if you like, the creation of homosexuality as a separate category haunts the history of societies for a long time, like a fantasy. I should make clear that we are talking about discrete homosexuality, Oedipal, guilty. In Plato's *Symposium*, it's not about that.

— Hmm!

— Let's get this right, once and for all: I don't call a text that describes pederastic relationships between males homosexual. This is what I'm saying: homosexuality haunts humanity, like the guilty conscience of sexuality, a bit like Oedipus is the guilty conscience of the family (the group inside of which the processes of oppression develop). Of course, just as Freud discovered Oedipus in Greek tragedy, you can also talk to me about homosexuality in the Bible. If you just hitchhike your way back through the streets of the past, you'll think: the first time I went through, I didn't notice it. You will read history in another way!

HOMOSEXUALS AND CRIMINALS

— You also speak in your book about the police repression of homosexuals and the relationship between criminality and homosexuality. Could you say more about this?

— I began with a rather simple thought: every time we try to make homosexuality respectable, we push up against the same obstacle: how to remove fags from criminality, without ruining the libidinal or erotic relationship between fags and criminals? We mustn't be naive: there is a relation of desire between the two. It's not a coincidence that people in the FHAR have named their journal *Social Plague*.[24] They have reclaimed their criminality. What's the meaning of the Mirguet subamendment?[25] It's the passing of a law that puts homosexuality into criminality. Of course, at that time the National Assembly was unusually weak. Still, we mustn't turn a blind eye. Even for us, the criminal aspect of homosexuality offers an opportunity. And it's all to the homosexuals' credit.

— What do you mean?

— Let me make it clear: firstly, homosexuality is not subject to a lesser repression in France today. I gave some statistics in the book, I mentioned the laws that were passed after 1945—and even before! Sometimes we need a reminder. In addition, the attempt to make homosexuality dignified, respectable, or honorable, like what happened with the COC in Amsterdam,[26] or in France with Arcadie[27]—that's a joke; it's hopeless. I don't want to attack André Baudry, for whom I have infinite respect. But when I say it's a joke, what I mean is: it doesn't allow homosexuals to integrate into society, but makes the uniqueness, the specific character of homosexuality disappear. They reduce it to a more general problem: faithfulness, conjugality, etc. That is also why I insisted on giving the book the title *Homosexual Desire*. And it's a hopeless attempt: if you think about it, homosexuals will just move from the level of the criminal to that of the diseased. This step has already been gleefully taken by some psychiatrists. According to them, homosexuals shouldn't be punished, but treated. Not for us! The cop and the psychiatrist go hand in hand anyway, that's well known.

— Arcadie never asked to turn homosexuals into diseased people. Quite the opposite!

FROM GUILT TO ILLNESS

— Of course not! That's not the issue. Their dream is not to send their members to psychiatrists or psychoanalysts. But it's still no less obvious that if you want to help a friend escape the criminal cycle, in the case of police repression, it's unfortunately only to help them fall into the hands of psychiatrists instead. For a comrade not to go to prison, a medical authority has to intervene to declare them unfit. This is why an organization like Arcadie is hopeless. Getting the public at large, the press, etc. to adopt the attitude that entails saying, these poor people are not guilty, but diseased—this attitude could in fact represent an interesting step (see the Simon Report on this subject).[28] Indeed, as for me, I think that it is extremely dangerous and very bad for us, at least in the long term. And then, to come back to it, there is a quite clear relationship, in Genet for example, between homosexuality and criminality. And why are homosexuals attracted to prisons, to shady places? Let's go even further: it's this relationship between fags and criminals that makes homosexuals a group of people beyond redemption for society, a quite amazing revolutionary movement.

— Just like the whole Gérard Grandmontagne case.[29] Why did you dedicate your book to him, by the way?

— First, he was a friend of a friend. Second, he was a homosexual who hustled at Saint-Germain-des-Prés.[30] He had a proletarian upbringing (his parents were workers). From the age of seventeen, he did time on a regular basis, purely for small offenses. In all, six years. At thirty-one years old, he came to accept himself as homosexual and to become accepted by his prison friends, which is very hard. He was even able to gain respect from them—which is even harder. He was imprisoned as a drug dealer following police entrapment. He was thrown in solitary (the prison's dungeon), following another entrapment by the prison administration, for . . . homosexuality! And he hung himself. More exactly, he was found hanged. In Saint-Germain-des-Prés, at a sidewalk café, you see a bunch of guys like him who cruise, they have years of prison in front of or behind them, with suicides as the outcome. That's all.

"MANLY" FRIENDSHIP

— It is generally said that homosexuals are paranoid and have a persecution complex. You flip this idea: in the end, the others are the paranoid ones?

— I began with the example of the psychoanalyst Ferenczi in his psychopathology.[31] He specifically mentions the case of a city employee in a little German provincial town. This guy spent his time writing letters of complaint to the German authorities. He wrote: "It's outrageous! Across from my house, there are officers shaving in their underwear." These are the kinds of letters that still pile up today in the police stations of France. There is thus a widespread antisexual paranoia. But there is another kind due to a repressed homosexuality, which is also widespread. All the psychoanalysts know it well. But for them, it isn't freakish: this paranoia matches quite well with the general organization of a society that is itself paranoid. On the other hand, I found something striking in Genet: the relations of desire that develop between people who find themselves inside repressive institutions and these institutions themselves (prison, court, police, army, church, sport, etc.). When you see the comics on sale in Amsterdam, you notice that the cop, for example, plays a very strong erotic role, just like the paratrooper, the sailor, the SS. We could speak of a widespread phenomenon of inversion of the relations of desire, that is, the transformation of an object of love into an object of hate.

— Namely?

— Most of the cruelest and the most paranoid repressive institutions of this society are loaded with an extremely strong negative homosexuality. I gave examples of it in the book: army, police, sports, church . . . All of these institutions are male clubs where you find, on the one hand, this very strong charge of homosexuality, and on the other hand, they develop a fascist, anti-effeminate ideology against overt homosexual relationships. They protect themselves from their homosexual desire by means of sublimation ("manly" friendship). For if an erotic relationship were established between this or that member of the institution, a short circuit in the group's system of sexual energy would occur. Every hierarchical institution would collapse. Imagine two priests, two soldiers sleeping together. If that became widespread, why keep projecting their homosexual love onto the General or God the Father?

CURING THE HETEROSEXUALS

— What do you make of the case of Röhm in Germany?[32]

— How did it end? The bloodbath of the Night of the Long Knives, that's it, sort of the true start of Hitlerism. I didn't say it was better before. Röhm was a bastard, of course. We must demystify the old myth of fascist homosexuality: if there was any regime that threw fags in a concentration camp, it was Hitler's. But the physical extermination of Röhm's homosexual gang played a key role in the mythical and psychological genesis of Nazism. They had to get rid of those people in order to focus all Nazi homosexual desire on Hitler's person, and thus avoid any short-circuiting! That's why the institutions that repress overt homosexuality the most brutally are the same that contain the most explosive charge of homosexuality.

— To finish, is your book the end of a phase, like, for example, your participation in the FHAR?

— It's the end of the phase of vindication. It is an ambiguous book. I say there is no longer any reason to speak about homosexuality except to ask, Why on earth do heterosexuals have problems with us? I had said that homosexuality ought to be allowed. I would say now: why do heterosexuals remain paranoid? Our concern today is to cure heterosexuals; it's no longer to assert or to justify ourselves.

INTERVIEW CONDUCTED BY GEORGES DANJOU,

PUBLISHED IN S, NO. 2, JANUARY 1973

06 Motorcycles

Motorcycles, bikers, rocker (English for culbuteur),[1] *in order to speak your rum-blings of revolt and of jouissance, we must free you from the whole getup of simple explanations.*

....

THESE STRANGE DESIRING MACHINES

They interpret us, manipulate us, claim to explain us, to reduce us to their dirty little stories of mommy-daddy . . . They've almost pulled off giving us guilty consciences.

They are the psychologists, sociologists, psychoanalysts, educators, from *France-soir* to the commissions on juvenile delinquency. All those who see the motorcycle above all as compensation, Oedipus complex, anything except what it obviously is: a beautiful machine that roars, lunges, transmits energy to our bodies finally rid of guilt.

All those who invoke Humanity and its psychology, the Person and their repressions: all of those who think climbing on a bike is *showing off*: as if they don't show off in their own way, with their big words—and with fewer risks.

They say that we don't know what we desire, that they know in our place, that our desire tapped into our beautiful machines is only the expression of something else, which they know: the "deep structures of personality," our childhood, our parents, women, men . . .

Because, their first fear, their first concern is mainly that our desires are not what they are, but substitutes for something else, compensations for what they claim to be able to offer us.

According to them, our desires must really be the result of lacks—if not, where would we be? In an era when the young would be able to do without those who claim to teach them what they must desire?

Holy humanists who believe "worshipping a machine alienates the human person" and who protect a society where the worker is the slave of their labor machine.

Who condemn the young who love motorcycles as "victims of consumer society," but who would rather make us guzzle their cars, their detergents, their supermarkets, their organized leisure, their cultural centers.

Pathetic leftist sociologists, who want to see in our motorcycles a desire for transgression, a deviant feeling of revolt, and who don't see that our machines are neither for nor against the *law*: they pass it by; our desire knows no law, even if it were just a matter of accepting it shamefully. We hop on our bikes, not even to piss off the bourgeois, not even to scare mommy-daddy: purely because we want to.

We don't rev up to drown ourselves out, but to vibrate.

You thought you pinned us down by saying: "But all of that (motorcycles, leather jackets, the noisy, sputtering meetups) is sexual, it's because . . . you have problems with girls or with boys, with your masculinity or with your femininity."

Yes, it's sexual but not the way you mean; not like a heavy, shameful secret of poisoned affairs where you've locked up sexual desire; not like in your families where, according to you, the son hops on a motorcycle because the father is too weak or too strict (you aren't even consistent in your explanations).

It's sexual because sexual desire isn't confined to your sad accounts that endlessly repeat family complexes.

The motorcycle is sexual because nothing is more sexual than a machine: not as a substitute, not "in place of," but on its own. A less stuffy philosopher recently described the world of desire to you in this way: "A world of explosions, rotations, vibrations . . ." And elsewhere, the same thing: "Desiring machines pound away and throb in the depths of your unconscious . . ."[2]

When we played and got off with little trains, little bicycles, you were already there, you psychologists, psychiatrists, and psychoanalysts, to tell us: "The little train is daddy's genitals, the tunnel is mommy's genitals . . ." You continued by saying: "Your big motorcycles are daddy's big penis, which you want to have in order to make love with mommy . . ."

And of course, by ramming this type of stuff into our skulls in every way, you have ended up making us believe it. You tell the young that what they love about bikes is seeming super-manly, cruising chicks, specializing in beatdowns among real men. Now of course, plenty of young guys get caught up in this and honestly believe this whole sales pitch about manliness, and end up playing the roles prepared for them, the silly stereotypes of a bleak and narrow sexual universe.

No, motorcycles are not more masculine than feminine; you invented these labels. And then you come back to slap them on our faces, happy to rediscover what you created.

A desire machine does not mean manliness; it means pleasure, an unclassifiable and unmotivated pleasure that your psychological classifications will never exhaust, even if you force us to live by them.

Ours is a group machine, because we only experience it as a group. Our motorcycles are tuned to each other, our desire is communicable because we spread it among us through our relationships with machines. Not as consumers, but as desire machines, ours only work by breaking down; if we wanted machines without problems, we would buy your bullshit "practical" cars, where desire hides itself under the assassin's mask of the good family man, sure of his rights.

You claim that we must choose between machines and humanity.

We answer: we don't care about your old idealist crap, humanity. But against your crushing labor machines, your watch and time clock, your car and your subway, your social machine that crushes lives, we have chosen to vibrate in tune with our desire machines.

CULBUTEUR, NO. 2, APRIL 1972

Contradictions of a polymorphous cultural revolution: April 22, 1972, we had a bike demonstration in Paris against car pollution. Meeting pop ecology with rock 'n' roll's roar. Sometimes violent clashes . . .

CAR

PARIS   MOTORCYCLE

BICYCLE

April 22: thousands of bicycles rode across Paris, from Porte Dauphine to the Bois de Vincennes.[3] Thousands of youth stuck the well-known "for sale" sign on cars they blocked. For sale, or for smashing. The car, capital of neurosis, traveling family, confined space (close the door! don't speak out the window!) where the public housing on wheels becomes a killing machine. Everyone who piles up high in the towers and housing blocks is thrown into the mad charge of streets and highways. Shoulder to shoulder in apartment buildings (neighbors don't speak to each other), facing off on the road, bumper to bumper, just watch Godard's *Weekend*, if it ever comes back to theaters.[4]

Against that, thronging bikes, huge avenues filled all at once with the country tinkling of silver bells, finally heard through the smog. Saying hello saddle to saddle instead of slinging insults wheel to wheel. And our motorcycles in all of this?

Everything about us seems to conflict with the April 22 demonstrators. Everything, on the surface. And yet . . . we feel like we agree. Of course, motorcycles aren't particularly quiet. They even have the tendency to backfire. And then, above all, environmentalists and avid cyclists are a rather nonviolent type, flowers and little birds, peace and love. Motorcycles seem more aggressive, violent, helmeted, booted, studded leather, and so on. Culturally, it's a bit like the Beatles (Lennon) against MC5's rock.[5] Sociologically, students and ex-students against hoodlums and dropouts. It's guitar and drums, collectives and bands. And yet, as we know, we want the youth movement not to be in conflict or divided.

Pollution? Everyone agrees. Noise? We all know that the same person who protests against the noise of cars lets their stereo wail at night with their friends. Of course, no one is for or against "Noise," as Poujade,[6] minister of the environment and its surroundings, would have us believe. We are against the dictatorship of the only allowed noise, the only legal noise, the noise of four wheels. Just as we are not against the TV, but against the legal violence it creates by being the only centralized and authorized mode of audiovisual expression.

What do we all agree that we are against? Against the horrible sameness that resolves the question of who gets to use the streets with the victory of the biggest and strongest. It's not just an issue of transportation. Transportation is not chiefly moving from one point to another. For a start, transportation is a social space and a space of desire. But there are two types of transportation: the imperialist, controlled kind, tied to the big producers of fuel and cars, and the marginal kind, young people on the run or meeting up, looking for something, or wandering around. Car transportation is imperialist, utilitarian, attached to work even in the organized leisure of weekends. It gobbles up the city: riverside expressways, beltways, parking lots. It gobbles up the countryside: who will declaim the dreary two-lane highways in deadlock? The car is the reign of the useful, of jobs, of structure. Only the car has every right. First off, the right to kill. The road belongs to the car and no one else. Bikers know it better than anyone, since they are tolerated yet chased down by the big hulking cars.

The revolt of bicycles and motorcycles, of pedestrians and scooters, of youth and kids, confronts the common enemy: the father of the family at the wheel of his clear conscience. Bikers greet each other. Drivers insult each other. Drivers constantly repeat the rigged journey: job—sleep—weekend. The youth ramble, go out to meet up, drift on the machines of their desire.

CULBUTEUR, NO. 3, MAY 1972

07 MLF—FHAR

Toward What End?

Sex versus feelings, the head and the crotch, this sticky debate can only finish with the end of the fighters—the end of rigid sexual identities.

....

WOMEN AND FAGS

A hideous spawn. Shaky couple. Badly married: what is there for them to do together, fags and dykes, since they don't want to make love with each other?

This partnership is not obvious at all. Fags come off like misogynists, that's well known. They have the cult of the cock and of manliness. Ah, women! Horrible, vindictive, stealing our men . . .

But don't fags ask to be dealt with like women, while women, rightly, are sick of it?

And yet: in the USA, since the beginning of the Gay Liberation Front in June '69[1] after the death of a young fag during a police raid on a "gay bar," Women's Lib[2] supported them. In France, it's even clearer: the lead comes from women. From the MLF, first: since its beginning, it set the stage for a new understanding of what we call *the struggles*. The political field has been sexualized; or rather, it has become possible to unite the struggle of people concerned with the same "private" condition. One is a woman before being a Trotskyite or Maoist, so why not the same for fags? The private life—that is, deprived of political meaning—has now become a site of struggle. The signs flipped: privately, fags hate women. In the struggle, they find themselves side by side. For that matter, women also took the lead on the homosexual issue. There was already a homosexual club in France, but hushed and secretive: Arcadie. The women who were part of it joined together with the MLF: they copied the fags, and in March '71 this particular group demonstrated consecutively at the Mutualité,[3] attacking a meeting against abortion, then sabotaging a broadcast by Ménie Grégoire about homosexuality.[4] The term *hetero-cop* popped up. Then *Tout!*, issue 12, came out during the discussion about abortion in the *Observateur*, to which fags and women actively contributed.[5] It was the dykes who started it: most of the MLF was actually reluctant, or even openly critical of this newly arrived little runt,[6] the FHAR, which copied the way the MLF worked (weekly general assembly at the Beaux-Arts), mimicked the style (songs, weekend gatherings, love among ourselves, war against misogynists). Even *Tout!*, issue 12, contained a manifesto of 343 sluts who had been fucked in the ass by Arabs . . .[7]

A new political logic emerged: up until then, relationships between fags and women had been marked by guilt, entailed by a concept of desire founded on lack and castration. In the end both groups said, screw castration, we can get off [*jouir*] without following or breaking the law of the phallus. And then there were shared targets: the reproductive heterosexual family, etc. We joined together to condemn this role. On the MLF side, they got used to finding fags at each demo. It seemed only natural. At heart, they didn't really know why except that in principle "they aren't like other men" since we have the same enemy: misogyny, those macho show-offs who beat up fags and catcall chicks. At the risk of caricature, you could say that the women in the MLF were the real butches of the FHAR,[8] politically speaking. They were the ones in charge.

Within the little leftist world, fags continued to enjoy the desirable—and desired—position of being the only men to talk with the women in the MLF. A position that was important to protect. On the flipside, working with fags, women showed their ability to speak to men—or at least people physiologically pronounced as such. Living side by side while planning actions, during little group discussions, some fags and some women end up making genuine—though completely platonic—declarations of love. Having removed the dreadful relationship of penetration on either side, and since we hadn't found—actually, we still haven't found—how to enact our relationships, we came to mix up collaboration against a same enemy and a true libidinal relationship.

The FHAR has always maintained an irresponsible side; an inability for thinking strategically. Not the MLF. Women, half of humanity, a real community, are hardly similar to the Brownian motion of a few hundred fags.[9] The MLF looms large over the FHAR. For women, fags speak too much about sex and little about love. They are sexually obsessed, their fantasies revolving around what is sleazy or abject, cruising the public bathrooms or the bushes in the Tuileries.

Women, on the contrary, fly the flag for true love, for emotional warmth, for big, deep feelings that they find missing in the world of men. Women fight in the name of love, fags in the name of sex. The debate comes back a thousand times, and namely during the last weekend that a few FHAR friends and a few MLF friends spent together. "Your stories of buggery are sadomasochistic, we want to hear about love. Rise above the zipper," they say. To which the fags respond, "But that's all they've ever wanted to make us do: sublimate, perform the assumption of homosexual sex in order to transform it into a purified feeling; we have no room for that." Problem: the girls explained that they were fed up with being catcalled by guys in the street. The fags responded that they only asked for that: to be catcalled, to have someone slap their ass. They go to Morocco and Tunisia for that. Perhaps it would be better to walk in pairs, a fag + a woman, and they could deflect the compliments given out from one to the other . . . But above all, the inhibiting aspects of these identities, of these institutional meetings of different groups, of these relationships of power have increasingly appeared to us. Fags, women, dykes: we are not simply that.

Yes, fags and chicks are more or less willingly stuck together: perhaps there is no need to maintain this separation of sexes, which is just the child of heterosexual domestic society, forever. Fags, dykes, women, women-fags, fag-dykes: the less we have identities and roles among ourselves, the better off we'll be. To each their genders, and to everyone all the genders. And all the hookups. That is, once misogynists are eliminated, of course.

ACTUEL, NO. 25, NOVEMBER 1972

A SHAMELESS TRANSVERSALISM

Let's invent slits and slopes that slice hierarchies and the specializations according to new layers. We cut up "social reality" how it suits us; risking confusion, we systematically pass from one order to another (aesthetics, politics, turn-ons, theory); we transversalize by transposing what happens here somewhere else without rhyme nor reason, not in order to make everything the same—for we need potential differences to power our cut. We don't seek to create hybrids, to marry everything through limp mediations, but to make everything intersect, to "interpellate"[10] as they say, fags with motorcycles, Fourier with "drugs," leftism with cash.

Money: it's sort of the bourgeois transversalism, this universalization that is the simplest way to pull everything down to the same scale. Our movement responds to this: instead of putting everything in the same key, leveling it all out to make anything exchangeable, we transmute from one order to another practically. It's not a matter of saying: love, family, profession, science, war, everything is revalued or devalued according to a single scale. We can't expect anything from a "universal exchange," even though its reign has made everything possible for us; but we have everything to desire from the unmediated transmutation of one "nature" into another. Not what's exchangeable, but transformable, or replaceable bit by bit. Transgender, for example, is not the middle between man and woman, or the universal mediator (man into woman, woman into man); it's one part of a world transferred into another like we pass from one universe to another universe parallel to the first (or perpendicular, or askew . . .); or rather, it's a million inappropriate gestures, transferred features, events (growing breasts, removing hair) happening in as untimely a way as the appearing or disappearing of a feline smile in *Alice in Wonderland*.

We aren't looking for new material. We produce the unexpected. The new only ever appears wherever the old assigns it its place. Producing the unexpected, the improper[11]—a flying carpet that rescues us from taking root in shame and propriety—this transversalization provides a response to the mobile warfare of capital (its fluid and instantaneous displacement from one continent to another by the forces of multinationals), a response to its slipperiness. In the battle led by capital, territorial defenses (the political and moral defense against capitalist cynicism; the theoretical defense, truth against formalism; the syndicalist defense, labor force against the shape-shifting vampire; the sentimental defense, against dehumanization by machines) are just like the Maginot Line facing German tanks.[12] Humanist progressivism is still fighting the last war. It blames capital for being stateless, without family, without morals, whereas all this baggage disables us, delivers us unarmed and tied up to the shape-shifting circulation of money.

Transversalism, transgender, versatility. Slide from one order to another, following the rifts. Social surfaces, smoothed over by the waves of repetitions without jouissance, no longer show us anything but the usual scenery to look at, a flat horizon of dull convictions without adventure. But if a crack appears, a split: let's go to a new layer, cut into the raw tissue, and suddenly, a freely flowing vein will open, new smells bubbling up with unimagined desires. But theory will never break or crack its own glass, not any more than the flow of cash will cut through the ocean of the monetary system. Throwing a tomato works against someone making a speech, as we discovered in May, but so does a very specific kind of touch against political attacks.

Enough with the well-behaved scientific and interdisciplinary transversalities, with institutional analysis used to confirm all the fears, or to spice up restructuring and reforms. Journey through the institutions: Dutschke already spoke about it.[13] Does this just mean adding a new kind of tourism, beyond nations and countries, in the air-conditioned buses of new institutional-internship assignments, training, professional audits— where the windshield of analysis protects the researcher?

Not here. A shameless, slutty transversalism, having lost all modesty— i.e., all sense of what's appropriate—that endlessly tries to put square pegs in round holes, losing its identity while gaining it, lewd when accepted as theoretical, "untimely." Fleeting. Spinning in a spiral. Like a journey through time: fully present at every instant, but cutting another path at the same time. Confusing the order of causes and consequences, because it tangles these big strings through determining first after, and then before. Carving up the worm of order.

And where is your landmark movement in all of this? A FHAR ball and chain attached to the token homosexual's foot, a heavy collar whose bells alert the entire Order of your movements at every moment. You must choose: remain motionless or signal where you are, where you are coming from, where you are going. Militant homosexual revolutionary here, ding dong ding; yet I had believed that at this level—it was so specific, so local, compared to the old organized politics—we would never be pinned down by social entomology.

The homosexual movements are done. Certainly, they will still develop, bring about changes in conditions for fags. But as *movements*, they are dead. The internal spring that makes them work is at the end of its life span; they've used up all the energy that could arise from the framework they were given.

Some indications: the issue of the magazine *Recherches* published before the summer of '73 by a group that would no longer agree to be seen as part of the FHAR, as well as some women not of the MLF persuasion, under the title "About the Shattered FHAR and MLF."[14] Even *Le nouvel observateur* mentioned that this issue broke with a FHAR. . . whose whereabouts no one knew any longer. In the USA, Gay Lib no longer exists as a centralized movement; it split into groups that either don't give a shit about homosexual liberation in general (trans people, sadomasochists . . .) or who violently attack the very idea of a homosexual movement. One example is the "revolutionary effeminists," newly born from the rubble of Gay Lib (since June '72). This is how they begin their Manifesto, which caused quite a stir: "We, the . . . effeminists . . . invite all like-minded men to join with us in making our declaration of independence from gay liberation and all the other male ideologies . . ."[15]

In any case, today the FHAR has fortunately split into more specific concerns than at its beginning. An American friend, attending for the first time what we still call a general assembly of the FHAR (a gigantic cruising site on six floors of a university building, probably the most considerable cruising space in Paris, if not in Europe) asked: *What is it supposed to be?*[16] He was hoping to launch a discussion that our answer—"it's the general assembly"—would have brought into militant terms. But this place is not supposed to be anything: it rejoins itself and rejoices in itself each week.[17] Thus the FHAR has really transformed Paris's homosexual geography— and that's already not so bad, having removed the police threat for the time being.

Meanwhile all kinds of indications allow us to imagine that a scope of homosexual movement, however narrow and fragile it might be, has recently emerged from the FHAR. It's as true for the news media as for public gardens—I've been surprised at nights in the Tuileries where fags armed with clubs handle "hooligans," or even the cops.

We can see it: thirsting for other modes of organizing than the FHAR doesn't mean giving up on all "homosexual militancy." In 1973, the pervasiveness of militant homosexual movements linked to leftism in Europe (Holland, Denmark, West Germany, Italy . . .) shows that a traditional "political space" is being taken over. But how sad is political space. A demo of fags down the Kurfürstendamm in West Berlin, chanting against sexual racism, like it's properly new and not at all untimely . . .

FAKE UNITIES

The very term *homosexual* gets in the way, with what it implies of guaranteed homogeneity.[18] It's too transparent, our movements are much more hetero than homo. We don't aim to be faithful to ourselves, in permanent self-sameness.

There was a rule in the FHAR and MLF that said that only women had the right to speak about women and only fags had the right to speak about fags.

This rule assigns one speech to one subject, forces acceptance of an identification, claims territories. A rule that had meaning when it aimed to block speech meant to oppress women and homosexuals, by identifying them as such all while keeping the benefits of the status of manly man for the speaker. A rule that becomes oppressive once it obliges me to restrict myself to the role of official fag, that is of speaking about fags as a fag, from a fixed and assigned place; once it obliges a comrade from the MLF to take on the nature of "woman," that narrows the scope of their desires and forbids them or me from becoming, for example, a fag-lesbian.[19] This rule died for me once it transformed itself into passport control for speech. Of course, we must say where we speak from, but we should be able to move. Thus it seemed to me that after three and a half years in the USA, and two years in France, the homosexual and women's movements turned out to be false alliances—or they became false. Yes, these movements broke off from oppressive wholes—political groups, ideologies, and to a limited extent social classes—but in order to establish others, big protest rallies, antisexist, antimale movements. But we don't live off antisexism. In order to set the guest molecules,[20] the little gears of jouissance, into motion,[21] we have to melt the ice of these big groups that restrain them, sever and break up these grand alliances where archetypes return at full speed.

What Marcuse wrote on this matter in his last book, *Counterrevolution and Revolt*, reflects rather well a certain inclination of the women's liberation movement and especially the effeminists: "That this image (and reality) of the woman has been determined by an aggressive, male-dominated society, does not mean that this determination must be rejected, that the liberation of women must overcome the female 'nature.'"[22] For the revolutionary effeminists, joining the women's side involves developing "feminine" qualities in themselves: love of the other and not the rough sexuality of *Gay Lib*, sensitivity, etc. A whole moral rearmament program against male capitalist inhumanity. Just as a certain MLF ideology forces woman to "take on her femininity" so as not to betray it . . .

The archetype of the liberated fag has fortunately never had enough power to impede the fragmentation of the homosexual movement, a fragmentation that the MLF resists better. But don't you feel, here too, the unease that cracks the clear consciences of the MLF, owing certain accepted forms of unity to the cost of a real psychological lockdown, to the blackmail of faithfulness or betrayal? The fact that a woman can gather around her a whole group of girls who have become her "patients," bathing in a mixture of political leadership and of affective-psychoanalytic submission, is not surprising once you've felt the power of the MLF ideological glue. The bonds of the FHAR were more practical—cruising—than ideological; their breakup is just as easy. The MLF isn't collapsing, but its ideology safeguards its cohesiveness in an oppressive way.

PRINCIPLE—WOMAN AGAINST SPLINTERED HOMOSEXUALS

Two sides in this new constellation that arises from the splintering of homosexual movements: one side is splintered practices, forming little groups around sex and life, such as trans groups, pedophiles, Arabophiles, who were described in an issue of *Recherches* ("Three Billion Perverts"), or the American sadomasochists. And the other side, demonstrated by American revolutionary effeminism, is the guilty conscience of being male and not female. One side acts in the body and blurs sexual definitions, the other side unifies everyone around intangible and simple sexual identities: we are men and therefore oppressors; how can you forgive our nature? The appearance in the issue of *Recherches* of innumerable erect cocks allowed a certain MLF ideology to classify immediately: these are men, misogynists. Similarly, the American effeminists haphazardly condemn masculine sadism, maso-transgender, rock-transgender, and Warholism as continuations of male ideology. In other terms, the movement is stretched between two extremes, one body with multiple organs (sado-maso, trans, etc.) and a new morality that aims to exclude the diversity and the polymorphism of the new perverts to the benefit of one and only one law, which draws a line between friends and enemies of the People—excuse me, of women. The revolutionary effeminists write (in "The Effeminist Manifesto"):

1 SEXISM. All women are oppressed by all men, including ourselves. This systematic oppression is called sexism.

2 . . . Sexism itself is the product of male supremacy, which produces all other forms of oppression . . . racism, classism, . . .ecological imbalance.

3 GYNARCHISM. Only that revolution which strikes at the root of all oppression can end any and all of its forms. That is why we are gynarchists; that is, we are among those who believe that women will seize power from the patriarchy.[23]

We recognize the style: this sort of Mao-feminism uses the whole operation of typical political discourse, just changing *proletariat* to *women*; this type of masochist delusion (for these guys don't doubt for a minute their untouchable male nature, they even glory in confessing it)—does it threaten us as well?

By wanting to discover the sexist enemy everywhere, we mistake the meaning of signs. The cocks in *Recherches* for example: they are only hijacked signs [*détournés*] that no longer occupy their transcendent signification, the grand Phallus that distinguishes man from women. These cocks are as fragmented as dildos or graffiti. Meanwhile, a new Phallus appears in the full sense, in this law that discriminates and excludes in the name of the Woman-Principle. Likewise for sadomasochistic practices: they are condemned by the ideology of a certain MLF or by the effeminists who read the signs of oppression, hijacked [*détournés*] by the pervert toward the aims of jouissance, as the reality of oppression.

But where does moral masochism stand, the kind based in submission, if not on the side of an ideology that replaces the Worker with the Woman in the role of Great Guilt-Tripper? Certain MLF groups are the worst enemies of trans people. The effeminists, who call it by the old psychiatric name of *eonism*,[24] write: "Certainly, sado-maso-eonism in all its forms is the very anti-thesis of effeminism. Both the masochist and the eonist are particularly an insult to women since they overtly parody female oppression."[25] Strangely enough, it's because the *Gay Lib* leaders had accepted trans people and sadomasochists into the ranks of the usual June parade that the effeminists announced their refusal to participate in the march. This is the "Woman-Principle" at work: everything that blurs the clear definition of the new law, everything that escapes grand classification, is the enemy. Everything that is a hijacked [*détourné*] sign, a perverse use, is dangerous. As if feminine qualities were not basically trans to begin with.[26]

THE GREAT UPENDING

Let's not fool ourselves[27]: "gender" is no more the grand signifier than anything else. And for that matter, sex can and should be challenged [*interpellé*] with violence, with art . . . The desiring fascism that marks the annals of the great libertines of the Western world is also the great big sense of being in one's place, dressed up to look like the most absolute radicalism and revolutionary apoliticism. Those who enjoy the most advanced perversions, lavish necrophiles of New York, or connoisseurs of Amsterdam's saunas and all of Europe's parks, terrify me in their perverse professionalism, having the power to rebuild everywhere (with the help of credit cards and the grand hotels) their territory from which any event is excluded ahead of time. There is a multinational power of sex as stateless as capital but also as nonchalantly oppressive and sure of itself, whose dividends are measured in cock strokes. Here, too, we get caught willingly, as if the whole journey since May could be summarized in the move from the world of slaves to the world of libertinized masters. But, breakthrough, we want to cut up the world of masters with the world of slaves, just like we want to cut up the world of slave territories painstakingly defended by narrow morals with the stateless jouissances of the world of masters.

Sade and the French Revolution—these two ruptures—and many others, meet here.[28]

The great upending imagines stronger emotions, more intense joys, deeper fractures, than the incomes of some perversions—fags, motorcycles, leather, drugs—whose capital is as off-limits as a big bank's.

Perversion first differentiates itself from normal pleasure in that it "costs" more, since for the social machine it amounts to a waste of forces in a quick potlatch carefully isolated from the production that works to accumulate these forces. This is its way of being integrated in society. But living out perversion in such a representation, as a shareholder who spends their income instead of investing it, somewhat narrows jouissance. In truth, perversion drags us along when its expenses are beyond the measure of the normal price range of our society. To say that the great upending corresponds with a luxury that "is very expensive" (Lyotard) is to play along with social integration of jouissance as "extra" or a supplement to the menu.[29] It means accepting the organization of the discourse shaped by the relation of oppressor-oppressed, the squabbling that gauges the jouissance of the masters by wasted fruits of labor, thereby giving it importance and prohibiting its use by the slaves.

So what? What if the oppressed did find out that what the masters pay a high price for could just as well be free? All the money in the world used up in buying the tiniest orgasm in the Gare du Nord bathrooms. To close the gap by paying for perverse jouissance according to the law of value, capital would be swallowed up in vain. The price of perversion is high enough, as gigolos know well, to break the financial balance of a world based exclusively on labor and capital. Precisely because it doesn't follow the laws of capitalist profitability or the laws of the defense of the labor force.

Let's upend ourselves, and declare the law of value bankrupt. In other words: luxury could be free because it has no price. Three billion perverts, three billion superstars . . . We always imagine that we need a fund of "fans" and normal people whose extorted surplus value bankrolls the star system or perversion.[30] Wrong: it's a matter of position, a matter of breaking out, not of linking explanation-exploitation, but rather of cutting.

Thus an old story of commitment dies. We no longer commit ourselves to just battles, we act through our positions; not out of a sense of men's battles, but through the breaking out of tiny obsessions for no reason: getting high, motorcycles, sodomy, being trans, all these ways of living aren't just an issue of how to be revolutionary, but are the absolute present of the untimely. We don't tackle the big questions that concern humanity head-on. We slip sideways between two layers of guilty conscience, crumbling the frameworks where they try to confine us from behind[31] into multiple quiverings of the social body in its infinite urgent places.

JULY 1973

Translator's Notes

TRANSLATOR'S INTRODUCTION

1 Hocquenghem, *Homosexual Desire*, trans. Daniella Dangoor (Durham, NC: Duke University Press, 1993). The other two are the novel *Love in Relief*, trans. Michael Whisler (New York: SeaHorse Press, 1986), and the posthumous novel *Amphitheater of the Dead*, trans. Max Fox (New York: Guillotine, 2019). A contentious text, *The Screwball Asses*, trans. Noura Wedell (Los Angeles: Semiotext(e), 2010), has been available in English for some time, but Hocquenghem's partner Roland Surzur has definitively debunked it as a single-author text by Hocquenghem. The text was part of the famous jointly authored "Three Billion Perverts," an issue of Félix Guattari's *Recherches* journal (Hocquenghem and René Schérer, eds., "Trois milliards de pervers: Grande Encyclopédie des Homosexualités," special issue, *Recherches*, no. 12 [1973]). The "true" author is Christian Maurel.

2 Hocquenghem's title, *L'après-mai des faunes*, refers to Stéphane Mallarmé's poem, "L'après-midi d'un faune" ("The Afternoon of a Faun"), which also inspired a symphonic piece by Claude Debussy and a ballet by Vaslav Nijinsky (with collaboration from Jean Cocteau)—giving it a queer lineage. Instead of a literal translation of Hocquenghem's title, which would lose all of this resonance, I gave a more descriptive title to this collection of works that catalog the rise and fall of French gay liberation in relation to the May '68 uprising. Hocquenghem's introduction was also the title of his dissertation, "Volutions: La revolution culturelle en Europe" (Volutions: The Cultural Revolution in Europe; Université Paris VIII Vincennes-Saint-Denis, 1972). His director was François Châtelet (1925–85), who spearheaded the Philosophy Department at Vincennes alongside Deleuze and Michel Foucault. The dissertation was accepted as part of the '68 reforms, *sur travaux*, which meant it contained work previously written or published. According to Antoine Idier, there is no record of the defense or even the makeup of Hocquenghem's committee. Idier states that René Schérer claimed that in addition to himself and Châtelet, Deleuze, Olivier Revault d'Allonnes, and Jean-Pierre Colin were present. Schérer also said that Deleuze's foreword contained here came out of the dissertation defense. Antoine Idier, *Les vies de Guy Hocquenghem* (Paris: Fayard, 2017), 141–42.

3 This volume, 12.

4 This volume, 12. Academic theory and political philosophy tend to enshrine the individual and align concepts with a singular name. Perhaps in this way, Hocquenghem's militancy disappears into the collective, which is a common element among anarchists whose names don't get solidified into a theory like Marx, Lenin, Trotsky, or Mao.

5 This volume, 12.

6 This volume, 12.

7 In Gilles Deleuze, *Desert Islands and Other Texts, 1953–1974*, ed. David Lapoujade, trans. Michael Taormina (Cambridge, MA: Semiotext(e), 2004), 284–88.

8 This introduction has also been translated at least twice into English: in *Baedan*, vol. 2, *A Journal of Queer Heresy* (New York: Contagion, 2014); and in Ron Haas, "Guy Hocquenghem's 'Volutions,'" *Radical Philosophy Review* 11, no. 1 (2008).

9 For some textual examples of current Black anarchist thinking, see Zoé Samudzi and William C. Anderson, *As Black as Resistance: Finding the Conditions for Liberation* (Chico, CA: AK Press, 2018); and Revolutionary Abolitionist Movement, *Burn Down the American Plantation: Call for a Revolutionary Abolitionist Movement* (New York: Combustion Books, 2017).

10 This volume, 117.

11 Idier, *Les vies de Guy Hocquenghem*, 132. Unless otherwise noted, all translations are my own.

12 Hocquenghem began railing against this betrayal already in *Gay Liberation after May '68*, but continued leveling his critique until his death, as in his 1986 *Lettre ouverte à ceux qui sont passes du col Mao au Rotary* (Open Letter to Those Who Gave Up the Mao Jacket for the Rotary Club) (Paris: A. Michel, 1986). For another contemporaneous perspective, see Jacques Camatte, "May–June 1968: The Exposure," where he names Marxism as "repressive consciousness [conscience repressive]." Jacques Camatte, "May–June 1968: The Exposure," *Fifth Estate* (November 1978).

13 Eventually the FHAR split around experiences of misogyny involving the gay men, the emphasis on sex acts and desire over love and care, and the splintering into narrower groups. Hocquenghem writes about the FHAR meetings becoming the biggest cruising site in Paris, which for him was also a revolutionary act.

14 Hocquenghem wrote a fictionalized account of this relationship in *The Amphitheater of the Dead*. In *Les vies de Guy Hocquenghem*, Idier points out that Schérer had been excluded from the Communist Party in the 1950s due to his sexuality, a repeated phenomenon in the traditional leftist formations that led to the gay liberation movement of the 1960s and 1970s. Hocquenghem and Schérer coauthored multiple texts, none translated into English, including *Co-ire*, which takes a frank approach to childhood sexuality as well as intergenerational relationships. There are important questions as well as periodic

scandals around the pedophilic nature of certain types of relationships and queer traditions, though many researchers are loath to explore these elements, except in distant times and cultures. Contrary to feeling like he was harmed, Hocquenghem maintained a relationship with Schérer (not always sexual) until Hocquenghem's death. In the 1970s, there was a political battle to lower the age of consent for homosexual acts from twenty-one (until 1974) and then from eighteen, since it was higher than the general age of consent (fifteen). This law served as a tool to criminalize queer sex. In *Gay Liberation after May '68*, Hocquenghem mentions youth sexuality and consent a few times, calling out the hypocrisy of expecting youth to be on the streets for militant movements without supporting their sexual autonomy but also critiquing groups like the FHAR for excluding "child lovers," a group that will never find "reintegration into the dominant morality" (this volume, 80). He treats trans people as another group that creates anxiety around inclusion/exclusion for militants, though there is no parallel with pederastic or intergenerational queer relationships. For further reading on the latter topics, see Kadji Amin's *Disturbing Attachments: Genet, Modern Pederasty, and Queer History* (Durham, NC: Duke University Press, 2017), which historicizes Jean Genet's support of pederasty in relation to radical politics and movements, and also explores Hocquenghem's shortcomings.

15   In his biography of Hocquenghem, Idier relates an anecdote about the response Hocquenghem got when he asked for an extra year of stipend for writing his thesis at the ENS in 1970. The director refused, telling him, "The state can't endlessly pay you to destroy it." Still, he was subsequently hired at Vincennes to teach a course named Revolution in the USA. Idier, *Les vies de Guy Hocquenghem*, 60.

16   Michael Moon, introduction to Guy Hocquenghem, *Homosexual Desire*, trans. Daniella Dangoor (Durham, NC: Duke University Press, 1993), 10. I want to express my gratitude to Michael Moon, who was an early supporter of this project and whose inspiration and influence guided me.

17   Tim Dean, "The Antisocial Homosexual," PMLA 121, no. 3 (2006): 826–28. The classic reference texts are Leo Bersani's "Is the Rectum a Grave?" (*October*, no. 43 [1987]: 197–222) and Lee Edelman's *No Future* (Durham, NC: Duke University Press, 2004).

18   Quoted in Dean, "The Antisocial Homosexual," 827.

19   Eve Kosofsky Sedgwick also provides a warm overview of Hocquenghem's utopian liberationism in a late text, "Anality," in *The Weather in Proust* (Durham, NC: Duke University Press, 2011), defending aspects of his project against a form of masculine protest embodied by Jeffrey Guss. Sedgwick, too, notes that Hocquenghem and his contemporaries always associated queer liberation with an antiracist, anticolonial, anticapitalist, antimisogynistic project, and these other "coalitionary" strands can fall off in the critiques of identity.

20   Amin, *Disturbing Attachments*, 16, 78–79, 95, 96, 189.

21 Amin, *Disturbing Attachments*, 79.

22 Jack Halberstam, *The Queer Art of Failure* (Durham, NC: Duke University Press, 2011).

23 Much of the legacy of French theory in general ends up performing a naturalizing move by shifting the critique from the realm of political or collective struggle to that of subjectivity. For more on the reactionary work of French theory, despite its aura of radicality, see Gabriel Rockhill, "The CIA Reads French Theory: On the Intellectual Labor of Dismantling the Cultural Left," *Los Angeles Review of Books*, February 28, 2017.

24 This volume, 57.

25 This volume, 57.

26 This volume, 57.

27 This volume, 56.

28 Fred Moten and Stefano Harney, *The Undercommons: Fugitive Planning and Black Study* (Brooklyn: Minor Compositions, 2013), 26.

29 Moten and Harney, *Undercommons*.

30 This volume, 116.

31 This volume, 116.

32 This volume, 1.

33 This volume, 112.

34 This volume, 6.

35 I give more detailed historical context in a footnote to the article, "Long Live Free Bengal," this volume, 136n23.

36 For analysis in this line, see Leila Shami, "The Anti-imperialism of Idiots," *It's Going Down*, May 4, 2018; and CrimethInc, "Why the Turkish Invasion Matters: Addressing the Hard Questions about Imperialism and Solidarity," October 12, 2019, https://crimethinc.com/2019/10/12/why-the-turkish-invasion-matters-addressing-the-hard-questions-about-imperialism-and-solidarity.

37 This volume, 31.

38 This volume, 31.

39 Ron Haas, "Utopia Aborted: May '68 in the Philosophy of Guy Hocquenghem," *Annual Proceedings of the Western Society for French History* 32 (2004): 417. For Hocquenghem, gay practices were revolutionary because of this clandestine factor, which created a space outside society. For similar writing in an American context, see Samuel Delany, who, in *Times Square Red, Times Square Blue* (New York: New York University Press, 1999), famously laments the loss of the porn theaters in the redevelopment of Times Square in the 1990s and uses his experience to theorize another utopian form of public sex, consent based and protected against masculine violence, within a class analysis. Delany's descriptions of the relations between men across racial and class divides, as well as relations among people of different genders, contain the formation of other worlds that already exist in the transversal gaps of this world.

40 This volume, 92. This uselessness is part of Edelman's elaboration of queerness as the "death drive" of society in *No Future*.

41 This volume, 97.

42 This volume, 37.

43 See, for example, James Penney's scathing assessment of Hocquenghem in *After Queer Theory* (London: Pluto, 2013).

44 This volume, 97.

45 This volume, 97, 98–99.

46 See Halberstam, *Queer Art of Failure*, for a possible lineage to the act of quitting.

47 Anonymous, "Against the Gendered Nightmare: Fragments on Domestication," *Baedan 2: A Queer Journal of Heresy*, 4–5.

48 "Against the Gendered Nightmare," 41.

49 Combahee River Collective, "The Combahee River Collective Statement," in *How We Get Free: Black Feminism and the Combahee River Collective*, ed. Keeanga-Yamahtta Taylor (Chicago: Haymarket Books, 2017), 15.

50 Combahee River Collective, "Statement," 18.

51 Combahee River Collective, "Statement," 23.

52 This volume, 90.

53 See Idier, *Les vies de Guy Hocquenghem*, 139.

54 When I say *gender abolition* I mean the destruction of the gender binary as a coercively assigned, policed typology of bodies that devolves from a hierarchy of masculine domination, compulsory heterosexuality, colonial rule, and anti-Blackness. It doesn't preclude the lived experience or expression of gender, whatever that would mean outside of this power structure.

55 This volume, 111.

56 Hocquenghem, *Homosexual Desire*, 150; translation modified.

57 This volume, 110.

58 Hocquenghem wasn't alone at the time in seeing transness as the horizon of queer liberation. Mario Mieli's 1977 book, *Homosexuality and Liberation: Elements of a Gay Critique*, trans. David Fernbach (London: Gay Men's Press, 1980), also envisions transness as the endpoint of liberation.

59 This volume, 111.

60 This volume, 2. Hocquenghem likely picked up the term *transversalism* from Guattari's notion of *transversality*, which was his modification of the psychoanalytic idea of *transference*. Guattari used the term to describe groups that were "more open, less hierarchical" (Eugene B. Young with Gary Genosko and Janell Watson, *The Deleuze and Guattari Dictionary* [New York: Bloomsbury, 2013], 148), which opens it to the anarchist inflections I am picking up in Hocquenghem. Of course, it has a mathematical connotation, as a description of intersection—an idea we have already discussed.

61 This volume, 5.

62 This volume, 91.

63 This volume, 116.

64 But Hocquenghem also disavows a group like the Revolutionary Effeminists, who split with US gay liberation in order to become "traitors to the class of men" (Steven F. Dansky, John Knoebel, and Kenneth Pitchford, "The Effeminist Manifesto" [1973], in *Burn It Down! Feminist Manifestos for the Revolution*, ed. Breanne Fahs [New York: Verso, 2020]). For Hocquenghem, this tendency, also present in other feminist movements, clings to a gender essentialism that he rejects and, like a liberal white guilt that sheds useless tears over anti-Blackness, only gives voice to "the guilty conscience of being male and not female. . . . We are men and therefore oppressors; how can you forgive our nature?" (this volume, 114–15).

65 C. Riley Snorton, *Black on Both Sides: A Racial History of Trans Identity* (Minneapolis: University of Minnesota Press, 2017), 5, 57.

66 Saidiya Hartman, *Wayward Lives, Beautiful Experiments: Intimate Histories of Riotous Black Girls, Troublesome Women, and Queer Radicals* (New York: Norton, 2019), 9–10.

67 Samudzi and Anderson, *As Black as Resistance*, 131.

68 This volume, 117.

69 This volume, 12.

FOREWORD

1 The FHAR is the Front homosexuel d'action révolutionnaire, or Homosexual Front for Revolutionary Action, a radical gay liberation movement started in 1971, with Hocquenghem as one of the most notable members. The FHAR was born in the wake of the events of May '68 and inspired by the MLF, Mouvement pour la libération des femmes, Women's Liberation Movement.

2 *For ever* is in English in the original.

3 "Volutions" is the title of Hocquenghem's introduction, which, along with the last chapter, makes the most comprehensive theoretical and political statement of the book. I leave *volutions* untranslated, since it is combined with various prefixes to form *revolution*, *evolution*, and so on. It has the sense of turning or spiraling.

4 Deleuze refers here to Hocquenghem's public "coming out," in an interview in which he details his mother's reaction to his sexuality: "La revolution des homosexuels," *Le nouvel observateur*, January 10, 1972. She responded in the magazine the following week, on January 17, 1972. This made Hocquenghem the first French person in the twentieth century to publicly come out in the press.

5 *Flux* is an important term for both Deleuze and Hocquenghem, indicating the movement of reality outside, through, and around the categories imposed on it by philosophy, capitalism, society, and so on. I keep the Latinate term rather than using the English word *flow*.

6 Deleuze uses the word *sexe*, which I translate here as "genital," "gender," or "sex," depending on the context.

7 *Anular* is Hocquenghem's spelling of *annular*, which means "ring-shaped," but which Hocquenghem uses to describe the "group mode" of the anus, "a circle which is open to an infinity of directions and possibilities for plugging in, with no set places. The group annular mode (one is tempted to spell it 'anular') causes the 'social' of the phallic hierarchy, the whole house of cards of the 'imaginary,' to collapse" (*Homosexual Desire*, 111). In other words, homosexual desire is not oedipal but instead "is the operation of a desiring machine plugged into the anus" (111).

8 Pierre Klossowski (1905–2001) was a French writer and translator who wrote about the Marquis de Sade, Friedrich Nietzsche, and Charles Fourier, among others. The source of this reference is unknown.

9 Deleuze is referring to three famous French homosexual writers. André Gide (1869–1951), who received the Nobel Prize for literature in 1947, and Marcel Proust (1871–1922) are perhaps the best-known French modernist writers, both of whom wrote about homosexuality. Roger Peyrefitte (1907–2000) was most celebrated for his first novel, *Les amitiés particulières* (1943), or *Particular Friendships* (a term referring to close relationships between men in seminary). This novel describes homoerotic encounters in boarding school. He was a proponent of relationships between older men and younger men (teenagers).

10 Deleuze is referring to William S. Burroughs (1914–97), Beat-associated author of books such as *Naked Lunch*, *Queer*, and *The Soft Machine*, which Hocquenghem references obliquely in "Volutions," and his son, William S. Burroughs Jr. (or III) (1947–81), who also wrote novels.

11 Tony Duvert (1945–2008) was a French novelist, well known in the late 1960s and 1970s, who wrote about homosexuality, sexual relationships between adults and children, and (critically) of the bourgeois family and child-rearing. In the 1980s, he withdrew from public life, specifically as tolerance for his sexual views waned.

12 Hocquenghem, *Homosexual Desire*, 11; translation modified.

13 This is a misremembered quotation from *Homosexual Desire*. The translation reads: "It is incomprehensible that the gay movement should be closely connected with the ecological movement. Nevertheless, it is so. In terms of desire, the motor car and family heterosexuality are one and the same enemy, however impossible it may be to express this in political logic" (142).

14 This volume, 92.

15 Hocquenghem, *Homosexual Desire*, 51; translation modified.

16 This volume, 86, 92; emphasis added.

17 This volume, 90.

18 Hocquenghem attended the École normale supérieure, one of the elite universities of France.

19 I am translating *sexe* as "gender" here, since it appears Deleuze is referring to

nonbinary gender. Above, I include both "sex" and "gender," as Deleuze catalogs acts and identities in both registers. Deleuze also references Charles Fourier (1772–1837), a utopian socialist who influenced Hocquenghem. See Hocquenghem's coauthored piece with René Schérer in this volume (32).

20 This volume, 110.

21 Hocquenghem, *Homosexual Desire*, 131; translation modified.

22 *Arcadian style* refers to the Arcadie Club, France's first homophile organization, predating the radical FHAR. Deleuze is referring to an assimilationist gay politics.

VOLUTIONS

1 "Les lauriers sont coupés" is a phrase in an eighteenth-century children's song and accompanying circle dance, "Nous n'irons plus au bois" ("We will go to the woods no more"). The song ends with the withering laurels already beginning to regrow. The phrase was also used as the title of an 1887 novel by Édouard Dujardin, which is sometimes considered to be the first novel to use stream of consciousness narration.

2 "Dress rehearsal" translates *répétition générale*, which contains the idea of repetition.

3 William Laws Calley Jr. (1943–) was a US Army officer convicted in a court-martial for murdering twenty-two unarmed South Vietnamese people during the Mỹ Lai Massacre in Vietnam on March 16, 1968. Over five hundred civilians were killed during the massacre. The trial took place in 1970, and his conviction led to widespread opposition. He was the only Army officer convicted for his role. He was initially sentenced to life imprisonment at Fort Leavenworth; in an appeal in 1971, President Nixon had him removed to house arrest at Fort Benning. The sentence was next reduced to twenty years and in 1974, his sentence was reduced to ten years, making him eligible for parole. This decision was overturned, and the sentence reinstated, but he was still paroled immediately.

4 *La matraque*, or police baton, was a symbol of state violence during May. See Kristin Ross's discussion of "matraquage" in *May '68 and Its Afterlives* (Chicago: University of Chicago Press, 2002), 27–39.

5 Adolphe Thiers (1797–1877) was a French politician who served as second elected president, and as first president of the Third Republic. During the Paris Commune in 1871, he built up army forces at Versailles and eventually led them to retake the city.

6 Pierre Viansson-Ponté (1920–79) was a French journalist. Hocquenghem is referring to his article of March 15, 1968, "When France Gets Bored," which some took to prefigure the events of May '68. The title echoes a pronouncement made about the July Monarchy before the 1848 Revolution.

7 Hocquenghem uses David Bowie (1947–2016), the English musician who at this time was in his "glam" phase, as an example of the bourgeois libertinage. Perhaps he was seen as counterrevolutionary in his cooptation of transness, as his glam persona came after his encounter with Andy Warhol's Factory and his trans superstars.

8 This was the challenge made by Sergei Diaghilev to Jean Cocteau in experimenting with ballet, then taken up as a motto for Cocteau's further works. Diaghilev (1872–1929) was the founder of the Ballets Russes, condemned by the Soviets after the revolutions as a bourgeois decadent, since he didn't return to Russia. He was famously a lover of the ballet dancer Vaslav Nijinsky (1889–1950), the star male dancer of the Ballets Russes. Jean Cocteau (1889–1963) was a French writer, artist, and filmmaker, who was openly homosexual and infused his writing and films with homoeroticism. Diaghilev hired Cocteau to write the scenario for the ballet *Parade* in 1917. This ballet brought together an assortment of modernist and avant-garde artists, with the sets by Pablo Picasso, libretto by French poet Apollinaire, and music by French composer Erik Satie. Diaghilev and Cocteau thus were important figures of a queer avant-garde landscape in France, with great influence over queer art to come.

9 Maurice Sachs (1906–45), a French Jewish writer, had relationships with Cocteau, André Gide, and Max Jacob, all homosexual writers. Sachs was discharged from the army during World War II due to homosexuality. He made money helping Jewish families escape during the Occupation but was also possibly a Gestapo informant. He was imprisoned and killed during an evacuation march. Sachs converted to Catholicism in 1925 and, despite his origins, had anti-Semitic views of what he saw as Jewish resignation to oppression.

10 This phrase is the literal translation of the French title of this book, which is a play on the titles of Stéphane Mallarmé's poem "L'après-midi d'un faune" ("The afternoon of a fawn"), a prelude by Claude Debussy, and a ballet by Vaslav Nijinsky. The ballet, inspired by Greek vases, presented controversial displays of (queer) sexual desire. This reference places Hocquenghem in a particular (queer) lineage of symbolism, decadence, and modernism.

CHAPTER ONE: BLACK NOVEMBER

1 Gilles Tautin (1950–68) was a militant Maoist high school student, member of the Union des jeunesses communistes marxistes-léninistes, who drowned in the Seine while fleeing police during an action at the Renault factory at Flins. Pierre Overney (1948–72) was a Maoist worker fired from the Renault factory, killed by a Renault guard while passing out pamphlets.

2 Moloch is the Canaanite god of child sacrifice, usually in war.

3 Père-Lachaise is the largest cemetery in Paris.

4　Donatien Alphonse François, Marquis de Sade (1740–1814), was a French aristocrat, known for his writings on libertine sex, leading to his name being used to describe a kind of erotic act of violence, sadism. Sade spent thirty-two years of his life in prison and mental institutions. He was a supporter of the French Revolution. His writings were taken up by many twentieth-century philosophers and thinkers, including Michel Foucault, Pierre Klossowski, and Simone de Beauvoir, and people have grappled with what his thinking might offer to revolutionary ideas.

5　Jacques Rigaut (1898–1929) was a French Dada poet who often wrote about suicide as the successful completion of life. He eventually died by suicide, using a ruler to make sure the bullet he shot pierced his heart. These lines come from his collected writings.

6　Guy Gilles (1938–96) was a French filmmaker who died of AIDS-related illness. *Absences répétées* (Repeated absences; Paris: Gaumont, 1972) is about a young bank clerk who finds his life empty, uses drugs, skips work, gets fired, and then overdoses.

7　Detained in the Fresnes prison, Gérard Grandmontagne died by suicide on September 25, 1972, after having been sentenced to the "hole" for "homosexual relations with his fellow prisoner." The latter, Éric, then died by suicide as soon as he was freed a few months later.

8　The tunic of Nessus comes from Greek mythology: it was the shirt, poisoned by the blood of the centaur Nessus, killed by Hercules, which ultimately killed Hercules.

9　I chose this translation, though there are political conceptions of voluntaryism (similar to American libertarianism), and voluntarism, with emphasis on noncoercive actions. But in this context, I didn't think Hocquenghem was being this specific.

10　In 1972, US president Richard Nixon made a visit to China, ending a twenty-five-year diplomatic isolation between China and the United States, where the United States only recognized the exiled government of the Kuomintang in Taiwan since the Chinese civil war. The visit marked the economic reforms in China, which opened it up to capitalist world trade. Houari Boumédiène (1932–78) was the chairman of the revolutionary council of Algeria from 1965 to 1976, seizing power in a coup, and then served as the second president of Algeria until his death. He also fought in the revolutionary war as a member of the Front de libération nationale, rising to the rank of colonel.

11　Gébé, born Georges Blondeaux (1929–2004), was a well-known French satirical cartoonist. *Year 01* was a comic strip made by Gébé, inspired by the anarchist utopian events of May '68. It was also made into a film in 1973, directed by Jacques Doillon with Alain Resnais and Jean Rouch.

12　Jacques Chaban-Delmas (1915–2000) was a French Gaullist statesman whose "new society" was a response to May '68, an attempt to mediate the conflicting social forces. Serving as prime minister during Georges Pompidou's presidency, he was eventually seen as too progressive and was forced to resign. He served again under François Mitterrand.

13 This is a translation of *ras-le-bol*, which I have translated previously as "frustration." It also has the sense of discontent. This reference could be to a banner or slogan, or perhaps a journal, but the source material is unknown.

CHAPTER TWO: THE CULTURAL REVOLUTION

1 Frank Alamo (1941–2012) was a French singer popular in the 1960s.

2 *Action* was a militant journal created in May 1968 by Jean Schalit, opening with the call for a "general strike and permanent insurrection." It was published through June 1969. Hocquenghem wrote "Why We Fight" for the first issue.

3 Jean-Luc Godard (1930–) is a French-Swiss film director, at first associated with the French New Wave cinema. His work fundamentally changed the way films are made. Many of his films are explicitly political, and in the years after 1968, he moved from his New Wave period to a more political understanding of filmmaking along with more political films. He has Marxist and Maoist tendencies, seen most clearly in *La Chinoise* (1967), which followed a group of Maoist students and captures a certain image of the political student culture leading up to May.

4 CRS-SS was a slogan that associated the CRS (Compagnies républicaines de sécurité, the French riot police) with the Nazi SS, first coined after the CRS murdered striking miners in 1948.

5 Katanga is a province in the Democratic Republic of Congo where there has been ongoing insurrection since independence in 1960.

6 Here, Hocquenghem lists important revolutionary dates: 1848 revolution (in France and elsewhere), 1871 Paris Commune, 1936 Spanish Civil War, May 1968 . . .

7 An action committee (*comité d'action*) was an organizing unit during May '68 (and is still used in various militant struggles, like the general assembly).

8 Georges Wolinski (1934–2015) was a cartoonist for *Hara-Kiri* and then *Charlie Hebdo*, both French satirical papers. He was killed in the *Charlie Hebdo* massacre in 2015.

9 This is a reference to a small radical faction (the *enragés*) that advocated for the poor and sans-culottes during the French Revolution. It was not a formal party, though it was associated with figures, including Jacques Roux, Jean-François Varlet, Jean Théophile Victor Leclerc, and Claire Lacombe, who were attempting to hold the Jacobin-dominated National Convention to the promises of the revolution. The term derived from the angry rhetoric used by speakers.

10 Alain Peyrefitte (1925–99) was a Gaullist (conservative) career politician and minister of education from 1967 to 1968 who resigned after the events of May,

as Georges Pompidou believed his decisions made the situation worse. Not to be confused with Roger Peyrefitte (1907–2000), a conservative gay writer and diplomat.

11 The Fouchet reform (proposed in 1963; protested, though finally implemented in June 1966), named for Christian Fouchet (1911–74), then minister of education, reorganized studies into two-year and four-year degrees, introducing new admission criteria, in order to address overcrowded classrooms. This reform was a precursor to the events of May. Alain Peyrefitte's suggestions were an attempt to quell student unrest by reforming the relationship with instructors, the methods of evaluation, and the way teachers were chosen and trained.

12 I translate *la matraque* (a billy club) as "beaten by the police." In *May '68 and Its Afterlives*, Kristin Ross devotes a whole section to the *matraque* as the symbol of the state and its violence. See Ross, *May '68 and Its Afterlives*, 27–39.

13 Nanterre is the site of the University of Paris campus where the events of 1968, culminating in what is known as May '68, kicked off. On March 22, following a suppressed demonstration against the Vietnam War, students occupied an administrative building to denounce class discrimination and the university bureaucracy. The university cleared the building without arrest, but summoned the assumed leaders of the movement to a disciplinary council and threated expulsion. This series of events was known as the Movement of March 22.

14 The Sozialistische Deutsche Studentenbund (SDS), or Socialist German Student League, began as the student wing of the Social Democratic Party (SPD), though it split off in 1961 over the rearming of West Germany. The SDS led the extraparliamentary opposition, due to the coalition of the SPD and the Christian Democratic Union.

15 Redon and Caen were locations of workers' strikes in 1968.

16 Charles de Gaulle (1890–1970) was a looming figure in French politics. Leader of the official Resistance during World War II and of the Provisional Government of the French Republic following the liberation, he was elected president in the formation of the Fifth Republic and served from 1959 to 1969. De Gaulle is associated with conservative, traditional French bourgeois values.

17 Alain Poher (1909–96) was a French centrist, longtime president of the Senate, and interim president after de Gaulle's resignation in 1969. Georges Pompidou was a conservative politician and de Gaulle aide, former prime minister of France, and president from 1969 to 1974 (his death).

18 The Grenelle Accords were an agreement negotiated among the government, the trade unions, and the corporations between May 25 and 26, 1968, in order to end the strikes. The agreements included increases in the minimum wage and average real wages. The workers rejected it, but after a pro-Gaullist counterdemonstration marched on the Champs-Élysées, the victory of the status

quo was evident. Thus, the Grenelle Accords represent a capitulation, a concession to the powers that be, and a betrayal of the revolution.

19 Raymond Marcellin (1914–2004) was a French politician. Interior minister under de Gaulle after Fouchet, he increased police repression against the revolutionaries of May '68. Marcellin was retained by Pompidou and continued to advocate for repressive measures. Edgar Faure (1908–88) was prime minister in 1952 and 1955. As minister of national education after May '68, he pushed through university reforms in an attempt to give concessions to the May actors.

20 *Youth Culture* appears in English in the original.

21 *Crèche sauvage* literally means "savage nursery" and refers to attempts by parents to rethink the care and early education of children outside of institutional authority, implemented during the events of May '68.

22 AG shortens *assemblée générale*, or general assembly; in other words, meetings held by organizations, unions, or political bodies.

23 Censier and Nanterre refer to two major sites of the Parisian university system where early May '68 demonstrations occurred.

24 The Unione dei Comunisti Italiani (marxisti-leninisti) or Union of Italian Communists (Marxist-Leninist) was a pro-Chinese communist group founded in Rome in 1968, which published *Servire il popolo* (*Serve the People*). Later the group moved to Milan and was then renamed the Italian (Marxist-Leninist) Communist Party (Partito Comunista [Marxista-Leninista] Italiano) in 1972. It was dissolved in 1978, with many of its members joining Autonomia Operaia and the autonomist movements.

25 Liu Shaoqi (1898–1969) was a Chinese communist political actor and theorist. In the 1960s, he came into conflict with Mao, especially in the power struggle over the Cultural Revolution.

26 Censier was a location for student demonstration and the Renault car factory at Boulogne-Billancourt, near Paris, was the site of a worker strike.

27 I thought of translating *groupe affectif* as "affinity group," referring to an anarchist organizing term that traces back to Mikhail Bakunin and the Spanish anarchists during the Spanish revolution of the 1930s (though it is still used currently). An affinity group might be dismissed by Marxist-Leninists for not being massive enough. However, the sense here is more the supposed depoliticization that comes from organizing around daily life, as the establishment communists separate life and politics. Hocquenghem seems to be alluding to something like a book club or even an emotional support group.

28 *S'établir*, "to settle" or "to take root," refers to a Marxist-Leninist tactic that Hocquenghem opposed. The idea was for militants to turn themselves into workers and peasants in order to build relationships with them, and thus to form a mass movement. Hocquenghem calls attention to the power dynamics inherent in the words *establishing* or *settling*. See Idier, *Les vies de Guy Hocqueng-*

hem, 72. I use the term *settle* as a reference to the settler mentality that occupies a space and establishes hierarchy within it. In fact, the term *colonization* had been used positively by communists in the past, along with other terms like *industrialization* and *salting*. My translation emphasizes Hocquenghem's critique of the practice as adhering to a masculinist worship of the image of the worker that is also the product of the bourgeois imaginary.

29 Here Hocquenghem takes another swipe at French Maoist groups, their workerism, their recovery of cultural and paternalistic norms under the cover of a cultural revolution, and their emphasis on the individual militant's development. Hocquenghem is referring to uncritical supporters of Nikita Khrushchev and Mao. See Idier, *Les vies de Guy Hocquenghem*, 71. Hocquenghem was certainly influenced by Mao—or at least by the idea of Mao in France at the time, which didn't grapple completely with the terrors he inflicted and uncritically championed "communist" China—but through his militant experience came to abjure parties and blueprints.

30 Following the May '68 uprisings, Italy experienced the "Hot Autumn" of 1969, where workers and students rose up together, with much of the focus on conditions and pay at the Fiat factories.

31 There was a Renault factory nearby at Flins.

32 CID stands for Centre informatique douanier (Customs Information Center). The reference to Nantes might be the workers' control of the city in 1968, which met with the support of employees in technology and shipping.

33 Hocquenghem pulls the first line from Mao's "Speech at the Lushan Conference" (July 23, 1959). I can't find a source for the second line. Zhu De (1886–1976) was a peasant adopted by a rich relative, a rebel warlord then communist who rose up in the Red Army. He was a founder and marshal of the People's Liberation Army in 1955. In the last year of his life, he was the head of state, chairman of the Standing Committee of the National People's Congress.

34 Charles Fourier (1772–1837), a French utopian socialist thinker and writer, inspired different communes and intentional communities; his ideas were influential during the revolution of 1848 and the Paris Commune. He was a critic of the positive sense of civilization, a thinker on education, a supporter of feminism, and a theorist of desire. His work has been particularly influential for anarchist thinking. He was also a favorite of Hocquenghem.

35 Hocquenghem refers here to a situationist intervention from March 10, 1969, that replaced the Fourier statue—originally set in place Clichy in 1896 by the anarchist sculptor Émile Derré, then taken down by the Vichy government, supposedly due to being a bronze statue. The new statue had written on its base, "En hommage à Charles Fourier, les barricadiers de la rue Gay-Lussac." Once the police discovered it, they guarded it the rest of the day until they took it down. The situationists claimed responsibility for it in their journal, *Revue de la section française de l'I.S.*, no. 12 (September 1969).

36 Jean-François Revel, *Without Marx or Jesus* (New York: Dell, 1970), 32. Revel

(1924–2006) was a French journalist and thinker; he was a socialist, but eventually promoted liberalism and free market economics.

37 These dates are references to the 1848 revolution, the Paris Commune of 1871, and the Russian Revolution of 1917.

38 Fourier's term is *ordre sociétaire*, which is sometimes translated as "ordered society" or "societary order." The term refers to the organization of society that will replace civilization.

39 "When they see an associative community yielding a profit (other things being equal) three times as large as that produced by a community of isolated families, as well as providing all its members with the most varied pleasures, they will forget all their rivalries and hasten to put association into practice." Fourier, *The Theory of the Four Movements*, ed. Gareth Stedman Jones and Ian Patterson, trans. Ian Patterson (Cambridge: Cambridge University Press, 1996), 12.

40 "Association" echoes Fourier's cooperative social arrangement, an "associative community."

41 The aromal movement is one of Fourier's cardinal movements. It is a vital energy that serves as a means of communication among beings and things in this world and the universe as a whole.

CHAPTER THREE: AFTER-MAY POLITICS OF THE SELF

1 Huey P. Newton, "The Women's Liberation and Gay Liberation Movements," speech made in 1970. Newton (1942–89) was a cofounder of the Black Panther Party.

2 Raoul Vaneigem, *The Revolution of Everyday Life*, trans. Donald Nicholson-Smith (Oakland, CA: PM Press, 2012), 30. This volume was originally published in 1967, shortly before the events of May '68. Vaneigem (1934–) was at that time associated with Guy Debord and the Situationist International. However, by 1970 he had left the SI and was denounced by Debord. His slogans were written on the walls by students.

3 Georges Séguy (1927–2016) was a labor organizer and activist who served as general secretary from 1967 to 1982 of the CGT, Confédération générale du travail, or General Confederation of Labor, one of the larger French labor unions. During the 1960s, it was dominated by the French Communist Party (PCF), though it had anarcho-syndicalist origins.

4 Paul Lafargue (1842–1911) was a French revolutionary Marxist, and Émile Pouget (1860–1931) was a French anarcho-syndicalist, vice secretary of the CGT from 1901 to 1908. Lafargue was criticized by Karl Marx for sloganeering, leading Marx to quip to Friedrich Engels, "One thing is for sure, I am not a Marxist." Lafargue's most famous text is *The Right to Be Lazy* (1880). Pouget helped write the Charter of Amiens, an important text in revolutionary syn-

dicalism and class struggle. He edited the weekly journal *Le père peinard*. He is famous for advocating sabotage with the slogan "Bad work for bad pay!"

5 Alfred Willi Rudolf "Rudi" Dutschke (1940–79) was a militant in the German student movement in the 1960s who advocated for integrating into the institutions in order to work change from the inside. In the 1970s, he joined the Green movement. He died in 1979 from a seizure that resulted from a previous assassination attempt eleven years earlier. Daniel Cohn-Bendit (1945–) was a French-German militant and later a politician, as well as one of the best-known names associated with May '68, though he spent much of the time away from the fray in Saint-Nazaire, and then was expelled to Germany. Part of the Movement of 22 March leading up to May's events, Cohn-Bendit was a member of the Fédération anarchiste (Anarchist Federation). In the 1970s, he took up with the Green Party and, capitalizing on his visibility, has become a member of the European Parliament.

6 Philippe Gavi, a French journalist, published *Les ouvriers: Du tiercé à la révolution* (Workers: From placing bets to the revolution) in 1970. The book included testimony from French workers, demonstrating their distrust of politicians and union power, along with a radicalization of demands and of the means to gain them. The book looks at the proletarianization of the middle classes and the failure of workers to join forces with groups that come from different places.

7 DIM is a French underwear company.

8 *Tout!* was a radical Left biweekly journal published from 1970 to 1971. Hocquenghem played an instrumental part in the writing and dissemination of the journal. Its political sympathies were connected in part to Vive la révolution (VLR), a Maoist-Libertarian group, but were also more generally Maoist, spontaneist, and libertarian/anarchist. *Tout!* was famous for being one of the few underground journals published in color (bright, psychedelic ones, at that!). The twelfth issue, dealing with homosexuality, was described as pornographic. This led to legal action against Jean-Paul Sartre, who was named on the editorial page and helped disseminate the journal.

9 See note 3 on Paul Lafargue.

10 The "Celma story" refers to Jules Celma, a French teacher who, from October 1968 to June 1969, gave his students complete freedom in order to allow them free, uncensored expression. He published a book about this experience, *The Diary of an Educastrator* (Paris: Éditions Champ Libre, 1971), and made the short film *School's Out* (Paris: Groupe des Cinéastes Indépendants, 1975).

11 The Peugeot factory at Sochaux in eastern France was the site of a sit-down strike in May 1968. Though a majority of workers voted to return to work on June 10, a radical minority continued the occupation, ending in violent clashes with the police. The rest of the workers came to the aid of the group in confrontation with the state and the bosses.

12 Beaux-Arts (Fine Arts) is a grande *école* located in Paris. Its full name is the École nationale supérieure des Beaux-Arts. During May '68, it was a meeting point for radical students and workers to discuss liberated worlds. See Fredy Perlman, "Anything Can Happen," *Black and Red*, no. 1, September 1968.

13 *Do it* and *Youth Culture* are both in English in Hocquenghem's text.

14 Popular "women's" and fashion magazines.

15 André Malraux (1901–76) was a French novelist and France's first minister of cultural affairs during de Gaulle's presidency, 1959–69. The ministry was intended to help promote the glory of French culture. His early work was connected to the surrealists and the 1920s art scene. Though he fought fascists in Spain and served in the French army and then the resistance during World War II, Malraux was a relatively conservative Gaullist.

16 See notes 17 (Geismar) and 23 (Bengalis).

17 Alain Geismar (1939–) is a French politician, mining engineer, and solid-state physicist. He was a student activist on the Left in the 1960s, as a leader and representative of the Étudiants socialistes unifies (ESU; Unified Socialist Students) and the Parti socialiste unifié (PSU; Unified Socialist Party), groups countering the French Communist Party and its Stalinist dogma. He was deputy general secretary of the Syndicat national de l'enseignement supérieur (SNESup; National Higher Education Union), and was seen as a leader of May '68 alongside Cohn-Bendit and Jacques Sauvageot. After the events of May, he became a leader of the Proletarian Left, a Maoist group that took on antiauthoritarian struggle, though perhaps less libertarian/anarchist minded than Vive la révolution. On October 22, 1970, Geismar was sentenced to eighteen months in prison for his involvement in a protest that led to police violence. Later he became a politician with the Socialist Party.

18 *France-soir* is a French daily newspaper with high circulation in the 1950s and 1960s. Begun during the Resistance, it is now is an online, tabloid-style newspaper.

19 Jacques Sauvageot (1943–2017), an activist and art historian, was one of the faces of May '68. At the time of May '68, he was the vice president (later president) of the Union nationale des étudiants de France (UNEF), or socialist-leaning French National Student Union, as well as a member of the PSU. At the head of demonstrations during May '68, he was arrested during the first night of uprising in the Latin Quarter.

20 Alain Krivine (1941–) is a leftist activist and politician. Beginning in his school days, Krivine organized with the Communist Party. Eventually, he was kicked out of the party for his Trotskyism. He helped found the Jeunesse communiste révolutionnaire (JCR; Revolutionary Communist Youth), which played a role in the events of May '68. The government banned the JCR, leading to Krivine's imprisonment. On his release, he formed the Ligue communiste (Communist League) and ran for president over the next few years.

21 Yasser Arafat (1929–2004) was an Arab nationalist who led the Palestinian Liberation Organization from 1969 to 2004 and served as president of the Palestinian National Authority from 1994 to 2004.

22 Either a reference to Maurice Thorez, leader of the PCF from 1931 until 1964 (his death), or his son, Paul Thorez, who broke with the PCF in 1968 following the Prague Spring and his disillusionment with the PCF's support of Moscow.

23 The following article discusses the Bangladesh Liberation War, a revolution led by Bengali nationalists for self-determination in East Pakistan after the contested first national elections in 1970, where the Bengali Awami League gained majority, and the following Bangladesh genocide (Operation Searchlight) in 1971. This revolution eventually resulted in independence and the establishment of the People's Republic of Bangladesh. India joined the war on December 3, 1971, leading to a second front for Pakistan. Some of the areas of conflict stemmed from language, ethnic, and religious definitions. Though Bengali Muslims shared a religious affinity, Pakistan's official language was Urdu, not Bengali, leading to primary identification for some with Bengali culture over a shared Muslim faith. There were also economic factors, stemming from the dominance of West Pakistan.

24 East Bengal eventually became the independent nation of Bangladesh.

25 Yahya Khan (1914–80) was a Pakistani general and third president of Pakistan from 1969 to 1971. After the East Pakistan uprising in 1969, Yahya Khan took over the presidency from Ayub Khan, imposing martial law and suspending the constitution until he held the country's first elections in 1970. Following the election, he delayed the transfer of power to Sheikh Mujubur Rahman, the Bengali Awami League politician who was elected prime minister. Yahya Khan authorized the violent suppression of the rebellion, now considered the Bangladesh genocide. After secession and the transfer of power to Zulfikar Ali Bhutto, Yahya Khan resigned from the army in disgrace, was stripped of his honors, and was placed under house arrest until 1977.

26 China supported Pakistan. At this time, Richard Nixon was working on forging connections with China against the USSR, who supported Bengali liberation. Both the United States and China have been seen as complicit in the genocide. China didn't recognize independent Bangladesh for years after independence.

27 This dilemma continually faces leftists and antiauthoritarians whenever there are uprisings against the state leading to international intervention. Marxist-Leninists such as the Party for Socialism and Liberation will try to excuse genocidal actions of so-called Marxists or support the intervention of US imperial forces, depending on an outdated idea of geopolitics from the Cold War. The view Hocquenghem outlines here, which is more in line with an antiauthoritarian, anarchist view of international uprising, is to support the people fighting for freedom and not the state. Of course, each situation has its own complexities.

28 *L'idiot international* was a journal founded in 1969 by Jean-Edern Hallier and Bernard Thomas, funded by Sylvina Boissonnas, and originally supported by Simone de Beauvoir. It had a leftist tendency, though it was eventually supplanted by *Libération* in 1972. The journal's tactics were provocative.

29 *J'accuse* was a monthly magazine published from 1971 to 1973 in the wake of May '68 and the Maoists, associated with the Gauche prolétarienne (GP; Proletarian Left). André Glucksmann (1937–2015) was originally a Maoist activist and writer who later became a neoliberal defender. Glucksmann was active as a revolutionary writer in 1968 and after (*Action*), a defender of the Chinese Cultural Revolution, and a member of the GP. He took over *J'accuse* while Geismar was in prison. Glucksmann and Hocquenghem worked together in opposition to the Revolutionary Communist League and to leading figures of May '68, forming a new tendency. Hocquenghem was named along with Glucksmann as a "new philosopher" by Bernard-Henri Lévy in *Le nouvel observateur* (June 30, 1975). By 1981, Hocquenghem and Glucksmann had gone their separate ways politically, with Glucksmann ever more nationalist and warmongering.

30 The Willot brothers were part of a wealthy French industrial family in the textile business. In 1971, they started mass-producing disposable baby diapers, using the same technology as Pampers.

31 André Rives-Henrÿs (1917–90) was a French Gaullist politician and a legislative delegate from 1962 to 1972. In 1971, he was involved in a financial corruption scandal involving La garantie foncière, a French investment company. The discovery of this Ponzi scheme involving real estate investment led to his resignation from political office and eventually a four-month prison sentence and fine.

32 *Minute* is a far right-wing French newspaper. *Le canard enchaîné* (literally *The Chained Duck*, or *The Chained Paper*, *canard* being a term for a newspaper) is a French satirical weekly.

33 FLJ is the Front de libération de la jeunesse (Youth Liberation Front), announced in *Tout!*, no. 9 (February 18, 1971), in a text by Richard Deshayes of Vive la révolution, meeting every Wednesday at Beaux-Arts, and calling for an international "savage" festival in Montpellier, August 3–5. They emphasized life as a form of revolution, looking for ways to live together toward collective emancipation. Deshayes was famously hit in the face by a tear gas canister during a demo in 1971 when he was helping another militant. He was blinded and his face seriously wounded. The photo of his bloody face was on the cover of this same issue of *Tout!*

34 *Midi libre*, or *Free South*, is also the name of a newspaper based in Montpellier.

35 *Actuel* (*Now*), where the following article first appeared, was a French magazine founded in 1967 that ran until 1994. With the events of May '68, it became a left-leaning magazine of the counterculture.

36 I translate *des étrangers pénétreurs et pénétrés* as "unknown tops and bottoms."

37 *Bye, bye* appears in English in the original.

38 *Underground* appears in English in the original.

39 For Krivine, see note 20. Jean-Edern Hallier (1936–97) was the editor of *L'idiot international*, created after May '68. Hallier was eventually seen as *rouge-brun*, or red-brown, mixing far-right and communist tendencies.

40 Gérard Gélas (1947–) is a French playwright and director, founder and director of the Chêne noir theater in Avignon. The theater's name is a reference to the anarchist black flag. Gélas participated in events in Avignon during May '68 and in the annual Avignon theater festival. Henri Lefebvre (1901–91) was a French Marxist philosopher and sociologist, best known for his critique of everyday life, the city, and social space. His book *The Right to the City* came out in 1968 before the uprising. He was a respected and influential professor during the events. Edgar Morin (1921–) is a French philosopher and sociologist known for his concept of "complex thought." Morin replaced Lefebvre as professor at Nanterre in 1968. Morin also took part in the student uprisings, writing a series of articles for *Le Monde* on "The Student Commune," as well as coauthoring a book with Cornelius Castoriadis and Claude Lefort titled *La brèche: Premières réflexions sur les événements* (*May '68: The Break*; Paris: Fayard, 1971), one of the early books trying to understand the events.

41 Philippe Gavi founded the daily newspaper *Libération* along with Sartre, Bernard Lallement, Jean-Claude Vernier, Pierre Victor (Bény Lévy), and Serge July in the aftermath of May '68. The first edition came out in February 1973. At first, the paper was run without hierarchy.

42 Jean-François Bizot (1944–2007) was a French journalist and writer. He founded *Actuel*, to which Hocquenghem frequently contributed.

43 *France dimanche* is a weekly French celebrity magazine covering gossip and scandals.

44 Colette Magny (1926–97) was a French musician who became famous in the 1960s for writing political music to accompany the texts of radicals, as well as her own political songs.

45 Raymond Marcellin (1914–2004), an anticommunist and repressive French politician, was minister of the interior after May '68 under de Gaulle and then Pompidou, replacing Christian Fouchet. He believed the militants had been fooled by Cuban propaganda and acted accordingly. He increased the number of police, dissolved political groups equally on the Right and the Left, banned the magazine *Hara-Kiri Hebdo* for running a satire on de Gaulle's death, tried to pass laws against association and meetings where "violence took place," and finally resigned after police were caught bugging the offices of *Le canard enchaîné*, though he was a senator until 1981.

46 Daniel Guérin (1904–88), an important French queer anarchist writer, took part in May '68 and the gay liberation movements.

47 Gébé, born Georges Blondeaux (1929–2004), was a well-known French satirical cartoonist.

48 Pierre Clémenti (1942–99) was a French actor, arrested in 1971 for drugs. Jean-

Pierre Kalfon (1938–) is a French actor who was close to Clémenti. They were part of a group of actors associated with the director Marc'O (Marc-Gilbert Guillaumin [1927–]).

49 Eight hundred francs is about $600 in today's dollars.

50 *Un studio style cité universitaire*, or academic housing.

51 CNRS stands for Centre national de la recherche scientifique (French National Center for Scientific Research), the largest government research organization in France.

52 Four to five thousand francs would amount to about $3,000–$3,800 in to-day's dollars.

53 MLF stands for the Mouvement de libération des femmes, or Women's Liberation Movement, born out of May '68. The MLF fought for access to abortion and contraception, as well as against misogyny and patriarchy in general. The first meeting of the MLF was in spring 1970 at Vincennes. It was a single-sex group, but eventually the question of sexuality led to the founding of the FHAR, and then the lesbian group, Gouines rouges (Red Dykes).

54 Alice says this at the tea party in *Alice's Adventures in Wonderland*: "'You should learn not to make personal remarks,' Alice said with some severity; 'it's very rude.'"

55 *Leaders* appears in English in the original.

56 In some depictions of the nativity, the ass and the ox make up part of the iconography, with the ox at Christ's head and the ass at his feet, perhaps representing Israel and the Gentiles, the clean and the unclean, being yoked together.

57 "Jerking off" is my translation of the slang phrase *la veuve poignet*, literally "the widow fist."

CHAPTER FOUR: YOUTH CULTURE / POP HIGH

1 In the title, *Youth Culture* appears in English in the original. "High" translates *défonce*, which is a term for the effects of drug use. *Flashback* also appears in English.

2 *Okay* appears in English in the original.

3 The Isle of Wight hosted music festivals from 1968 to 1970, with 1970 estimated to be the largest human gathering in the world (over six hundred thousand people in attendance). In response, Parliament passed an act banning overnight gatherings of more than five thousand people without a special license. The Altamont Free Concert took place at Altamont Speedway in California in 1969. The Hells Angels bike gang was hired to guard the stage. There were multiple deaths during the concert, including most notably the stabbing of a young black man, Meredith Hunter, by a member of the Hells Angels. Culturally, Altamont was seen as the comedown from the hippie positivity of

the 1960s, the end of the Summer of Love. Aspects of this murder were captured in the documentary *Gimme Shelter* by the Maysles brothers (1970).

4 *Rock 'n' roll suicide* appears in English in the original. This is most likely a reference to the David Bowie song from *The Rise and Fall of Ziggy Stardust and the Spiders from Mars* (1972).

5 Saint-Laurent-du-Pont was the site of the Club Cinq-Sept nightclub fire on November 1, 1970; 146 people died at a rock show.

6 *Hara-Kiri Hebdo* was a monthly satirical magazine. This headline was their reference to de Gaulle's death, in juxtaposition with the deaths at Club Cinq-Sept. Minister of the Interior Raymond Marcellin banned its advertisement and sale to minors. Afterward, the name was changed to *Charlie Hebdo*, perhaps in honor of the dead Charles.

7 Gamal Abdel Nasser (1918 – 70) was the second president of Egypt from 1954 to his death from a heart attack immediately following an Arab League Summit where he negotiated a cease-fire in a war over land taken by Israel. Nasser led the overthrow of the monarchy, made Egypt fully independent from British influence, implemented socialist measures, like nationalizing the Suez Canal, and worked toward pan-Arab unity. As he attempted to gain these liberal measures, he also cracked down on individual freedoms, with surveillance, media censorship, and electoral suppression.

8 François Mauriac (1885 – 1970) was a French Catholic writer, Nobel Prize winner, and member of the Académie française who was also awarded the Légion d'honneur. Mauriac opposed Franco, worked with the resistance, opposed French rule in Vietnam, and condemned torture in Algeria. He also wrote a biography of de Gaulle.

9 Apomorphine was a treatment for heroin addiction developed by Dr. John Yerbury Dent and championed by William S. Burroughs, who claimed he wouldn't have written his well-known books if he hadn't been cured through this treatment by Dr. Dent in 1956. Apomorphine's effectiveness against heroin addiction has been discredited, but now it is used to treat a variety of other issues. As Hocquenghem mentions, many argue that Dent's attempt to cure heroin users was countered by the medical and pharmaceutical establishment. Incidentally, in a footnote in *Homosexuality and Liberation*, Mario Mieli discusses the use of apomorphine in the Soviet Union in forms of aversion therapy to "cure" homosexuals by creating a sense of nausea attached to homosexual desire (235n40).

10 In French, *expérience* connotes both "experience" and "experiment."

11 The Monterey Pop Festival was a three-day concert held in California from June 16 to 18, 1967, the first major appearance of the Jimi Hendrix Experience and of Janis Joplin. The festival was seen as a landmark in the development of the counterculture and the Summer of Love. D. A. Pennebaker made a concert film of it: *Monterey Pop* (1968).

12 In Hocquenghem's text, the title of this section is *Overmorts*. He takes the English prefix from *overdose*, which is also a borrowed word in French.

13 Admittedly, Hocquenghem isn't totally adept in the racial complexities of American pop music. Nor does he fully convey the history of expropriation or appropriation of Black cultural forms, whether for mass production and the financial benefit of white elites or as the basic blueprints of American culture. Additionally, he overlooks the racist aspect of Hendrix's death, as he was transported to a hospital farther away from where he was living because he was Black.

14 Or, rather, the national anthem is sung at the beginning of baseball games.

15 *Détourner* was given the sense of "repurposing bourgeois or hegemonic forms for revolutionary means" by the Situationists. It is sometimes translated as "repurposed." I use "hijack" to preserve a political meaning.

16 Here again the revolutionary extent of this gesture could be questioned.

17 The Democratic National Convention was held in Chicago in 1968, a turbulent year of political assassinations and uprisings in the United States. On August 28, ten thousand people showed up to protest the convention and were met by heavily armed, violent police, with much of the police violence being broadcast on television. Eight militants were charged with conspiracy and incitement to riot, with convictions eventually overturned. To open the convention, Aretha Franklin sang the national anthem, with her performance garnering racist criticism in news coverage.

18 "Smashed the gates" is my translation of *défoncé la barrière*.

19 These nonsense pop lyrics are also perhaps a reference to a song by the Italian singer and pianist Renato Carosone.

20 This is probably a reference to the Force de libération internationale de la pop, which was formed in October 1970 to merge radical movements and pop music. Their manifesto was printed in leftist papers as well as pop music magazines.

21 Sun Ra (1914–1993) was an experimental jazz musician and an Afrofuturist. His first European tour started at Les Halles in Paris on October 9, 1970. The concert perplexed much of the audience since it departed so fully from expectations of jazz (or from music in general). Recordings were made of the concert and subsequently released as *Nuits de la Fondation Maeght*, vols. 1 and 2 (2003).

22 *Shit* appears in English in the original.

23 *Joint* appears in English in the original.

24 "A poorly sealed concept" is my translation of *un concept mal joint*.

25 I am translating *pédérastes* here not as the slang "fag" but as a term designating older men who have relationships with teenagers. As noted above, I translate *travesti* as "trans"/"transgender"; though the term was also used to designate "transvestite," I have adopted the terminology now used by a majority of the people Hocquenghem is describing.

26 R. Crumb (1943 –) and Gilbert Shelton (1940 –) are both American underground cartoonists.

27 I'm translating *le shit* as "dope."

28 The French poet Charles Baudelaire (1821 – 67) wrote positively about his experiences with drugs. Hocquenghem is referring to tracing drug use to non-Western "authentic" cultures or to high art/literary culture.

29 *Deal* appears in English in the original.

30 In French, the title is *Stupéfiants; Stupéfiant!*, turning the term for drugs into an adjective that could be talking about the effects of the drugs on the user just as well as the hype around them, both positive and negative.

31 In 1969, a young girl in Bandol overdosed from heroin, leading to a press uproar and the law passed in 1970. In 1971, President Pompidou and Interior Minister Raymond Marcellin increased attention on fighting addiction and swelled the ranks of the narcotics brigade.

32 Claudine Escoffier-Lambiotte (1923 – 96) was a Belgian journalist who wrote on medical news for *Le Monde* from the 1950s to the 1980s.

33 Bernard Muldworf (1923 – 2019), a French psychoanalyst and sexologist, belonged to the PCF and was a frequent target of Hocquenghem's ire.

34 Francis Crick (1916 – 2004) was a British molecular biologist known for his work with James Watson on the double-helix structure of DNA.

35 Hocquenghem invents a noun from the author's name to describe the kind of writing he is criticizing. Throughout the piece, Hocquenghem plays on Escoffier-Lambiotte's name. *Escoffier* is an archaic verb meaning to kill, with an etymology tracing back (perhaps) to decapitation. We might see him playing on her hack job as a journalist, as well as his own attempt to delegitimize her authority.

36 Toluene is found in airplane glue, contact cement, and paint thinner, and is often sniffed.

37 I translate *épreuve de vérité* as "acid test" here in reference to Ken Kesey and the Merry Pranksters' coinage of the term for their parties centered on LSD, where "acid test" refers to both lysergic acid and the gold miner's testing of their discoveries. The French term could also be rendered as "litmus test" or "moment of truth."

38 Robert Boulin (1920 – 79) was a French politician in the cabinets of de Gaulle, Pompidou, and Valéry Giscard d'Estaing; he served as minister of public health and social security from 1969 to 1972. Boulin was involved in a real estate scandal and died under mysterious circumstances.

39 UDR stands for Union des démocrates pour la République (Union of Democrats for the Republic, renamed from Union for the Defense of the Republic), a Gaullist political party from 1968 to 1976.

40 The verb *défoncer*, which I translate here as "smash," contains the same word that I have rendered as "getting high" or "smashed." In French, Hocqueng-

hem adds a pronominal *vous*, so an alternative translation could read "repress your desire to get smashed the system"—which would reflect the grammatical strangeness of the phrase.

41 Louis XVIII was the constitutional monarch for a ten-year period known as the Bourbon Restoration; this period coincided with what is known as the Romantic period.

42. This is a line from André Gide's lyrical novel, *Nourritures terrestres* (*Fruits of the Earth*, 1897). Gide (1869–1951) was a prominent French writer who wrote about his love for other men. In particular, Gide wrote about his experiences with young Arab boys in North Africa. His career spanned the period from decadence to modernism.

43 François Guizot (1787–1874) was a historian and liberal politician who served as minister of education, minister of foreign affairs during the July Monarchy (under King Louis Philippe), then prime minister from 1847 until the revolution of 1848.

44 Philippe Pétain (1856–1951), also known as Marshal Pétain, was a World War I hero, then head of state for the Nazi-collaborationist Vichy regime during World War II. He was convicted of treason and served a life sentence.

45 L'Union des femmes françaises (Union of French Women) is a liberal feminist group, organized around equality of rights.

46 "Families live off good soup and not off beautiful language." *Humanité* responded to Pompidou by quoting Molière (*L'humanité*, December 7, 1970).

47 Georges Marchais (1920–97) was the head of the French Communist Party from 1972 to 1994.

48 Michel Debré (1912–96) was a French Gaullist politician, first prime minister of the Fifth Republic, "father" of the constitution of the Fifth Republic, and overseer of the forced removal over two decades of thousands of children from the French colonial holding, Réunion, to France to repopulate rural areas. These children are known as *Enfants de la Creuse*. Debré's father was Roger Debré (1882–1978), the "father" of pediatrics.

CHAPTER FIVE: FAGS

1 Wilhelm Reich (1897–1957) was an Austrian psychoanalyst, a former student of Freud's, known for his thoughts on sexual liberation and character analysis. His book, *The Mass Psychology of Fascism* (1933), which read fascism as an effect of sexual repression, was influential on the *soixante-huitards*, who wrote Reichian slogans on the walls during the uprising. Importantly, Reich's theory of sexuality imagined that in a liberated world there would no longer be the need for homosexuality, which for him was still a form of deviancy.

2 Hocquenghem is referring here to the Declaration of Rights of Man and of

the Citizen, written in 1789. This is one of the foundational texts, along with the US Declaration of Independence and the US Constitution, of liberal/bourgeois republican democracy.

3 *Le nouveau monde amoureux* is the title of a text by Charles Fourier. It was written in the early nineteenth century, but not widely read until after 1967.

4 The scandal of Hocquenghem's apparent defense for child love, including his experience with teacher and collaborator René Schérer and their coauthored book, *Co-Ire* (1976), resurfaced in 2020 when the Parisian mayor wanted to dedicate a plaque to Hocquenghem. The resistance came in large part due to Hocquenghem's friendship with Gabriel Matzneff (1936–), a French author who has written widely of his pedophilia, sex tourism, and rape, and was summoned to appear in court in a criminal investigation in 2020. This aspect of gay history still haunts contemporary homophobic stereotypes as well as liberationists, and deserves fuller treatment. Kadji Amin has written on this in *Disturbing Attachments*. The history of pedophilic sexual tourism is tied to colonialism, with writers cited earlier such as André Gide commonly traveling to Algeria to live out their sexuality more freely, at the expense of Algerian boys. (This wasn't solely a gay phenomenon, as straight men also sought out young girls in colonial spaces.) This history is also connected to the history of modern art, which is in part what Hocquenghem critiques in "Volutions" regarding the sexual libertines of the bourgeoisie. However, fuller reckoning with Hocquenghem's thoughts on pederasty must come. The main point that Hocquenghem defends in this book is the idea of adolescent self-determination, especially since teens were actively participating in the insurrections of the day. And he did lament their straight sexuality.

5 L'Affaire Dreyfus was a galvanizing moment in European politics, not only in France. The scandal went on from 1894 until 1906 but had long-lasting implications in relation to statecraft and antisemitism, as Hannah Arendt argues in *The Origins of Totalitarianism* (New York: Schocken, 1951). An army captain of Jewish descent, Alfred Dreyfus was accused of treason in 1894 and was sentenced to life imprisonment on Devil's Island, French Guiana, for trading secrets with Germany. Within two years, evidence came to light proving Dreyfus's innocence. The real spy, Ferdinand Walsin Esterhazy (1847–1923), a French officer, was acquitted of treason, and more charges were leveled at Dreyfus. An enormous response in defense of Dreyfus, emblematized by novelist Émile Zola's *J'accuse*, pressured the government to reopen the case. The next trial still found him guilty, though he was released with time served, only being exonerated in 1906. The split between the Dreyfusards and the anti-Dreyfusards dominated French politics, around both antisemitism and military support. This time period also found the French republic cracking down on anarchists and then communists, with repressive laws that enabled suspected dissidents to be charged and held on suspicion. In other words, as Hocquenghem is saying, the Dreyfus affair was not external to class war, the

violence of the state, colonial expansion, racism, and patriarchy—these all work together.

6 *Les avortées* could also just mean people who have failed. Given the feminized ending, I translated this with a political understanding, since the MLF and the FHAR found some of their initial momentum in protesting antiabortion measures. As Hocquenghem's biographer, Antoine Idier, writes, these lines show "all the tension in homosexual liberation's genealogy," simultaneously a rejection of and inscription within leftist politics. Idier, *Les vies de Guy Hocquenghem*, 89.

7 This issue dedicated to gay liberation and the FHAR made a huge impact and resulted in a legal complaint lodged against Jean-Paul Sartre, who was on the editorial board.

8 This analogy of homophobia with racism was not uncommon during the time Hocquenghem was writing, but the textural differences of gender and sexual oppression as opposed to racial oppression—and more importantly the way these all work together—has been rethought extensively, making Hocquenghem's locution here sound quite dated.

9 Jean Genet (1910–86) is a huge figure in French literature and revolutionary movements. He was unabashedly gay and lauded the criminality of homosexuality. He spent time in prison and wrote about sex and prison in *Un journal de voleur* (The thief's journal) (Paris: Gallimard, 1949). He also spent time with the Black Panthers in 1970 during Huey Newton's trial and traveled to meet Arafat and support Palestinian freedom. He had great influence on queer writers and also pop cultural references by the likes of Bowie (who keeps appearing here), with his song "The Jean Genie" (1972). Hocquenghem later discussed the opportunity that criminality gives queers as a revolutionary position.

10 Here, Hocquenghem parrots the Reichian view. Reich, though antifascist and on the side of sexual liberation, was inherently homophobic, perhaps due to his roots in psychoanalysis.

11 The French may contain a reference to René Descartes's *larvatus prodeo*.

12 Eve Kosofsky Sedgwick elaborates on the unevenness of the closet, the "open secret," in comparison to Jewishness, in another important queer theoretical text, *Epistemology of the Closet* (Berkeley: University of California Press, 1990), 67–90.

13 I find it important to note that Hocquenghem here is explaining the misogynist homophobic view, not defending biological or anatomical sex as essential.

14 "Crève salope" was a pamphlet published in April 1968 in Bordeaux. It was also made into a song by Renaud (1952–) that became an anthem of May '68. The title means "Die, Bitch." It could also be translated as "Fuck Society."

15 Martha Altman or Shelley (1943–) is a lesbian feminist activist who was part of Daughters of Bilitis and an original member of the Gay Liberation Front. She was downtown during the Stonewall uprising. Shelley was not a lesbian separatist but worked at the intersection of different struggles.

16 Wilhelm Dilthey (1833–1911) was a German philosopher, influential in the field of hermeneutics, who also theorized different types of Weltanschauungen (worldviews). He emphasized the act of interpretation of the world, a kind of embedded empiricism.

17 This is my translation of Hocquenghem's quotation. The line comes from Antoine de Saint-Exupéry, *Terre des hommes* (Wind, sand, and stars) (Paris: Gallimard, 1939).

18 Hocquenghem is referring to the participation of the FHAR and the MLF at the May Day demonstration in 1971, where they declared their position among leftists, disturbing the stately procession with dancing, touching, and singing. (See Idier, *Les vies de Guy Hocquenghem*, 84–85). Incidentally, some feminist militants critiqued *Tout!*, no. 12, for sticking to a masculine understanding of sexuality that excluded women's relationships. This is symptomatic of the trouble with women that Hocquenghem keeps alluding to.

19 "Male domination" is my translation of the French *phallocratisme*.

20 This is an obscure reference. Hocquenghem could be referring to Margaret Mead, the cultural anthropologist, but she wrote positively of bisexuality.

21 See Wilhelm Stekel, *Onanie und Homosexualitat* (Onanism and homosexuality) (Berlin: Urban and Schwarzenberg, 1921). Stekel (1868–1940) was a psychoanalyst who wrote on perversions. Once a student of Sigmund Freud's, he eventually broke with him.

22 Hocquenghem, *Homosexual Desire*.

23 The *Simon Report* on the "sexual behavior of French people" was published in 1972 by Dr. Pierre Simon (1925–2008): *Rapport Simon sur le comportement sexuel des Français* (Paris: Gallimard, 1972). The report looked at sexuality from a sociological and political point of view, toward a liberation of values. It was limited to adult conjugal sexuality, though it aimed to investigate "contraceptive" sex. Simon was part of the move toward legalization of birth control and abortion in France.

24 *Social Plague* refers to *Fléau social*, a Situationist-influenced journal published from 1972 to 1974 by Group 5 of the FHAR.

25 Hocquenghem is referring to an amendment named after deputy Paul Mirguet that classified homosexuality as a social plague, with enhanced punishments for homosexual acts. It was adopted in 1960 and remained on the books until 1980. This amendment also linked homosexuality and pedophilia.

26 Cultuur en Ontspanningscentrum (COC; Center for Culture and Leisure) is a Dutch LGBT organization founded in 1946, making it the oldest active LGBT organization in the world. The COC fought for rights and acceptance and also provided social and cultural space for LGBT people, becoming more public in the 1960s. In 1971, article 248-bis in the Dutch criminal code, which criminalized homosexual acts between sixteen (the heterosexual age of consent) and twenty-one, was finally struck.

27 Arcadie was a French homophile organization started in the 1950s by André

Baudry (1922–2018). Just as Hocquenghem states, its aim was to gain respectability for homosexuals. Arcadie disbanded after the laws criminalizing homosexuality were no longer different than heterosexual criminal offenses. Baudry also edited a journal named after the group.

28 See previous note (23) on the *Simon Report*.

29 Gérard Grandmontagne died by suicide in the Fresnes prison at the age of thirty-one. He was sentenced to eight days in solitary for "homosexual relations" with his cellmate, who also died by suicide a few months later. See Idier, *Les vies de Guy Hocquenghem*, 106–7, for the effect of this episode on the anti-prison and gay liberation movements, particularly involving Michel Foucault and Hocquenghem.

30 Saint-Germain-des-Prés was considered a hip postwar Parisian neighborhood.

31 Sándor Ferenczi (1873–1933) was a Hungarian psychoanalyst and acolyte of Freud's, who developed theories of sexuality.

32 Ernst Röhm (1887–1934) was a Nazi officer, cofounder of the SA, and friend of Hitler's who was purged during the Night of the Long Knives due to the increasing influence of the SA. Röhm was homosexual, with a masculinist view of manly love and social health. His homosexuality was well known, though after the purge it was used to tarnish his and his officers' reputations further.

CHAPTER SIX: MOTORCYCLES

1 Hocquenghem uses the word *rocker* in English, and then translates it as *culbuteur*, a term for the rocker arm of an internal combustion engine.

2 Gilles Deleuze and Félix Guattari, *Anti-Oedipus*, trans. Robert Hurley, Mark Seem, and Helen R. Lane (Minneapolis: University of Minnesota, 1983), 44, 54.

3 This route is about a fifteen-kilometer ride across the city from west to east.

4 *Weekend* (1967) is a film directed by Godard that shows the murderous desires that circulate in heterosexual coupling and families. The film is set as a weekend car trip to the country and features traffic, accidents, kidnapping, and more.

5 Hocquenghem takes a few shots at the Beatles, who mostly represented a vapid "peace and love" version of the cultural revolution that Hocquenghem wanted to be more militant. On the other hand, Detroit's MC5 was overtly political; members lived as a collective, stockpiled guns, and were part of a White Panther Party in solidarity with the Black Panthers. See, for example, the group's cover of John Lee Hooker's "Motor City Is Burning" about the Detroit riots of 1967. MC5's version talks about joining in the cause for freedom as white people rebelling against the state.

6 Robert Poujade (1928–) was a Gaullist French politician and cabinet member as well as a member of the Anti-Noise League. From 1971 to 1974, under Presi-

dent Pompidou, he was the minister tasked with the protection of nature and the environment, creating the Ministry of the Environment, now the Ministry of Ecology. He led campaigns against noise pollution and poor air quality.

CHAPTER SEVEN: MLF—FHAR

1 In the text, Hocquenghem translates *Gay Liberation Front* as *front de libération homosexuelle*. The event he is referring to is the Stonewall uprising.
2 *Women's Lib* appears in English in the original.
3 Hocquenghem is referring to a demonstration at the Maison de la Mutualité, a conference center owned by a mutual insurance company. In order to start a revolutionary homosexual movement, women Arcadie members joined with the MLF to interrupt a pro-life meeting put on by Laissez-les vivre (Let Them Live) and the doctor Jérôme Lejeune on March 5, 1971.
4 Ménie Grégoire (1919–2014) was a journalist and writer who hosted a radio show called *Allô, Ménie*. On March 10, 1971, her show was devoted to "this painful problem, homosexuality." The disruption to her show, along with the pro-life meeting, are seen as the birth of the FHAR.
5. This is a reference to the publication in *Le nouvel observateur* (April 5, 1971) of the "Manifeste des 343 salopes" ("Manifesto of 343 Sluts"), written by Simone de Beauvoir and signed by people who claimed to have had an abortion, thereby opening themselves up to punishment by the legal system. At the end of the manifesto, the MLF demanded free abortion access.
6 The French word is *avorton*, which is playing off the abortion issue.
7 It's worth noting here that, though the FHAR claimed to be antiracist, some of its publications and imagery used racist representations of Arabs. See Idier, *Les vies de Guy Hocquenghem*, 115–20, for a discussion of this in relation to Hocquenghem. There is also a longer history at play here between French men and Arab boys; see for example Todd Shepard, *Sex, France, and Arab Men, 1962–1979* (Chicago: University of Chicago Press, 2018); and Kadji Amin, *Disturbing Attachments*.
8 The French term is *Jules*, which for a lesbian is akin to *folle* ("queen") for a gay man.
9 Brownian motion is the random movement of particles suspended in liquid or gas, also called *pedesis* in Greek, which means leaping—and has an interesting echo of *pédé*, as well as the leaping fauns of Hocquenghem's French title.
10. Hocquenghem could be referring to Louis Althusser's notion of interpellation, which he analyzes as the process by which the subject is called into ideology, a form of identification or calling out to, emblematized by being stopped by the police on the street. See Althusser, "Ideology and Ideological State Apparatuses," in *Lenin and Philosophy*, trans. Ben Brewster (New York: Monthly Review Press, 2001), 85–126.

11 *Déplacé* could also be translated as "displaced," but since I translated it above in the context of transness as "inappropriate gestures," and it is juxtaposed with the following term *du bienséant*, or "propriety" ("seemly," "decorous"), I kept that inference. However, Hocquenghem then uses the cognate noun *déplacement* to talk about capital's movement and exchangeability; I translate this use of the term as "displacement."

12 The Maginot line, named after French minister of war André Maginot, was an extensive line of fortifications to defend against German invasion in the 1930s. Germany ended up invading from a different angle. The term refers to the intensive effort of creating false security. It also fits into Hocquenghem's repeated idea that revolutionaries are always "behind one war," as he says in the next sentence. The Maginot line would have made sense in World War I but not World War II. Thus, we would have to ditch revolutionary strategies of the past toward an unknowable future—and also give up the assumed value of civilization and humanity, products of capital, the state, and colonialism.

13 Hocquenghem is referring to Rudi Dutschke's slogan of "the long march through the institutions," a revolutionary strategy of infiltrating or integrating into institutions and professions in order to change society.

14 Hocquenghem is most likely referring to the spring issue (no. 12) of *Recherches*, a journal directed by Guattari. Hocquenghem was one of the editors and writers of this famous issue, "Three Billion Perverts: Grand Encyclopedia of Homosexualities," at a time when the FHAR was dissipating. Like *Tout!*, no. 12, the police seized this magazine, resulting in a trial and fine for Guattari. The text itself has been subject to critique, from its portrayal of Arabs to its overly masculine sexuality.

15 I replaced Hocquenghem's French version with the opening text from "The Effeminist Manifesto," published in 1973 by Steven Dansky, John Knoebel, and Kenneth Pitchford, three former Gay Liberation Front members.

16 The italicized text appears in English in the original.

17 This is my attempt to convey Hocquenghem's playful use of language in the original: "il se recrée et se récrée de lui-même chaque semaine."

18 Hocquenghem's "Unités factices" in the heading to this section could also mean a "decoy unit," a group deployed to mislead an enemy.

19 Hocquenghem writes, "une-un pédélesbienne," mashing together the binary genders and binary same sexualities.

20 "Guest molecules" is my translation for "les molecules prisonnières." The terminology comes from chemistry, describing complexes made up of multiple molecules or ions that are held together through noncovalent bonding.

21 Here the original French, "se mettent en branle," also has the connotation of "jerking off."

22 Herbert Marcuse, *Counterrevolution and Revolt* (Boston: Beacon, 1972), 77–78.

23 Dansky, Knoebel, and Pitchford, "Effeminist Manifesto," in *Burn It Down*, 47.

24 *Eonism* is a term coined by the American psychologist Havelock Ellis in his

study of trans people. Ellis created this term in distinction from Magnus Hirschfeld, another early sexologist, who used the term *transvestite*, though he recognized its limitations. Hocquenghem's French uses the language of transvestism, which I've replaced with *trans/transgender/trans people*. *Eonism* comes from the name of the Chevalier d'Éon (1728–1810), a French noble, diplomat, and spy, who anachronistically could be considered trans. According to D'Éon herself, though, she was a woman.

25 Dansky, Knoebel, and Pitchford, "Effeminist Manifesto," 48.

26 I chose to translate this provocatively. The sentence is "Comme si les attributs féminins n'étaient pas d'abord fondamentalement un travestissement," which could also be rendered, "As if feminine qualities were not essentially cross-dressing [or dress-up] to begin with."

27 Hocquenghem's section title is "Le grand Dessalage." *Dessalage* has the immediate sense of "desalting," also "capsizing," but the verb *dessaler* figuratively means "to disabuse." In the context of the splintering of the movements, we could assume that both "capsizing" and "a sudden realization of the ways of the world" would be appropriate, which I tried to convey with "upending."

28 Sade supported the revolution, despite his aristocratic background. However, this made him suspect to revolutionaries. He was on the more radical side of things, and his support for Marat and critique of Robespierre found him imprisoned during the Terror. After Napoleon seized power, Sade was arrested for his pornographic literature. Hocquenghem is highlighting these two ruptures that he sees as intersecting transversally, with contingent and disparate legacies. Sade's later influence would show him to be more revolutionary than the French Revolution, which inaugurated the bourgeois republic. Similarly, Sade's writings are in the spirit of sexual liberation and provide a foothold for critiquing Enlightenment ideology and moralism. Jacques Lacan as well as Theodor Adorno and Max Horkheimer have written on this: see Lacan, "Kant with Sade," trans. James B. Swenson, *October*, no. 51 (1989): 55–75; and Horkheimer and Adorno, "Excursus II: Juliette or Enlightenment and Morality," in *Dialectic of Enlightenment: Philosophical Fragments*, ed. Gunzelin Schmid Noerr, trans. Edmund Jephcott (Stanford, CA: Stanford University Press, 2002), 63–93. The antigay rhetoric of communist revolutionaries of the twentieth century associated sexual liberation with decadence and libertinage. For Hocquenghem, sexual freedom (which was often touted by the early anarchists) dislodges the kind of moralism that keeps so-called revolutionaries reactionary and hampers them in their fight against capital and the state.

29 I believe Hocquenghem is referencing the French philosopher Jean-François Lyotard (1924–88) and his 1974 book, *Libidinal Economy* (trans. Iain Hamilton Grant; Bloomington: Indiana University Press, 1993). He discusses there a Sadean jouissance: "If it is true that pleasure has no price, the torturing and putting to death of all Europe by the silver wars is not too expensive to sus-

tain the glory of the king, that is to say his *jouissance*" (194–95). The libidinal economy is an attempt to combine Freudian and Marxist thought. In this paragraph, Hocquenghem is pulling also from French sociologist Marcel Mauss's 1925 *The Gift: The Form and Reason for Exchange in Archaic Societies* (trans. W. D. Halls; New York: Routledge, 1990), which provides an alternative economy through an analysis of the Northwest coast Indigenous practice of potlatch, where wealth is created through destroying items of luxury. The French philosopher and pornographer Georges Bataille developed this theory further with his idea of "expenditure" as the fundamental principle of economics—that reciprocal exchange relies on a more general perspective of waste. See Bataille, "The Notion of Expenditure," in *Visions of Excess*, trans. Allan Stoekl with Carl R. Lovitt and Donald M. Leslie Jr. (Minneapolis: University of Minnesota, 1985), as well as *The Accursed Share*, vol. 1, trans. Robert Hurley (New York: Zone, 1988). As opposed to Deleuze and Guattari, both Lyotard and Bataille could be seen as apolitical or amoral. The idea of expenditure can be taken up both by the bourgeoisie in their destruction of the poor, and the poor in their uprising against the ruling class. Hocquenghem here elaborates an explicitly revolutionary—or more accurately volutionary/transversal—perspective that reimagines luxury and jouissance outside of the structure of exchange, class, and the state. This perspective is necessarily queer, another element left out of all these thinkers' work.

30 *Stars, fans*, and *star system* all appear in English in the original.

31 "Par derrière" can also have the connotation "up the ass."

Index

abolition, abolitionism, xii–xiii, xxiv, xxviii, 123n54. *See also under* gender

abortion and abortion rights, xiii–xiv, 80–81, 108, 139n53, 145n6, 146n23, 148n3, 148nn5–6. *See also* feminism; Mouvement de libération des femmes (Women's Liberation Movement); Simon, Pierre

Absences répétées (Repeated Absences; Gilles), 14, 128n6

Action (militant journal), 17, 38, 129n2

action committee (*comité d'action*), xiii–xiv, 18, 21, 129n7

Actuel (Now; left-leaning magazine), 14–16, 49, 51–61, 137n35, 138n42

Adorno, Theodor, 150n28

Affaire Dreyfus. *See* Dreyfus Affair

AG (*assemblée générale*). *See* general assembly

agriculture, 35–36

Alamo, Frank, 17, 129n1

Algeria, 15, 128n10, 144n4. *See also* Boumédiène, Houari; colonialism; Gide, André; pedophilia

Alice's Adventures in Wonderland (Carroll), xxiv, 10, 57, 110, 139n54

Altamont Free Concert, 63, 139n3

Althusser, Louis, 31, 148n10. *See also* interpellation

Altman, Martha, 145n15

American Indian Movement, xvi

American Revolution. *See under* United States

Amin, Kadji, xv, 120n14, 144n4

anarchism, xii–xiv, xvi, xxi–xxiii, xxviii, 15, 43, 132nn34–35; and Black radical tradition, xxv–xxvii, 120n9; and *groupe affectif* (discussion group), 26, 131n27; and individualism, 120n4; and queer and trans liberation, xxiv–xxvii. *See also* anticapitalism; communism; Hocquenghem, Guy; leftism

Anarchist Federation. *See* Fédération anarchiste

Anderson, William C., xxvi, 120n9. *See also* anarchism; Black radical tradition

anti-Arab racism, 71–72, 108–9, 148n7, 149n14. *See also* Arabophilia

anticapitalism, xii, xiv–xv; and homosexual desire, xv, 121n19; and queer theory, xi; and student protests, 20–21. *See also* capitalism

anti-institutionalism, xi

antihomosexual laws. *See* homosexuality, laws against

antisocial thesis. *See under* queer theory

antistatism, xi, xv–xvii, xx, xxvi–xxix, 19, 21–23

antiwar, xx

anus, xxviii; anular structure, 2, 125n7

"L'après-midi d'un faune" ("The Afternoon of a Faun"; Mallarmé), 119n2, 127n10

apocalypse. *See under* crisis

Apollinaire, 127n8

apomorphine, 63, 140n9. *See also* drugs; heroin

Arab Spring, xxvii

CGT. See Confédération générale du travail (General Confederation of Labor)

Chaban-Delmas, Jacques, 15, 128n12

Charlie Hebdo. See *Hara-Kiri Hebdo*

Châtelet, François, 119n2

Chêne noir theater, 51, 56, 138n40. *See also* Gélas, Gérard

children, 95; and childhood sexuality, 42, 77, 95–96, 120n14, 144n4; and early education, 131n21. *See also* pederasty; pedophilia; youth and youth culture

China, xx, 15, 28, 47; and Bangladesh, 46–48; economic reforms, 128n10. *See also* Bangladesh; Cultural Revolution; Maoism

Chinoise, La (Godard), 129n3

CID. See Centre informatique douanier (Customs Information Center)

circulation, 35–37

civilization, 8, 32–37

class, 34–35; and desire, xix, 93, 122n39, 150n29; dominant, 24; struggle, xxii–xxiii, 21, 90, 134n6; working, 25–26, 28–29. *See also* bourgeoisie; desire; workers

Clémenti, Pierre, 56, 138n48

clothing, 57–58

Club Cinq-Sept nightclub fire, 63, 140nn5–6

CNRS. See Centre national de la recherche scientifique (French National Center for Scientific Research)

COC. See Cultuur en Ontspanningscentrum (Center for Culture and Leisure)

Cocteau, Jean, 119n2, 127n8

Cohen, Leonard, 76

Cohn-Bendit, Daniel, 40, 45, 51, 134n5, 135n17

Colin, Jean-Pierre, 119n2

collective (collectivity), xi–xii; as liberation, xxiii; and experiments in living, x, xiv, 23–24, 26. *See also* Combahee River Collective

colonialism, xv, xix, xxiv, 143n48; anti-colonialism, xv, xxvi, 121n19; and communism, 131n28; global decolonial movement, xvi, xxi; and pedophilic sex tourism, 144n4, 148n7. *See also* Algeria; Arabophilia; Debré, Michel; *Enfants de la Creuse*; Gide, André; imperialism; pedophilia; Réunion

Combahee River Collective, xxiii. *See also* Black radical tradition; collective, liberation

commune, 11, 15, 23, 66, 75, 85, 132n34. *See also* collective and collectivity, and experiments in living; Paris Commune of 1871

communism: and anti-gay rhetoric, xxiii, 150n28; formations of, xiii; groups, 131n24; ideal militant, 25–26; and piety, xvii. *See also* anarchism; French Communist Party; leftism; Maoism

community. See collective and collectivity, and experiments in living; commune

compromise, ix–x

Confédération générale du travail (CGT; General Confederation of Labor), 76, 133n3

confusion, xxiv, 76, 110–11

consent, 80, 120n14, 146n26. *See also* children, and childhood sexuality

consumerism, 12

continuity, 31, 34, 40, 42–43; and discontinuity, 18. *See also* transition

cops. *See* police

"Cosmic Blues" (Joplin), 65

Counterrevolution and Revolt (Marcuse), 7, 114

COVID-19 pandemic, xxvii

Crick, Francis, 142n34

criminality. See *under* homosexuality

crisis, x, xxvii, 20, 22–23, 28; and apocalypse, 8–11; and boredom, 10; and enjoyment, 11; and perverts, 10

cruising, xiii, xviii, xx, xxvii, 2, 99, 109, 112, 114, 120n13. *See also* public, sex in; sex and sexuality, public sex; sodomy

Crumb, R., 67, 142n26

Cultural Revolution (China), 21–23, 30, 46–47, 131n25. *See also* Maoism; revolution, cultural; Shaoqi, Liu

culture, 43–44

Cultuur en Ontspanningscentrum (COC; Center for Culture and Leisure), 98, 146n26

Customs Information Center. *See* Centre informatique douanier (CID)

cynicism. *See* pessimism

de Gaulle, Charles, xxiii, 21, 62–64, 78, 130n16, 131n19, 138n45, 140n6, 142n38

De, Zhu, 132n33

Dean, Tim, xv, 121n17

death, 13, 16. *See also* suicide

death drive. *See* psychoanalysis: death drive

Debord, Guy, 133n2

Debré, Michel, 78, 143n48

Debussy, Claude, 119n2, 127n10

decadence, xxiii, 10, 73, 127n8, 127n10, 150n28. *See also* Bowie, David; communism, and anti-gay rhetoric; desire; Gide, André

decolonial movement, xvi, xxi. *See also under* colonialism

defeat. *See* pessimism

Delany, Samuel, 122n39

Deleuze, Gilles, xi–xii, xix, xxiv–xxv, 1–5, 32, 49–50, 52, 55–56, 119n2, 150n29. *See also* Guattari, Félix

Democratic National Convention, 141n17

Derré, Émile, 132n35

Deshayes, Richard, 137n33

desire, x, 15, 32–37, 83–84; compensation, 102; and connections, 2; and critique of homosexual identity, xi; and liberation, xxv, 79–80; to live, 48–49; as luxury, xix; as mobile and disruptive, xi; and motorcycles, 102–4; and normalcy, 94; and politics, 38–42; and production, xx–xxi, 5, 32–37; and psychoanalysis,

1–2; and revolution, 12; and sublimation, 100; and utopianism, xxi–xxii. *See also* anticapitalism; bourgeoisie; Hocquenghem, Guy, works by: *Homosexual Desire*; homosexual desire

Detroit riots of 1967, 147n5

deviancy, xviii–xix, 69, 74, 96, 143n1. *See also* drugs; homosexuality, and criminality; Reich, Wilhelm

Diaghilev, Sergei, 127n8

dialectics, xix, xxi, 4, 9, 11, 31. *See also* temporality

Dilthey, Wilhelm, 88, 146n16

disappointment. *See* pessimism

discipline. *See under* police

discontinuity. *See under* continuity

discussion group. *See under* anarchism

division, 26–28

Doillon, Jacques, 128n11

domesticity, 23, 77

Dreyfus Affair (Affaire Dreyfus), 80, 144n5

drugs, 62–75; criminalization of, 68–70; and marginalization, 67–68; and revolution, 74–75; as social necessity, 71–72; and youth culture, 73. *See also* deviancy; Hendrix, Jimi; heroin; Joplin, Janis; youth and youth culture: and drugs

Dujardin, Édouard, 126n1

Dutschke, Alfred Willi Rudolf "Rudi," 40, 111, 134n5, 149n13

Duvert, Tony, 2, 125n11

East Bengal. *See* Bangladesh

École normale supérieure (ENS), xiv, 4, 125n18. *See also* Beaux-Arts

Edelman, Lee, xv, 121n17

education, x, 131n21. *See also under* children; May '68 uprising

effeminacy. *See under* femininity

"Effeminist Manifesto, The" 115, 149n15

Enfants de la Creuse, 143n48. *See also* colonialism; Debré, Michel; Réunion

enjoyment. *See* crisis: and enjoyment

ENS. *See* École normale supérieure

New World of Love, The (Fourier), 79

Nijinsky, Vaslav, 119n2, 127n8, 127n10

Nixon, Richard, 15, 48, 126n3, 128n10. See also Mao Zedong

noise, 105

nominalism, 3–4. See also Hocquenghem, Guy: critique of identity; identity and identity politics: critique of

normalcy and normativity, xviii, 81–82, 85–88, 91, 94. See also assimilation; recuperation

"Nous n'irons plus au bois" ("We will go to the woods no more," children's song), 126n1

nouvel observateur, Le (weekly news magazine), 84, 108, 112, 137n29, 148n5

occupation, ix. See also student movement

Occupy movement, xxvii

octopus (metaphor), 10

Oedipus, 16

Oedipus complex. See under psychoanalysis

oppression, xvi, xix, xxii, xxv, 29, 64, 77; and bourgeoisie, 24–25, 28; and homosexuality, 80–81, 82–83, 86, 90–93, 113–17, 124n64, 145n8; and imperialism, 20; and justice, 6; and patriarchy, 24, 30, 80–81, 124n64; systems of, xxiii, 28, 145n8

Overney, Pierre, 13, 127n1

Pakistan, xx, 46–48, 136n23, 136n25. See also Bangladesh; China

Palestine, 136n21, 145n9

Parade (ballet), 127n8

paranoia, 99–100

Paris Commune of 1871, 129n6, 132n34, 133n37. See also commune

Parti communiste français. See French Communist Party (PCF)

Parti socialiste unifié (PSU; Unified Socialist Party), 135n17, 135n19

passion. See desire

Pauwels, Louis, 9

PCF. See French Communist Party

pederasty, 67, 80, 97, 120n14, 125n9, 125n11, 141n25. See also children, and childhood sexuality; Guy Hocquenghem; pedophilia

pedophilia, 114, 120n14, 144n4, 146n25. See also Algeria; Arabophilia; children, and childhood sexuality; colonialism, and pedophilic sex tourism; Gide, André; Hocquenghem, Guy; pederasty

performativity, xxv

Perlman, Fredy, 135n12

perverts and perversion, 10, 116–17; and pleasure, 95

pessimism, xvi, 15, 18, 25, 60. See also Hocquenghem, Guy: pessimism; militancy; revolution

Pétain, Philippe, 76, 143n44

Peugeot (factory), 134n11

Peyrefitte, Alain, 2, 5, 18–19, 129n10, 130n11

Peyrefitte, Roger, 125n9

phallocentrism, 3

Picasso, Pablo, 127n8

Pink Floyd, 63

Plato, 97

Poher, Alain, 21–22, 130n16

police and cops (policing), 29, 43, 59, 63, 66–67, 72–74, 129n4, 132n35, 148n10; and clashes with leftists, ix–x, 19, 134n11, 141n17; and discipline, xxv, 123n54; and homosexuality, 79, 82–83, 97–100, 107, 112–13, 149n14; and matraque (police baton), 9, 126n4, 130n12; and violence, xxvii–xxviii, 19, 131n19, 135n17, 138n45, 141n17

politics: and daily life, 26; and desire, 38–42

pollution, 104–106

Pompidou, Georges, 21–22, 75–78, 128n12, 129n10, 130n17, 131n19, 138n45, 142n31, 142n38, 147n6

pop (music), 62–64, 141n20; and leftist movements, 66–67; and race, 65

Pop Liberation and Intervention Force, 66

Potlach, 10, 151n29

Pouget, Émile, 39, 133n4

Poujade, Robert, 147n6

power, 91

prison, 13–16, 98–99. *See also* suicide

private life, 23, 51–61

production: relation to desire, xx–xxi, 5, 32–37; food, 57–58

productivity, 58

profit, 34

Proletarian Left. *See* Gauche prolétarienne

proletariat, 28–29. *See also* class; worker

property, 58

Proust, Marcel, 2, 4–5, 125n9

psychoanalysis, 1–2, 123n60; death drive, 10, 16, 123n40; and desire, 102–4; and homosexuality, 83–84; and negativity, xv; Oedipus complex, 96–97, 102. *See also* Amin, Kadji; Bersani, Leo; Dean, Tim; desire: and psychoanalysis; Edelman, Lee; Freud, Sigmund; homosexual desire: and psychoanalysis

public, 23, 51–55; sex in, xviii

purity politics. *See under* queer and queerness; revolution

queer and queerness: art, 127n8, 127n10; and death drive, 123n40; and liberation, xii–xiii, 121n19, 123n58; militancy, xii; and purity, xvii; reading, xx–xxi; and transness, 123n58. *See also* anarchism; Hocquenghem, Guy; homosexuality; transness, transgender, and trans people

queer theory, xi; and anticapitalism, xi; antisocial thesis, xv, 121n17; and English reception of Hocquenghem's work, xiv; and failure, 123n46; and militancy, xiv–xvi; and negativity, xv; and utopianism, xxi. *See also* anticapitalism; French theory; Hocquenghem, Guy; homosexuality; Marxism; queer and queerness; transness, transgender, and trans people

race and racism, xxv–xxvii, 141n13, 145n8; Black radical tradition, xvi, xviii, xxv–xxvi; and pop music, 65. *See also* anarchism; Black radical tradition; Combahee River Collective

Recherches (magazine), 112, 114–15, 149n14. *See also* "Three Billion Perverts"

recuperation, xvii–xx, 57. *See also* assimilation; bourgeoisie; liberalism; reform; respectability

Redding, Otis, 65

Red Dykes. *See* Gouines rouges

redistribution, 34

reform, xvii. *See also* recuperation

Reich, Wilhelm, 79, 143n1, 145n10

Renault (factory), 16, 23, 127n1, 132n30

Repeated Absences (Gilles), 14

repetition (figure), 31–32

repression, xvi, 9–10, 22, 24, 25–26, 71–73, 75, 144n5; of desire and sexuality, xv, xxi, 3, 18, 81–83, 93–94, 96, 97, 99–100, 102, 143n1; and self, 26, 30, 42; and violence, 13, 17, 19–21, 98, 99–100, 131n19. *See also* desire; homosexual desire; homosexuality; police violence

Resnais, Alain, 128n11

respectability, 88, 97. *See also* assimilation; bourgeoisie; liberalism; recuperation

return (figure). *See* repetition

Réunion (French colonial holding), 143n48. *See also* colonialism; Debré, Michel; *Enfants de la Creuse*

Revault d'Allonnes, Olivier, 119n2

Revel, Jean-François, 132n36

revolution and revolutionary: betrayal of, xvii–xviii, 130n18; critique of work, 29; cultural, 7, 21–31, 48, 132n29; death and, 13; drugs and, 74; family and, 6; and femininity, 114–15; as fusion, 25–28; generalizations, 90; living, 40–42; moralism of, xviii, 6–7; pessimism and failure, 8–10; and purity politics, xvii, 7; as reactionary, 6; relationality of, 6; universalism of, 7–8; set of principles; 46–68;

revolution and revolutionary (*continued*)
as strategic project, 25; subject of, xiii,
7–8, 40–41. *See also* China; Cultural
Revolution; desire; drugs; family;
Hocquenghem, Guy; leftism; Marxism;
work; worker
Revolutionary Abolitionist Movement,
120n9
Revolutionary Communist Youth. *See* Jeu-
nesse communiste révolutionnaire (JCR)
Revolutionary Effeminists, 112, 114–16,
124n64, 149n15
Revolution of 1848, 18, 126n6, 129n6,
133n37, 143n43
Rigaut, Jacques, 128n5
Rives-Henrÿs, André, 48, 137n31
rock (music), 62–63. *See also* pop (music)
Röhm, Ernst, 100, 147n32
Rolling Stones, 63
Rouch, Jean, 128n11
Russian Revolution of 1917, 133n37

Sachs, Maurice, 10, 127n9
Sade, Marquis de, 13, 79, 116, 128n4,
150n28
sadomasochism, 4–5, 114–16, 128n4. *See
also* Sade, Marquis de
Saint-Exupéry, Antoine de, 89
Samudzi, Zoé, xxvi, 120n9. *See also* anar-
chism; Black radical tradition
Sartre, Jean-Paul, xiii, xviii, 51, 56, 134n8,
138n41, 145n7
Satie, Erik, 127n8
Sauvageot, Jacques, 45, 135n17, 135n19
Schalit, Jean, 129n2
Schérer, René, xiv, xx–xxi, 119n2, 120n14,
144n4. *See also* Hocquenghem, Guy;
pederasty
SDS. See Socialist German Student
League (Sozialistische Deutsche
Studentenbund)
Sedgwick, Eve Kosofsky, 121n19, 145n12
Séguy, Georges, 39, 133n3
self, 52, 54. *See also* individualism; subject

settlement (*l'établissement*), 27. *See also* un-
der militancy
sex and sexuality, x; and capitalism, 116;
and deviancy, 81–82; ethics of, xix; and
liberation, xviii, 92; and objectifica-
tion, 86–87; and phallocentrism, 3; and
politics, 107–9; public sex, 122n39; and
repression, 93–94, 99–100; and society,
3; and children, 42, 77, 95–96, 120n14,
144n4. *See also* children; desire; homosexual desire; pederasty; pedophilia
shame (shameful), xxiv, 4, 8, 42, 52,
56–57, 81, 86, 103, 110–11. *See also* guilt;
transversalism
Shaoqi, Liu, 26, 131n25
Shelley, Martha, 88
Shelton, Gilbert, 67, 142n26
Simon Report (France), 96, 98, 146n23
Simon, Pierre. *See* Simon Report
Situationist International, xiii, 42, 132n35,
133n2
SNESup. *See* Syndicat national de l'ensei-
gnement supérieur (National Higher
Education Union)
Snorton, C. Riley, xxv–xxvi
Social Plague. See Fléau social
Socialist German Student League (So-
zialistische Deutsche Studentenbund;
SDS), 19–20, 130n14
sociality, xv–xvi. *See also* homosexual
desire
sodomy, xiii, xx, 93, 117
solidarity, xvi
Sozialistische Deutsche Studentenbund
(SDS). *See* Socialist German Student
League
Spanish Civil War, 18, 129n6, 131n27
spiral (trope), 1
standardization, 29. *See also* assembly
line
"Star-Spangled Banner, The" (national an-
them), 65, 141n17. *See also* Franklin, Aretha; Hendrix, Jimi
Stekel, Wilhelm, 96, 146n21

universalism, 7, 110

university: as site of protest, 17–22, 25–28; regulations, ix. *See also* student movement

utopianism, xv–xvi, xviii–xxi, xxvi, xxvii 16, 121n19, 122n39

utterances, 2–5. *See also* Deleuze, Gilles

Vaneigem, Raoul, 39, 133n2

Vernier, Jean-Claude, 138n41

Viansson-Ponté, Pierre, 126n6

Victor, Pierre (Bény Lévy), 138n41

Vietnam, 15, 48, 130n13

Vive la révolution (Long Live the Revolution), 38

voluntarism, 128n9

volution, xix–xxi, xvii, 1–5, 6–12, 124n3. *See also* revolution, cultural

war, 47

Warhol, Andy, 127n7

Watson, James, 142n34

Wayward Lives, Beautiful Experiments (Hartman), xxvi

Weekend (Godard), 105, 147n4

wildcat strikes, ix

Willot brothers, 48, 137n30

Wolinski, Georges, 18, 129n8

women: and liberation, xvi, 107; and revolution, 38. *See also* feminism; gender; Mouvement de libération des femmes (MLF)

Woodstock (music festival), 65–66, 75, 93. *See also* Hendrix, Jimi

work: critique of, 29–30, 39–40, 57, 73; dignity of, 39–40; as a site of protest, 22. *See also* factory; leftism; militants; Peugeot; Renault; revolution, critique of work; student; worker

worker: defining, 28–29; laziness as idealized, 38, 42; movement, ix, 134n6; as revolutionary subject, xiii; relation to students, 26–27; strikes, 130n15, 130n17, 131n26, 134n11. *See also* leftism; militants; Peugeot; Renault; student movement; work; *and* labor unions by name

Workers (Gavi), 40

Year 01 (comic, Gébé), 15, 128n11

youth and youth culture, xiii, 14, 20–21, 24, 43–44; and aging, 14; and class struggle, 93; and drugs, 65–66, 67–75; and environmentalism, 104–6; and family, 75–78; and music, 62–67, 93. *See also* children; drugs; Hendrix, Jimi; student movement; *and* student unions by name

Youth Liberation Front. *See* Front de libération de la jeunesse (FLJ)

Zapatista movement, x

Zedong, Mao. *See* Mao Zedong

Zola, Émile, 144n5